fMRI Study of Japanese Phrasal Segmentation

Hituzi Linguistics in English

No.1	Lexical Borrowing and its Impact on English	Makimi Kimura-Kano
No.2	From a Subordinate Clause to an Independent Clause
		Yuko Higashiizumi
No.3	ModalP and Subjunctive Present	Tadao Nomura
No.4	A Historical Study of Referent Honorifics in Japanese
		Takashi Nagata
No.5	Communicating Skills of Intention	Tsutomu Sakamoto
No.6	A Pragmatic Approach to the Generation and Gender Gap in Japanese Politeness Strategies	Toshihiko Suzuki
No.7	Japanese Women's Listening Behavior in Face-to-face Conversation
		Sachie Miyazaki
No.8	An Enterprise in the Cognitive Science of Language
		Tetsuya Sano et al.
No.9	Syntactic Structure and Silence	Hisao Tokizaki
No.10	The Development of the Nominal Plural Forms in Early Middle English
		Ryuichi Hotta
No.11	Chunking and Instruction	Takayuki Nakamori
No.12	Detecting and Sharing Perspectives Using Causals in Japanese
		Ryoko Uno
No.13	Discourse Representation of Temporal Relations in the So-Called Head-Internal Relatives	Kuniyoshi Ishikawa
No.14	Features and Roles of Filled Pauses in Speech Communication
		Michiko Watanabe
No.15	Japanese Loanword Phonology	Masahiko Mutsukawa
No.16	Derivational Linearization at the Syntax-Prosody Interface
		Kayono Shiobara
No.18	fMRI Study of Japanese Phrasal Segmentation	Hideki Oshima
No.19	Typological Studies on Languages in Thailand and Japan
		Tadao Miyamoto et al.

Hituzi Linguistics in English No. 18

fMRI Study of Japanese Phrasal Segmentation
Neuropsychological Approach to Sentence Comprehension

Hideki Oshima

Hituzi Syobo Publishing

Copyright © Hideki Oshima 2013
First published 2013

Author: Hideki Oshima

All rights reserved. Except for the quotation of short passages for the purposes of criticism and review, no part of this publication may be reproduced, stored in a retrieval system, or transmitted in any form or by any means, electronic, mechanical, photocopying, recording or otherwise, without the written prior permission of the publisher.
In case of photocopying and electronic copying and retrieval from network personally, permission will be given on receipts of payment and making inquiries. For details please contact us through e-mail. Our e-mail address is given below.

Hituzi Syobo Publishing
Yamato bldg. 2F, 2-1-2 Sengoku Bunkyo-ku Tokyo, Japan
112-0011

phone +81-3-5319-4916 fax +81-3-5319-4917
e-mail: toiawase@hituzi.co.jp
http://www.hituzi.co.jp/
postal transfer 00120-8-142852

ISBN978-4-89476-595-5
Printed in Japan

Contents

Preface	ix
Acknowledgements	xi

Chapter 1 Introduction — 1
1.1 Segmentation Problem: its Issues — 2
1.2 Goals Achieved — 8
1.3 Direction of the Study — 9
1.4 Relevance to the Field — 12
1.5 Limitations and Delimitations — 14
    1.5.1 Limitations of the Study: Methodological Constraints — 15
    1.5.2 Delimitations of the Study:
        Scope of Inquiry and Approach to the Study — 16
1.6 Definition of Terms — 18
1.7 Organization of Chapters — 25

Chapter 2 Why Phrasal Segmentation? — 29
2.1 Linguistic Intuitions and Empirical Evidence — 29
2.2 Possible Considerations about Phrasal Segmentation — 34
    2.2.1 Issues on Modeling Sentence Processing — 35
        2.2.1.1 Processing Properties: Incrementality and
            Compositionality — 35

  2.2.1.2 Core Linguistic Information in Language Processing 36
  2.2.1.3 Designing Distinction in Modeling Sentence
     Processing 38
  2.2.1.4 Neurophysiological Evidence for Modeling Sentence
     Processing 40
  2.2.1.5 Neurophysiological Models of Sentence Processing 46
 2.2.2 Premises of the Research of Phrasal Segmentation 55
2.3 Summary 57

Chapter 3 Human Language Processing in the Brain 59
3.1 Human Language Processing 60
 3.1.1 Functional Brain Imaging: its Techniques 61
 3.1.2 Mapping of Language in the Brain 66
 3.1.3 Language Specificity in the Brain 71
3.2 Functional Relationship between Language and the Brain 75
3.3 Sentence Comprehension and Phrasal Segmentation 79
3.4 Rationale for the fMRI Experiments of Phrasal Segmentation 82
3.5 Summary 85

Chapter 4 Search for Phrasal Segmentation: Visual fMRI Study 87
4.1 fMRI Experiment 88
 4.1.1 Participants 88
 4.1.2 Stimuli and Task 88
 4.1.3 Procedure 91
 4.1.4 fMRI Data Acquisition and Preprocessing 93
 4.1.5 fMRI Data Analysis 94
4.2 Results 96

4.2.1 Behavioral Data	96
4.2.2 fMRI Result	98
4.3 Discussion	109
4.3.1 Cortical Area Involved in Phrasal Segmentation	110
4.3.2 Cortical Area Involved in Semantic Violations	115
4.4 Summary	118

Chapter 5 Search for Phrasal Segmentation: Auditory fMRI Study — 121

5.1 fMRI Experiment	122
5.1.1 Participants	122
5.1.2 Stimuli and Task	122
5.1.3 Procedure	125
5.1.4 fMRI Data Acquisition and Preprocessing	128
5.1.5 fMRI Data Analysis	129
5.2 Results	131
5.2.1 Behavioral Data	131
5.2.2 fMRI Result	133
5.3 Discussion	144
5.3.1 Cortical Area Involved in Phrasal Segmentation	145
5.3.2 Cortical Area Involved in Semantic Violations	148
5.4 Summary	150

Chapter 6 What Happens with Phrasal Segmentation in the Brain, Then? — 153

6.1 Phrasal Segmentation in the Brain	154
6.1.1 Effect of Phrasal Segmentation in the Brain	154
6.1.2 Nature of Phrasal Segmentation in the Brain	157

6.2 What is Phrasal Segmentation?   160
6.3 Summary   168

Chapter 7 Conclusion   169
7.1 Concluding Remarks   169
7.2 Summary   173

References   177
Appendix A: List of Sentence Stimuli   195
Appendix B: Sample List of Stimulus Presentation
         (Event Related Design)   203
日本語の読者のための内容紹介   213
Index   227

Preface

Language is unique to humans. We have the gift of language in the brain. As speakers of language, we produce and understand language. Words, phrases and sentences support and reflect our ability to produce and understand language. Sentences are made up of words and phrases. Words and phrases are sequenced into sentences. In production, we build up sentences by combining words and phrases. In comprehension, we understand the meaning of sentences that are made up of words and phrases. We are further able to decompose each sentence into words and phrases, and at the same time, we are able to take out the meaning of individual words and phrases in each sentence. We have such ability of language in the brain.

This book takes up the issue of how the human brain copes with language when we produce and understand sentences. Among others, this book places our major focus of the study on the ability of how we group words into phrases, and how we decompose each sentence into phrases. We intuitively know how to group individual words together into phrases within a sentence. We are also able to intuitively detect individual phrases within a sentence. In production, we do not build up a sentence at one time from individual words. In comprehension, we do not understand each sentence at one time from each individual word. Rather, it is likely that, using phrases, we group individual words into a sentence when we produce and understand each sentence. Phrases seem to serve as the intervening units to group individual words into a sentence. This book investigates the role of phrases during sentence comprehension.

To understand the meaning of a sentence, we do not place a word boundary one by one within a sentence and work out the meaning of each word one at a time. Instead, we intuitively group each word into phrases. However, we do not group words in a sentence in haphazard, arbitrary ways. We group each word into grammatically structured, meaningful phrasal units, although we have never learned the way to group words in such ways. We intuitively do such phrasal grouping correctly in grammar and meaning. For instance, in comprehension, we never group the words, 'a', 'beautiful', and 'city', into 'a beautiful' and 'city'. We usually group these words into the phrase of 'a beautiful city'. We can group words in a sentence properly into phrases. We can also detect each phrase within a sentence in proper manners. We can do such grouping of words and detecting of phrases as our ability of language.

Then, how and where do we carry out such grouping and detecting? To answer this question, we need to investigate the processing behaviors in the brain. This book tackles the issue of how and where the processing operation of grouping words and detecting phrases is executed in the brain, using functional magnetic resonance imaging (fMRI) techniques. Therefore, the aim of this book is to investigate how and where that processing operation is instantiated in the brain in the course of sentence comprehension.

In this book, we refer to the processing operation of grouping words and detecting phrases in a sentence as phrasal segmentation. Prior to starting our study, we set up two goals of the study of phrasal segmentation in the following. The first goal is to explore the neural substrates of phrasal segmentation during sentence comprehension. The second goal is to argue possible roles of phrasal segmentation to sentence processing, in particular, for further discussion to create proper models of sentence processing. In addition, in the course of our study, this book introduces necessary information to start the study of language in the brain, showing and explaining the terms and the techniques of brain imaging. This book is also an attempt to contribute our study to researchers who are interested in language research, using brain imaging.

Acknowledgements

The idea for this book started about ten years ago. At that time, I had a chance to visit Professor Naoyuki Ono, a distinguished scholar of linguistics and also my mentor when I was doing my master work. He kindly suggested to me to start my PhD work in Tohoku University in Sendai. I was wondering whether I could continue my PhD work, because my work place was in Kochi at that time, far in the south from Sendai. Finally, I decided to start my PhD work there. In my first year of my study, Professor Tadao Miyamoto came back to Japan from University of Victoria, Canada, as a specialist of psycholinguistics and he became my supervisor of my PhD work. Professor Takeshi Nakamoto, a specialist of phonology and linguistics, and Professor Heiko Narrog, a specialist of Japanese linguistics, kindly supported my PhD work in Sendai. There I decided to conduct research to investigate unresolved human linguistic behaviors.

In the autumn of my first year in Sendai, I had an opportunity to visit the laboratory of Professor Ryuta Kawashima, a prominent, pioneering scholar and a great contributor in the neuroimaging study in Japan, and to know the research using fMRI. Professor Ryuta Kawashima kindly supported my research in his laboratory. There I joined the research team of Professor Motoaki Sugiura, a well-known scientist of neuroimaging. Dr. Yuko Sassa and Dr. Hyeonjeong Jeong, the senior members of the team, kindly and patiently helped my research step by step until midnight. Professor Motoaki Sugiura coached me on the methods and techniques of brain imaging studies with patience and eagerness. Actually, I was a sheer layman in the research field of brain imaging when I started my study. I needed a lot of effort to continue my research. However, my stay in Sendai was enjoyable and I met a lot of respectable people there. When I became unsure of my study, many people cheered me up for my continuing research work. My supervisor, Professor Tadao Miyamoto, patiently and kindly, watched over my study and I benefited enormously from his cordial, enlightening comments and advice through my work. Professor Wanner Peter John, as a specialist of psycholinguistics, patiently read through my work and gave me insightful comments and advice. I was surrounded by a rich and fulfilling environment in which I could pursue my work. Also, the support from the members of the department of linguistic communication is greatly acknowledged. Thus, my PhD work in Sendai owes a great deal to overwhelmingly warm and kind people.

However, because of my laziness, it took another several years to publish my work after I finished my study in Sendai. The idea to publish my PhD study took its shape from a lovely, enjoyable lunchtime conversation with Professor Ken-ichi Takami, Professor Fuminori Matsubara, and Professor Shizuya Tara in Kochi. Professor Ken-ichi Takami, a world-renowned linguist, kindly encouraged me to publish my PhD work. I deeply appreciate Professor Ken-ichi Takami to give me great courage to publish this book. In addition, I am deeply indebted to the colleagues and staffs in Shiga University for assisting and supporting me in the completion of this work. I am greatly privileged to have the colleagues and staffs at the same working place in Shiga.

Finally, it has been a great pleasure to work with the people at Hituzi Press. I especially want to thank my editor Isao Matsumoto and my editorial assistant Eri Ebisawa at Hituzi Press for their every warm effort and kind help in making this book. Lastly, I am grateful to my family, Ritsu, Sao, and Kaoru, for their tolerance and understanding of my continuing my work and publishing this book. A final word of gratitude must go to all the people I introduced here. Any deficiencies are of course my responsibility. In particular, I apologize to anyone whose work I have failed to cite or cite sufficiently in spite of its relevance to this book.

Chapter 1

Introduction

In a sentence, words are structured together into phrases, and phrases are organized together into a sentence. In sentence comprehension, people have the ability to perceive phrasal units from a string of words in a sentence, deducing their syntactic organization and structure. The present study aims at the clarification of the perceptive behavior of phrases, which is referred to as the phrasal segmentation, from the perspective of neuropsychology. Eventually, this study seeks to investigate and understand the issue of how the phrasal segmentation is instantiated in the brain, using functional brain imaging techniques.

This study is a neuropsychological approach to bridging the gap between human behaviors and underlying neural events through the measurement of changes in brain blood flow during mental activities by using the task of functional brain imaging (fMRI). This premise is on the basis of the neuropsychological fact that brain circulation changes selectively with neural activity and quantitative changes in regional blood flow in the brain are related directly to brain function (Raichle, 2006). Functional brain imaging techniques provide the opportunity to observe and validate real-time in vivo mental activities such as perceptions, memory, language, emotions, skill learning, and human development. By adopting functional brain imaging techniques, this study seeks to identify the network of regions of the brain and their relationship to the performance associated with the task of current interest, with particular focus on the mental activities of segmentation of heard and read phrasal units during sentence comprehension. This study further argues possible contributions to theories and models of language processing through the systematic investigation of key areas driven by the task in the healthy human brain.

1.1 Segmentation Problem: its Issues

As speakers of language, people have sensitivity to words and phrases (Anderson, 2000; Gleitman, 1986; Pinker, 2000). Linguistically, words and phrases are defined as linguistic units that constitute a sentence. Words are grouped into phrases, and phrases are grouped into a sentence. However, words and phrases emerge as continuously connected strings in speech. Usually, they are not separated by spaces or slashes. Nevertheless, people have no difficulty decomposing such continuous strings and discerning the boundaries of individual words and phrases in a sentence. People intuitively know that a sentence is not analyzed as simply a sequence of words and phrases, but rather it is regarded as certain ordered strings of words and phrases governed by regularities of language (Jackendoff, 2002; Lasnik, 1995; Pinker, 1999). The problem of how people detect such linguistic units as words and phrases as ordered strings in a sentence is referred to as the segmentation problem (Cutler, 1994; Ingram, 2007; Saffran, Newport, et al., 1996). The behavior of detecting words and phrases in a sentence is referred to as the segmentation of words and phrases in a sentence. The present study investigates and argues the problem and the behavior of segmentation using functional magnetic resonance imaging (fMRI).

In order to solve the segmentation problem, considerable attempts have been undertaken with a long history of study (see, Cutler et al., 1997, for an extensive review of the previous studies). However, most studies have converged on two aspects of its process: the way of how people can find and recognize individual units of words from strings of words (word level segmentation, henceforth word segmentation), and the way of how people can chunk and group individual units of words into phrased units of words (phrase level segmentation, henceforth phrasal segmentation). In both levels of the studies, it has been assumed that the segmentation of words and phrases is performed with the assistance of prosodic information such as stress, rhythm and intonation (Cutler, 1999; Cutler et al. 1997; Ingram, 2007). The stress patterns and the statistical regularities of syllable occurrence have been mainly thought to support the word segmentation. The prosodic patterns of relative prominence of the sentence constituents are primarily involved in phrasal segmentation. The hypothesis that people use prosodic information to solve the segmentation problem is called prosodic bootstrapping (Ingram, 2007).

At the word level, in the studies of psycholinguistics, from the observation of the phenomena that pre-verbal infants are attempting to segment speech into words or word-like chunks, researchers have proposed that people may employ prosodic features of language to solve a search of word boundaries (Cutler, 1990; Friederici & Wessels, 1993; Jusczyk & Aslin, 1995; Jusczyk et al., 1999; Saffran, Aslin, et al., 1996). On the basis of this proposal, several behavioral studies have shown that infants and adults predict word boundaries from prosodic information such as the stress patterns and the statistical regularities of syllable occurrence (Curtin et al., 2005; Johnson & Jusczyk, 2001; Johnson et al., 2003; Shukla et al., 2007).

In a similar way, in the studies of neurophysiology and neuroimaging, by adapting the same paradigm from the psycholinguistic studies, research has been conducted on the on-line ability to extract individual words from continuous word strings. Neurophysiological research using event-related brain potentials (ERPs) has provided evidence from the brain responses of on-line segmentation that the stress patterns and the statistical regularities of syllable occurrence are employed to detect individual words from speech streams (Cunillera, Gomila, et al., 2008; Cunillera, Toro, et al., 2006; Kooijman et al., 2005; Sanders & Neville, 2003; Sanders et al., 2002) and letter strings (Carreiras et al., 2005). Neuroimaging research using fMRI has also shown evidence of the exploitation of prosodic information while looking for word boundaries (McNealy et al., 2006). At the word level, empirical evidence has justified the proposal in the process of segmentation for explaining the behaviors of assigning boundaries by prosodic information.

However, above the word level, the prosodic bootstrapping hypothesis does not sufficiently account for the problem and the behavior of segmentation. A number of studies have empirically pointed out that people do not exclusively use prosodic information to gain evidence about identifying syntactic phrase boundaries: every syntactic phrase boundary is not reliably signaled by prosodic information such as rhythm and intonation (Bybee, 2001; Chomsky & Halle, 1968; Inkelas & Zec, 1990; Jackendoff, 1987; Pinker, 1987; Selkirk, 1984).

To see how this might happen, consider the following examples. The assignment of prosodic phrase boundaries to a sentence basically depends on the way the sentence is segmented into intonational phrases, in which words are grouped together into phrases by their rhythmic and durational properties as well as their tonal pitch (Frazier et al., 2006). The sentences illustrated in (1a) and (1b) show that intonational units of the sentence (1a) correspond to syntactic units of the sentence (1b).

(1) a. [Angela] [gesticulated].   (two intonational units)
     b. [Angela] [gesticulated].   (two syntactic units)
        [Noun Phrase] [Verb Phrase]

However, in another different case, no segmentation can be assigned into the same sentence, as indicated in the sentence (1c).

(1) c. [Angela gesticulated].   (one intonational unit)

Another example is the sentences (2a) and (2b), where prosodic segmentation is produced in conflict with syntactic segmentation, when a sentence is segmented into the full set of phrasal constituents.

(2) a. [The man in the yellow coat] [gesticulated].
                                          (two intonational units)
      b. [The man] [in the yellow coat] [gesticulated].
                                          (three syntactic units)
           [Noun Phrase] [Prepositional Phrase] [Verb Phrase]

The following example also shows the inconsistency between the intonational and the syntactic structure, as provided by the sentences (3a) and (3b) (Chomsky & Halle, 1968).

(3) a. This is the cat [that caught the rat [that stole the cheese]].
                                 (two intonational units in the predicate)
      b. This is [the cat [that caught [the rat [that stole [the cheese]]]]].
                                 (five syntactic units in the predicate)

Thus, the examples show that the correlation between prosody and syntax is not perfect: the intonational units of a sentence do not correspond to syntactic units of the sentence.

The problem is due to the fact that prosodic phrase boundaries do not necessarily coincide with syntactic phrase boundaries: a certain string is segmented into a prosodic phrase that conforms to a syntactic phrase, while another similar string is not (Bybee, 2001; Inkelas & Zec, 1990; Pinker, 1987). As the examples indicate, prosodic information does not exactly specify phrase boundaries. Except some obligatory cases such as at the end of a sentence or after a preceding subordinate clause, syntactic structures do not necessarily require prosodic boundaries.

Rather, empirical evidence has indicated that there is considerable optionality in how a sentence can be prosodically phrased (Frazier et al., 2004; Frazier et al., 2006; Schafer, et al., 2000). In a linguistic sense, a sentence can be freely divided into prosodic phrases, as long as the resulting phrases are semantically coherent and they do not conflict with syntactic phrase boundaries or they do not break up a syntactic phrase (Jackendoff; 1987; Selkirk, 1984). In a behavioral sense, the correlation between prosodic and syntactic units is not perfect, and prosodic information is not sufficient to assign every syntactic phrase boundary positions (Beckman & Edwards, 1990; Ferreira, 1993; Gerken et al., 1994; Suci, 1967). Thus, above the word level, there exists the disparity between prosodic phrasing and syntactic phrasing, which makes it difficult to deal with the segmentation problem.

Therefore, in order to circumvent the issue of this inconsistency in segmentation above the word level, researchers have mainly focused their attention on the perception of larger units, in which prosody and syntax coincide. In the perceptive behaviors of these larger units, prosody has reflected major syntactic constituents as in the form of clauses and sentences, which are closest in size to intonational phrases as phonological units. Using these perceptive phrasing units as the experimental stimuli, a number of researchers have attempted to explain the issue of segmentation above the word level in different fields: psycholinguistics (Christophe et al., 2003; Clifton et al., 2002), neurophysiology using ERPs (Pannekamp et al., 2005; Steinhauer et al., 1999; Steinhauer & Friederici, 2001; Van Pattern & Bloom, 1999) and neuroimaging using fMRI (Ischebeck et al., 2008). As a consequence of their experimental studies, the researchers have showed that there is a possible mediating role for such larger prosodic units in grouping individual words into a set of perceptual units in sentence processing.

Yet, beyond the word level, these studies still have not successfully specified the perceptive behaviors of how people group words into phrases and how we segment sentences into their constituents, and also they have not explained the on-line ability well enough that underlies these behaviors. On the contrary, other different empirical studies have confirmed that people show a stronger preference and sensitivity to syntactic boundaries than to prosodic boundaries, when decisions are made to phrase connected strings of words into the individual phrasal constituents within a sentence (Geers, 1978; Wingfield, 1975). Their evidence shows indications that the perceptive behaviors of segmentation into phrases are determined primarily based on syntactic phrasal boundaries given by syntactic structure. These predictions are certainly the case with written language, where prosodic information is entirely missing, as well as spoken language. So far, the results of previous studies of segmentation above the word level have temporarily suggested that prosodic information plays a supporting role, rather than a leading role, for segmenting the group of words into the phrasal constituents in a sentence.

Currently, the prosodic bootstrapping hypothesis does not seem to hold true for the segmentation behaviors above the word level, at least, at the minor phrase level (i.e., at the syntactic phrase level), even though it can explain the phrasing behaviors partially at the level of larger syntactic unit such as clauses and sentences. Thus, despite all the indications that prosodic information has some influence on the sensitivities of phrase boundaries, exactly how phrasal segmentation is implemented is still a matter of considerable debate, especially, within the overall design of sentence processing.

The disparity of units between prosodic phrasing and syntactic phrasing seems to make it more difficult to clarify and specify the issue of segmentation above the word level than to explain the same issue at the word level. Indeed, at the phrase level, research into phrasal segmentation has been limited to date. There have been only a few behavioral studies that have dealt with the issue in particular attention to the relationship between the behaviors of segmentation and the perception of syntactic units (Aaronson & Scarborough, 1977; Gee & Grosjean, 1983). However, these studies have not clearly illustrated the behaviors of phrasal segmentation and their underlying mental activities. For now, the segmentation problem above the word level has not been settled, in particular, at the phrase level, and appears to be still an unresolved question. The segmentation problem at the phrase level seems to remain subject to further close scrutiny.

1.2 Goals Achieved

To the knowledge, there is no attempt in the field of neurophysiology and brain imaging so far that seeks to directly investigate the on-line processing behaviors of phrasal segmentation and their underlying neural correlates. The present study, hence, attempts to do the following:

1. To directly investigate the on-line processing operation of phrasal segmentation and its underlying neural correlates, using fMRI techniques, and ultimately to clarify the processing domain and region of phrasal segmentation in the brain.
2. To characterize the on-line processing operation of phrasal segmentation within the overall framework of sentence comprehension by arguing its position in theories and models of sentence processing (i.e., serial vs. parallel theories and models of sentence processing).

In the present study, in order to accomplish the task, two sets of fMRI experiments have been carried out, particularly focusing on the issue of the perceptive behaviors of grouping words into phrases and segmenting strings of words into constituents of a sentence in the course of on-line sentence comprehension. The experiments have been conducted with two different modalities in the same experimental paradigm: one is the experiment of phrasal segmentation in the visual sentence comprehension task and the other is the experiment in the auditory sentence comprehension task. The present study hypothesized that if phrasal segmentation is universally associated with language processing, the similar cortical areas and networks will be activated independently of the input modality (visual in reading comprehension and aural in speech comprehension); if it is not so, the activations will become an inconsistent relationship between the two different modalities of the study.

1.3 Direction of the Study

In the following subsection, the study will offer a glimpse at the direction the present study is taking.

To closely look into the processing behaviors of phrasal segmentation and its neural substrates, the study has schemed and implemented fMRI experiments of phrasal segmentation with two different modalities: the visual experiment and the auditory experiment of phrasal segmentation. In the visual experiment of phrasal segmentation, in designing the task, Japanese Kana sentences were adopted as the stimuli to control the involvement of prosodic information in segmentation. Japanese has the regular metric structure described by the subsyllabic unit, the mora (Cutler & Otake, 1994; Otake et al., 1993). In Japanese language, the speech stream and hence the words can be phonologically segmented and chunked by every unit of the mora. For instance, the word *toori* (street) has three morae: *to-o-ri*. Each mora in that word is shown by the following vowel and consonant sounds: [CV]-[V]-[CV]. Further, each mora is represented by the Japanese phonogram, Kana, with one-to-one correspondence. For example, the word *toori* consists of three Kana characters: とおり (*to-o-ri*). Phonologically, each mora can be separated freely between any boundaries. Therefore, segmental cues to signal word boundaries can be equally controlled at each mora (Inagaki et al., 2000).

However, there is an exception to such one-to-one correspondence between mora and Kana. Japanese language has a group of palatalized consonants, which are known as the contracted sounds, [CjV] (or [CCV]). For example, the word *kyaku* (guest) has two morae: *kya-ku* ([CjV]-[CV]), while the same word is made up of three Kana characters: きゃく. The word has the different correspondence status in phonology and phonogram. In きゃく (*kyaku*), きゃ (*kya*) and く (*ku*) respectively correspond to each mora. Thus, the word constitutes two mora units with three Kana characters. As for the issue of whether the basic linguistic unit for the segmentation is letter-based or mora-based in Japanese, a number of experimental studies have demonstrated that the mora is recognized as the basic segmentation unit in reading as well as in speech (Dairoku, 1995; Inagaki et al., 2000). Hence, the present study adopted the mora as the basic linguistic unit for the segmentation. In the experiment, not the number of Kana but the number of morae was controlled to equalize the segmenting effect of each mora in each sentence stimulus: the number of the morae was equally justified into 15 mora pieces.

In the visual experiment, the stimuli were visually presented in Japanese Kana in the form of Japanese canonical basic simple sentences. In choosing the sentence stimuli, the canonical simple sentences of Japanese were selected for the task stimuli to control the possible effects of the processing demands dues to the difference of sentence structure. As for the issue of the sentence structure influence on sentence processing, research has found that people are sensitive to the canonical sentences of their languages, which promote their correct grasp of syntactic relations, when processing sentences (Caplan, 1987).

In the auditory experiment of phrasal segmentation, the same task design was adopted as the task design employed in the visual experiment of phrasal segmentation. Except that the auditory stimuli carried prosodic information, the same task design was introduced between the visual and auditory experiments. The difference of the modality in the task design was motivated by the desire to investigate whether the mental operation of phrasal segmentation would be influenced by the difference between the visual and auditory sentence comprehension tasks or not. Consequently, two sets of the fMRI experiments were carried out under the different modality conditions to investigate and compare the neural basis of phrasal segmentation in the course of written and spoken Japanese sentence comprehension.

The present study attempts to explain localization of the neural correlates involved in phrasal segmentation and the governing factors of phrasal segmentation. Therefore, the fMRI experiments compare neural activation during sentence comprehension between two different conditions: the segmented and the non-segmented condition. In the segmented condition, phrasal boundaries were spaced visually or paused auditorily noticeably, and in the non-segmented condition, no noticeable phrasal boundaries were provided visually or auditorily. When the sentence comprehension task was performed, it was hypothesized that the on-line processing of phrasal segmentation would be more strongly reflected in the non-segmented condition than in the segmented condition. Figure 1.1 shows examples of sentence stimuli presented in the non-segmented and the segmented condition of the visual experiment of phrasal segmentation.

In the auditory experiment, stimuli were aurally presented in the similar manner in the two different conditions. By comparing the neural activities shown in fMRI signal's difference between the two conditions, two of the

> **Non-segmented sentence stimulus:**
> おばがおじにでんごんをつたえた
> (o-ba-ga-o-zi-ni-de-N-go-N-o-tu-ta-e-ta)
> (aunt-Nom uncle-Dat message-Acc delivered)
> (My aunt delivered the message to my uncle.)
>
> **Segmented sentence stimulus:**
> おとこが　かべに　らくがきを　かいた
> (o-to-ko-ga　ka-be-ni　ra-ku-ga-ki-o　ka-i-ta)
> (man-Nom　wall-Loc　graffiti-Acc　wrote)
> (The man wrote graffiti on the wall.)

Figure 1.1. Examples of sentence stimuli: Non-segmented sentence vs. Segmented sentence.

experiments will make it possible to directly investigate the on-line processing behaviors and the neural correlates of phrasal segmentation. In doing so, the present study will finally aim for the clarification and the explanation of properties and factors of neural computation that underlie the processing operation of phrasal segmentation. Then, the study will further argue the on-line properties of phrasal segmentation in sentence comprehension, discussing their connection to theories and models of language processing, through the systematic investigation of key areas driven by the task in the healthy human brain.

1.4 Relevance to the Field

In neurophysiology as well as linguistic and psycholinguistic studies, it has been generally agreed that three distinct sources of linguistic information are invoked in human language processing: phonological, semantic, and syntactic information (Démonet et al., 2005; Friederici, 2002; Hagoort, 2008; Harley, 2001; Jackendoff, 1992). Most commonly, it is acknowledged that the three different forms of linguistic information contribute to human language processing. During the comprehension of language, linguistic information is processed and integrated in a particular way in order for the meaning of a sentence to be obtained. However, the issue has still remained unresolved on how available linguistic information becomes integrated and unified into an interpretation of a sentence, especially under the conflict of the explanation provided by serial vs. parallel perspective of sentence processing (Friederici, 2002; Hagoort, 2003b). In terms of the segmentation problem, the issues have not been solved on how individually segmented words are grouped into several sets of phrases and on how these phrases are combined and create a meaningful sentence.

Empirical evidence has indicated that people process a sentence phrase by phrase. When people produce a sentence they generate it a phrase at a time. When they comprehend a sentence they pause at each phrase and put a boundary between the phrases. The behavior is extensively observed by a number of studies of sentence generation and comprehension (Boomer, 1965; Gee & Grosjean, 1983; Grosjean et al., 1979, in sentence generation; Aaronson & Scarborough, 1977; Jarvella, 1971; Just & Carpenter, 1980, in sentence comprehension). The results of these studies suggest that the phrase is the semantic unit of the sentence as well as the structural unit of the sentence. These studies have pointed out that the phrasal unit plays a key role in the production and comprehension of the sentence. However, in what way and to what extent the unit is involved in sentence processing has remained unknown so far.

The present study will give primarily attention to the study of mental activities concerning phrasal segmentation during sentence comprehension. This study deals with the neuropsychological point of view by introducing brain imaging techniques. Thus, the primary objective of the study is to clarify how the phrasal segmentation is instantiated during sentence comprehension. It will investigate brain activity involved in phrasal segmentation through auditory and visual sentence comprehension of Japanese. In so doing, the study tries to shed the light on the on-line processing properties of phrasal segmentation in sentence comprehension. In order to closely investigate the neural correlates concerning phrasal segmentation, two sets of experiments were conducted by employing the techniques of the fMRI study. These fMRI experiments were carried out to identify which brain regions would be specifically implicated in phrasal segmentation by the systematic comparison of the brain regions engaged in the sentence comprehension task. Hence, this research seeks to explore the neural correlates underlying the behaviors of phrasal segmentation and to clarify the on-line mechanism in question. Then, based on the research results, this study argues the on-line properties of phrasal segmentation in sentence comprehension. Finally, this study provides arguments for possible solutions to the unresolved issues regarding phrasal segmentation and sentence comprehension stated earlier in this section (see, Section 1.1), in the hope that this research attempt gives a new perspective on the issues of phrasal segmentation. Thus, the present study contributes to the construction of theories and models about sentence processing.

1.5   Limitations and Delimitations

The present study explores the brain mechanisms regarding phrasal segmentation in order to investigate unresolved issues of phrasal segmentation. In this regard, the following sections will present the limitations and the delimitations of the study. In the limitations of the study, a statement on the methodological constraints of the study is introduced, giving considerations to the philosophy behind the experimental design of functional neuroimaging. In the delimitations of the study, specification of the scope of the inquiry and the approach the study takes throughout the present study are presented.

1.5.1 Limitations of the Study: Methodological Constraints

The present study deals with the issue of phrasal segmentation by introducing functional neuroimaging techniques. Functional neuroimaging is the techniques that investigate brain function by measuring signal changes in functional brain activation associated with a number of specific stimuli and tasks of interest (Raichle, 2006). However, brain activation in a particular brain area usually depends on many factors. In functional neuroimaging, for controlling potential confounds of these factors and extracting informative activation to make use of, brain activation is measured on the basis of the subtraction method (Culham, 2006). Brain activation levels in one condition are usually considered relative to another condition rather than considering the absolute level of signal on its own. Thus, functional neuroimaging research generally measures the difference in activation rather than the absolute levels of brain activations per se.

Methodologically, the subtraction method requires the two different conditions that differ in only one critical component of processing, usually either in the stimulus or the task (Culham, 2006). As a consequence, neuroimaging research must focus more narrowly on the issue of one particular aspect of processing between the two conditions to be compared. In a similar vein, the present research has focused on the issue of phrasal segmentation of only one aspect of processing operations during the sentence comprehension task: the issues of the processing of phrasal segmentation in the comparison conditions between the non-segmented and the segmented conditions (see, Figure. 1.1).

Neuroimaging techniques make it possible to identify the neural activity that underlies a number of different human cognitive behaviors, showing which specific brain areas will be differentially activated. The temptation is always to include as many conditions as possible to expect meaningful activation in the data. However, poorly considered experiments without optimizing the design may fail to find any possible outcomes about the process in question (Culham, 2006). With this admonition in mind, the research will seek out a list of areas in which significant activation differences are observed in the mental operations of the performance of phrasal segmentation.

1.5.2 Delimitations of the Study:
Scope of Inquiry and Approach to the Study

The primary concern of the present study is with the mental activity of phrasal segmentation during sentence comprehension. This study seeks to investigate the links between the segmentation behavior of phrase and the brain mechanisms underlying the behavior, hoping to provide insight into the study of sentence processing. Above all, this study focuses on the functional brain mechanisms of phrasal segmentation in sentence comprehension. In this study, two sets of fMRI experiments were conducted to explore the mechanisms of phrasal segmentation. To avoid overlapping and confounding with other processing operations concerning sentence processing, the experiments were designed to more stringently control the comparison conditions such as those implicated in the stimulus, the task, and the procedure of the experiment. We will also add the control conditions in the separate sessions in the experiment to control the possible influence of other factors such as working memory constraints subject to the finite processing resources.

Therefore, the current focus of the inquiry is on the study of mental processing activity per se while phrasal segmentation is being performed during sentence comprehension. The task-induced brain activity will be directly observed and compared with the functional brain imaging techniques. The resulting imaging data will be evaluated and considered to clarify the brain mechanisms of phrasal segmentation. Then, the outcomes of the studies will be argued to generate plausible hypotheses of phrasal segmentation in sentence comprehension in the light of the neuropsychological understanding of the principles of the brain function. Finally, this study aims to adequately explain and specify the processing of phrasal segmentation.

As described earlier, it is commonly acknowledged that phrasal segmentation is the processing operation associated with sentence processing. Still at present, the relationship between phrasal segmentation and sentence comprehension, it is not clear in the studies of neurophysiology as well as psycholinguistics as reviewed in Section 1.1 and Section 1.2 in the present chapter. Phrasal segmentation is assumed to be based on linguistic sources of information. However, no attempt has been made to adequately explain phrasal segmentation thus far, addressing the issue based on an explicit model and a theory of language processing.

Usually, linguists and psycholinguists first define the criteria that an adequate theory of language has to meet in the form of a model and hypothesis. Then, they provide the data that are of relevance for specifications of their model and hypothesis to claim their adequacy. However, in the present study, it is not possible to adopt such a standard approach just as in regular studies of linguistics and psycholinguistics due to the limited previous studies of phrasal segmentation. An alternative is an approach that first focuses on well-established areas of language processing defined by their functional responses, and then evaluates activation in these areas independently to test a new hypothesis about the processing of phrasal segmentation. This approach employed is known as the region of interest (ROI) approach, one of the main approaches in neuroimaging studies (Culham, 2006). Thus, this study will first confirm the predictions that phrasal segmentation is one of the processing operations associated with sentence processing on the basis of anatomical criteria. Next, this study will test whether there is reliable activation for a particular comparison. The underlying assumption is that there is a systematic relationship between phrasal segmentation and sentence processing.

1.6 Definition of Terms

The following subsections will make explicit the definition of the terms used in a special or a technical sense in the present study. The meanings of the terms are explained and made clear. The terms that follow are listed in alphabetical order and their heading is shown in bold.

Blood-oxygenation-level-dependent (BOLD) response

It reflects the concentration of deoxygenated hemoglobin, blood flow, and blood volume. Increased neuronal activity leads to increased oxygen consumption, and hence to changes in BOLD response, which cause changes in magnetic differences between oxygenated and deoxygenated blood associated with regional changes in neural activity in the brain (Ogawa & Lee, 1990; Ogawa, Tank, et al., 1992). Thereby, BOLD response is used as a measure that indexes neuronal activity called BOLD signal for fMRI experiments.

Electroencephalography (EEG)

Electroencephalography (EEG) is the technique to measure the neuronal electrical fields at the scalp. It allows a registration of the brain's neuronal activity in the millisecond by measuring the patterns of electrical activity at the scalp (see, Kutas & Van Petten, 1994; Kutas et al., 2006). By using detectors outside the surface of the scalp, it assesses electrical activity of the brain.

Event related design

Event related design is a recently developed standard experimental design used in functional neuroimaging studies. It allows each trial of the stimuli to present in an unpredictable, randomized order. It enables the intermixed and the rapid presentation of trials of various types. Trials can be time-locked and averaged to extract the common signal change related to the event. Trials can also be categorized by subjects' performance across stimuli of various types. A sample of the event related design, which was used for the fMRI experiments in the present study, is listed in Appendix B.

Event related brain potential (ERP)

Event related brain potential (ERP) represents the electrical activity of the brain correlated with a particular stimulus event. It can vary as a function of a particular cognitive process in its latency, its polarity, its amplitude, and its topological distribution. The summation of the potentials registered at the surface of the scalp reflects the summation of post synaptic activities of neurons. Perceptual and cognitive regularities are mirrored in the modulations of electrical activity referred to as the event related brain potential (ERP) (see, Kutas & Van Petten, 1994; Kutas et al., 2006). The ERP has been used to investigate temporal aspects of information processing in the human brain, but it does not allow direct conclusions concerning the location of neural activities (Friederici, 1999).

The ERP waveform of voltage (i.e., amplitude of electrical potential) plotted against post-stimulus time usually consists of a series of positive and negative peaks. The ERP peaks are often labeled according to their polarity (negative [N] or positive [P]) and latency in milliseconds relative to stimulus onset (e.g., N100, P230, P300). Sometimes, the labels signify a functional description (e.g., mismatch negativity [MMN]) or its most reliable scalp location (e.g., left anterior negativity [LAN]) (see, Kutas & Van Petten, 1994; Kutas et al., 2006). On occasion, these ERP labels are used to denote the ERP components. In this case, the component refers to a particular ERP response evoked by the processing of any external stimulus over a period of time.

Neurophysiological studies using the event related brain potentials (ERPs) have been known as the main approach to investigate the temporal structure of the processing of linguistic information by registering the brain's reaction. ERP components called P600 (positivity at approximately 600ms from the onset), LAN (the left anterior negativity) and ELAN (the early left anterior negativity) are typically known for the components sensitive to syntactic manipulations, while negative ERP component called N400 (negativity at approximately 400ms from the onset) is well recognized as the component sensitive to semantic associate (Kutas et al., 1999).

The term ERP also sometimes refers to one of the electrophysiological methods for measuring the brain activity associated with human perceptive and cognitive functioning by recording the scalp electrical activity.

Functional neuroimaging (Functional brain imaging)

Functional neuroimaging (Functional brain imaging) is the approach of neuroimaging to understand the functional organization of the normal human brain underlying the human activity. Using PET (positron emission tomography) and fMRI, it seeks to relate the normal human behavior to the normal human brain function, to bridge the gap between descriptions of the human behavior and the underlying neural event, and to explain the human brain and its relationship to the human behavior.

Functional magnetic resonance imaging (fMRI)

Functional magnetic resonance imaging (fMRI) is the noninvasive neuroimaging method that enables functional exploration of the normal human brain with resolution at a fine spatial scale. It is observed that brain activity is associated with changes in blood oxygenation. By combining this observation with another observation that changing the amount of oxygen carried by hemoglobin changes the degree to which hemoglobin disturbs a magnetic field, it was demonstrated that in vivo changes in blood oxygenation could be detected as the MRI signal known as the blood-oxygen-level-dependent (BOLD) signal (Ogawa, Lee, et al., 1990). Later it was also demonstrated that BOLD signal changes in normal humans during functional brain activation (Bandettini et al., 1992; Ogawa, Tank et al., 1992). Using these findings, functional magnetic resonance imaging has been introduced into functional neuroimaging studies.

Magnetoencephalography (MEG)
Magnetoencephalography (MEG) is the technique to measure the neuronal magnetic fields at the scalp. The magnetic fields are generated by electric currents of the active neurons. The MEG makes it possible to record the neuronal magnetic signals in much the same way as the EEG, preserving the same temporal resolution as the neuronal electrical signals (see, Kutas & Van Petten, 1994; Kutas et al., 2006).

Magnetic event related field (MERF)/ Evoked magnetic field (EMF)
Magnetic event related field (MERF)/ Evoked magnetic field (EMF) refer to the averaged MEG responses adjusted to a particular stimulus event. The MERF/EMF peaks are often labeled according to their latency in milliseconds relative to stimulus onset (e.g., M170, M250, M300). Since bone is magnetically transparent, it is easier to estimate the location of the MERF/EMF source; in contrast, the ERP is sensitive to variations in skull thickness and electrical conductivity. The measurement of the MERF/EMF is one of the noninvasive methods that present the best combination of spatial and temporal resolution. However, the studies measuring the MERF/EMF are not very common, because the recording devices (superconducting quantum inference device [SQUID]) are expensive and not widely introduced to date (see, Kutas & Van Petten, 1994; Kutas et al., 2006).

Neuroimaging (Brain imaging)
Neuroimaging (Brain imaging) is the technique that permits us to monitor

human brain function in a safe yet increasingly detailed and quantitative way, using strategies to map local changes in brain circulation and metabolism associated with changes in brain cellular activity (Raichle, 2006). Particularly, positron emission tomography (PET) and magnetic resonance imaging (MRI) are known as main approaches to neuroimaging studies.

Optical topography (OT)
Optical topography (OT) is one of the brain imaging techniques to investigate neural functioning. OT uses smaller and less invasive devices than scanning devices such as PET and fMRI. OT devices emit infrared light at different wavelengths over the scalp. Then, changes in blood flow are estimated by changes in the reflected infrared wavelengths in a manner comparable with changes in blood oxygenation in fMRI (Strangman et al., 2002). OT recording is relatively limited to superficial cortical areas below the scalp.

Parsing (Syntactic parsing)
Parsing (Syntactic parsing) is a processing or a stage in the processing of written or spoken language at which people compute the syntactic structure of the sentence. In the course of sentence processing, every human being is required to analyze the grammatical structure of the sentence and to determine and assign the syntactic structure to a string of words. Parsing is considered to be a basis for computing semantic relations between individual words into sentence meaning (Anderson, 2000; Ferstl & d'Arcais, 1999; Fodor, 1995b). Parsing can serve as interface to mediate between word strings and sentential meanings.

Positron emission tomography (PET)
Positron emission tomography (PET) is one of the less invasive functional brain imaging techniques. PET is a technique used for the functional

mapping of brain activity in normal human subjects, exploiting the effects of local changes of neuronal activity on local blood flow. PET records changes in blood flow by using radiopharmaceutical ($H_2^{15}O$) as a radioactive tracer, causing gamma emissions provoked by the positron emitting ^{15}O isotope (Raichle, 2003, 2006). Just before performing an experiment, the participant is injected with a radioactive tracer, usually ^{15}O-labeled molecule, such as water or butanol (Hagoort, 2003a). Recently, PET has been replaced by fMRI, because fMRI provides superior spatial and temporal resolution compared to PET.

Phrase
Phrase refers to a group of words within a sentence that function as a unit. Usually, it is a unit above the word and below the clause level in a sentence. In the following example, the units in the blankets show the phrases given by the phrase structure: [The girl] [hit [the ball]]. Syntactically, a phrase is the constituent unit that constitutes a sentence. Semantically, a phrase is the unit that organizes words into meaningful groupings within the sentence (Gleitman, 1986). In a sentence, a phrase can be replaced by a single word without changing the overall structure of the sentence (Harley, 2001). The organization of a sentence into phrases is described by the phrase structure.

Phrasal segmentation
Phrasal segmentation refers to the intuitive human behavior to detect individual units of phrases in sentences. Linguistic intuitions and empirical evidence show that people have the ability to perceive the phrasal unit in sentence comprehension and production as argued in Section 1.2 in the present chapter and Section 2.1 in Chapter 2. However, the mechanism of phrasal segmentation has not been specified well.

Region of interest (ROI) approach
Region of interest (ROI) approach is one of the commonly accepted approaches used for analyses in neuroimaging studies. In particular, it is a useful approach for generating specific hypotheses in a novel experiment about well-established brain areas by prior studies (Culham, 2006). In the ROI approach, regions of interest (ROIs) are first identified based on prior studies. Activation in these ROIs is then evaluated in an independent line of experiments designed to test a new hypothesis. Arguing stimuli and tasks that drive activation in these ROIs, characterization of ROIs' responses is systematically investigated.

Segmentation
Segmentation refers to the metal operation to split up continuous word strings in sentences into individual words and phrases. The present study distinguishes the segmentation between the word and the phrase level: word segmentation and phrasal segmentation. In the studies of speech perception, the segmentation often refers to the operation to split speech up into constituent phonemes and other phonological units such as syllables and morae (Harley, 2001). In the present study, however, segmentation exclusively refers to the behavior that people separate connected strings of words in sentences into individual words and phrases.

Word segmentation (Lexical segmentation)
Word segmentation (Lexical segmentation) refers to the segmentation to find and recognize individual units of words from connected word strings in sentences. The issue of word segmentation has been extensively studied as the most active area of the study of segmentation in psycholinguistics, neurophysiology and neuroimaging as described in Section 1.2 in the present chapter.

1.7 Organization of Chapters

This study tries to approach the issues of phrasal segmentation from the perspective of neuropsychology. Eventually, this study seeks to investigate and understand the functional relationship between the behavior of phrasal segmentation and the relevant brain areas of its processing operation, using functional brain imaging techniques. The study is an attempt to characterize phrasal segmentation within the overall framework of sentence processing. The present section that follows will give an overview of this study.

Chapter 1 will make a statement of the issues and the goals of this study, reviewing the field of relevant studies. Then, the chapter will provide the methodological considerations for the validity of the study, specifying the scope of and the approach to the study. In the final part, the chapter will give the definitions of the terms used in a special or a technical sense in the study. They will show the explanations of the techniques and methods introduced in this book.

Chapter 2 will, first, look at the issues of phrasal segmentation in the light of our sensitivity of phrasal unit in sentence processing and our intuitive ability of phrasal segmentation. Then, the chapter will consider the problems and issues on the nature of human sentence processing, showing the fundamental concepts and views on the approach to modeling human sentence processing. Finally, the chapter will present the premises of the study of phrasal segmentation to test the behavior and its underlying neural correlates: those premises will call for research to resolve the issue of phrasal segmentation. Accordingly, the chapter will present the research perspective on the study of phrasal segmentation to justify the fMRI experiments presented later in the chapters that follow.

Chapter 3 will focus on the issue of the functional relationship between the language-related human behaviors and the place of language processing in the brain. First, this chapter will present current neuroimaging evidence on the human sentence processing. Then, the chapter will offer current view on the functional relationship between language and the brain. Finally, the chapter will give the verification of the study of phrasal segmentation, considering possible ways of research for brain imaging to solve issues of phrasal segmentation.

Chapter 4 will show the experiment using event-related fMRI on the visual Japanese phrasal segmentation. The experiment will investigate the neural activity regarding phrasal segmentation during Japanese visual Kana sentence comprehension, comparing the neural activation between segmented and non-segmented conditions. The experiment will seek to identify the localization of sources of phrasal segmentation in the visual sentence processing condition.

Chapter 5 will present the experiment using event-related fMRI on the auditory Japanese phrasal segmentation. The experiment will further try to test the effect of phrasal segmentation on the auditory sentence comprehension. In the experiment, this study will investigate the neural activation during the Japanese auditory sentence comprehension between segmented and non-segmented conditions. The experiment will examine the localization of sources of phrasal segmentation in the auditory sentence processing condition.

Chapter 6 will discuss the results obtained from visual and auditory fMRI experiments shown in the previous two chapters. First, the chapter will argue the issue of whether the cortical area specific and/or pertaining to phrasal segmentation exists in the brain or not. Then, based on the fMRI experimental findings here, the chapter will discuss the effect and the nature of the processing of phrasal segmentation. Finally, the chapter will consider the validity of approaches to modeling human sentence processing to formalize the results obtained from the fMRI experiments here.

Chapter 7 will summarize and review the study of phrasal segmentation, considering the future perspective of the study of phrasal segmentation.

Finally, the chapter will conclude the current study.

Chapter 2
Why Phrasal Segmentation?

The present chapter, as a preliminary of the study of phrasal segmentation, will first look at the related issues of phrasal segmentation on the basis of the intuitions of speakers of the language and subsequently of the evidence from behavioral studies, validating our sensitivity to units of phrases and our intuitive ability of phrasal segmentation. The chapter, then, will look into the relevant issues to understand the human sentence processing and the fundamental views on the approach to modeling the overall design of sentence processing, showing research findings from the current human sentence processing studies. Finally, the chapter will make mention of possible hypotheses about phrasal segmentation to test the behavior and its underlying neural correlates. Accordingly, the chapter will present the research perspective on the study of phrasal segmentation to justify the fMRI experiments presented later in the chapters that follow. This chapter will provide groundings necessary for the study of phrasal segmentation.

2.1   Linguistic Intuitions and Empirical Evidence

The basic task in sentence comprehension is to combine the meanings of the individual words to come up with the meaning of the overall sentence (Anderson, 2000; Crocker, 1999; Fodor, 1995a). As readers or hearers process sentences, they compute the meaning on the basis of the words that compose each sentence. However, the sentence meaning could not be established by just combining each meaning of the individual words haphazardly. The words in a sentence have to be organized in the particular way by which the syntactic and the semantic relations can be inferred from the words in a sentence and in the end they have to be structured into an interpretation of a sentence. Our knowledge of language guides us onto the right path of how to go from a string of words to a proper interpretation of a sentence. The present study will address the question of how the meanings of the individual words in a sentence can be guided into the whole meaning of the sentence by the knowledge of language.

To make our discussion more concrete, let us consider the following examples. So, for example, the following two sentences (4a) and (4b) are comprised of the same individual words:

(4) a.　この　おとこのこは　その　おんなのこが　すきだ
　　　　(ko-no o-to-ko-no-ko-wa so-no o-N-na-no-ko-ga su-ki-da)
　　　　(this　　　boy-Top　　　that　　girl-Acc　　　like)
　　　　(This boy likes that girl.)
(4) b. *すきだ　この　その　おんなのこが　おとこのこは
　　　　(*su-ki-da ko-no so-no o-N-na-no-ko-ga o-to-ko-no-ko-wa)
　　　　(*like　　this　that　girl-Acc　　　boy-Top)
　　　　(*Likes this that girl boy.)

When we read these sentences in the above, we immediately understand that the sentence (4a) is a grammatical and meaningful sentence, while the sentence (4b) is ungrammatical and meaningless or nonsense as a sentence. We intuitively tell the difference between a proper sentence and a haphazard series of words. This example shows that people have the intuition of language, which is often characterized as the competence of language or as the grammar. That competence is assumed to allow us to appreciate the way of how the words can be combined orderly into a grammatical and meaningful sentence (Chomsky, 1980; Pinker, 1999; Anderson, 2000; Jackendoff, 2002).

The next example presents another aspect of our intuitions of language. If we are asked to segment a sentence into several major parts in the most natural way, we will effortlessly provide the segmentation that corresponds to the constituent units referred to as the phrases.

(5) a. その　こどもが　この　ねこを　みつけた
      (so-no ko-do-mo-ga ko-no ne-ko-o mi-tu-ke-ta)
      (that   child-Nom   this   cat-Acc   found)
      (That child found this cat.)
  b. [そのこどもが [[このねこを] みつけた]]
      ([so-no-ko-do-mo-ga [[ko-no-ne-ko-o] mi-tu-ke-ta]])
      ([that child-Nom   [[this cat-Acc]   found]])
      ([That child][found [this cat]].)
  c. *[その] [こどもがこの] [ねこをみつけた]
      (*[so-no] [ko-do-mo-ga ko-no] [ne-ko-o mi-tu-ke-ta])
      (*[that]   [child-Nom this]   [cat-Acc found])
      (*[That] [child this] [cat found].)

The sentence (5a), therefore, will be segmented into the phrasal units shown by the brackets in the sentence (5b), not like the units in the sentence (5c). Each phrasal unit in the sentence (5b) has its own individual meaning that would conform to each unit, but the segmented unit in the sentence (5c) does not have any meaning that each unit in the sentence (5b) will present. This example shows that people have the intuition of language that a sentence is more than a linearly ordered string of words: each word in a sentence is structured into the constituent units called the phrases and hence each sentence is broken up into the phrases in the structured manner as presented in the sentence (5b). Every properly segmented phrasal unit provides its own meaning by itself as the meaningful unit of the sentence. In other words, every phrase that forms a syntactic constituent usually forms a semantic constituent as well in a sentence (Partee, 1975). Although the phrase structure is not overtly manifest in the sentence, people intuitively know the way of how to compose the words into the phrases and decompose the sentence into the phrases (Chomsky, 1980; Pinker, 1999; Anderson, 2000; Jackendoff, 2002). People can identify the phrase structure of a sentence and also find out the individual meaning of each phrase (Anderson, 2000; Jackendoff, 2002; Culicover & Jackendoff, 2005). The phrase is thus the unit that organizes individual words into meaningful groupings within the sentence (Gleitman, 1986).

The two examples stated above illustrate that people appear to determine the structure and the meaning of the sentence by considering how the individual words can be put together to make sense as phrases and finally as a sentence. When they process sentences, people recognize that the sentence like the sentence (6a) is made up of and segmented into the phrases shown by the brackets in the sentence (6b). They also make out that every individual phrase has respectively its own individual meaning as the meaningful unit of the sentence. Concurrently, they have the knowledge that the sentence (6c) is an ungrammatical sentence and that it doesn't give any sentence meaning without the syntax for constructing meanings, even though it is made up of the same individual phrases as given in the sentence (6b).

(6) a.　わたしは　つくえのうえに　そのやかんを　おいた
　　　　(wa-ta-si-wa tu-ku-e-no-u-e-ni so-no-ya-ka-N-o o-i-ta)

(I-Top   desk-Gen on-Lac   that kettle-Acc   put)
(I put that kettle on the desk.)
b. [わたしは [[つくえのうえに] [そのやかんを] おいた]]
([wa-ta-si-wa [[tu-ku-e-no-u-e-ni] [so-no-ya-ka-N-o] o-i-ta]])
([I-Top   [desk-Gen on-Lac]   [that kettle-Acc]   [put])
([I] [put [the kettle] [on the desk]].)
c. *[[そのやかんを] おいた] [つくえのうえに] [わたしは]
(*[[so-no-ya-ka-N-o] o-i-ta] [tu-ku-e-no-u-e-ni] [wa-ta-si-wa])
(*[[That kettle-Acc]   put] [desk-Gen on-Lac]   [I-Top])
(*[put [the kettle]] [on the desk] [I].)

The examples show that the meaning of the sentence is determined by the phrases that each sentence contains, and also by the way these phrases are put together. People can intuitively determine how individual words may be combined to yield phrasal structure which can be interpreted appropriately.

A number of empirical studies of sentence production and comprehension bring forward evidence for such explanations of intuitive knowledge of phrasal segmentation. In the study of the speech production, Grosjean et al. (1979) and Gee and Grosjean (1983) report that speakers produce sentences phrase by phrase, bundling the meaning of the words together into each phrase. They argue that their observation gives evidence to indicate that speakers tend to choose the phrase as the meaningful unit of speech: the phrase is the unit above the word, which enables speakers to put the individual words together into coherent semantic information. In the study of eye fixating times in sentence comprehension, Just and Carpenter (1980) show that their subjects spend more extra time at the end of each phrase. They argue that their subjects take their time wrapping up the meaning of the words in every phrase. They suggest that the meaning of the sentence is defined in accordance with the phrasal unit given by the phrase structure, by which a set of relationships could be drawn between a sentence as the whole and the parts as the individual words. These studies set it forth as the basic premise of sentence processing that, when producing and comprehending sentences, the meaning is provided from phrase to phrase in parallel with the generation and the detection of every phrase, and then the meaning of each phrase is built up together into the meaning of a whole sentence. Consequently, the premise argues for the importance of the phrasal unit in sentence processing in the sense that phrases would be the platform from where production and comprehension of sentences start.

The linguistic intuitions and the empirical findings mentioned so far stress the primary involvement of the phrasal unit in processing sentences. In the present work, the study will focus on our attention on the role of the phrase in sentence processing and investigate its executive function in sentence comprehension. In the next section, this study will take up possible considerations about phrasal segmentation, evaluating the model of sentence comprehension based on research findings in the studies of neurophysiology and neuroimaging as well as psycholinguistics.

2.2 Possible Considerations about Phrasal Segmentation

In the forecited discussion and examples in the previous section, the study has appealed to our linguistic intuitions and meta-linguistic judgments as native speakers to show a number of facts about phrasal segmentation. However, they are not sufficient measures and evidence to explicate a number of facts about our linguistic knowledge and its related behaviors of phrasal segmentation. Some clarification is also needed to deal with issues to infer the mental and neural operations that take place in the course of phrasal segmentation when we understand language. But before taking up possible hypotheses about phrasal segmentation, the present study will preliminarily clarify the issues regarding the relationship between the model of sentence processing and the processing of phrasal segmentation. In the following subsections, the study will first discuss kinds of characteristics of existing models in human sentence processing, with particular focus on models of sentence comprehension. This study will then evaluate insights that these models provide for our study of phrasal segmentation. Finally, the study will consider a number of issues in order to more adequately and concretely shape our proposals of the study.

2.2.1 Issues on Modeling Sentence Processing

In the following sections, this study will argue for the issues that matter when considering the problem of phrasal segmentation within the overall architecture of sentence processing. First, the study will look at the processing properties of human sentence processing. Then, the study will make mention of different types of core linguistic information generally involved in language processing. Next, the study will go on to the issue of architectural distinction in modeling sentence comprehension, and further this study will consider the issue from two different perspectives: perspectives of representation and processing. Finally, this study will consider framing the issue of modeling sentence processing in terms of the question of how precisely to specify the overall architecture of human sentence comprehension, based on recent neurophysiological studies on language processing.

2.2.1.1 Processing Properties: Incrementality and Compositionality

Literature has relied on behavioral, empirical evidence to establish scientific models of human sentence processing (Crocker, 2005; Cutler & Clifton, 1999; Ingram, 2007). Such evidence has contributed to developing the architecture of models by looking for a number of processing operations embedded in human sentence processing. In particular, evidence has shown the following processing operations, which have influenced current model development (Croker, 1999; Pickering, 1999). In processing language, it has been considered that people process sentences incrementally as their words are recognized in the linear order that they come into us from strings of written words or from utterances in the speech stream (Just & Carpenter, 1980; Just et al., 1982; Marslen-Wilson, 1973, 1975; Rayner & Duffy, 1986; Tyler & Marslen-Wilson, 1977). Sentences are processed by the particular way their words can be combined together in the sequential order (Croker, 1999). It has also been assumed that sentences are processed basically in a highly compositional fashion for merging and integrating their local constituents such as words into organized minor grouping of constituents such as phrases (Jarvella, 1971; Shieber & Johnson, 1993; Taraban & McClelland, 1988). Their words are integrated into a group of connected representations as the words are encountered (Crocker, 1996; Frazier, 1979). By these processing operations, syntactic relationships are established among individual constituents, and eventually syntactic structure is built up in sentences. The series of processing is technically known as syntactic parsing. It has been postulated that syntactic parsing further provides a basis for computing semantic relations between individual words in a sentence into a complete sentence meaning (Anderson, 2000; Ferstl & d'Arcais, 1999; Fodor, 1995b). For full semantic interpretation of sentence, syntactic structure to be assigned can serve as interface to mediate between word and sentential meaning. Virtually, models of human sentence processing are characterizing and modeling these processing properties (see, Crocker, 2005).

2.2.1.2 Core Linguistic Information in Language Processing

Currently, models of human sentence processing seek to account for the research results pertaining to the processing flow of the three different sources of linguistic information: phonological, semantic, and syntactic sources of information. As speakers of a language, we know facts about its sound structure (phonology), its meaning structure (semantics), and its sentence structure (syntax) (Lasnik, 1995). The study of language posits that a human language involves knowledge of these three different kinds of linguistic information. In production and comprehension of a language, the three distinct forms of information are considered to be invoked. Therefore, in the study of human sentence processing, it has been generally agreed that processing a language depends on the three different sources of linguistic information (Cutler & Clifton, 1999; Garrod & Pickering, 1999; Pickering, 1999).

With the advent of recent noninvasive neurophysiological and neuroimaging techniques, evidence has become available from healthy subjects providing insight into modeling in human language processing. Evidence has confirmed that phonological, semantic and syntactic information respectively but to the different extent contributes to human language processing (see, Caplan, 2004; Démonet et al, 2005; Vigneau et al., 2006; Wise & Price, 2006). Their findings are compatible with the view based on the behavioral, empirical evidence that the different types of linguistic information (i.e., phonological, semantic and syntactic information) are implicated in language processing.

Sentence comprehension is also a task that such linguistic information is processed and integrated in a particular way in order for the organization of a sentence to be detected and the meaning of a sentence to be obtained from concatenated strings of words. Hence, the central problem in the study of sentence comprehension is to unfold how people represent a string of words as the structured constituents of the sentence and how they provide the appropriate connections of meaning into the individual words. Keeping this problem in mind, the study of human sentence comprehension have been tackling and solving the issues of how people use the linguistic information in the course of interpreting sentences. Indeed, models of sentence comprehension are heavily motivated and shaped to account for the access and interplay of the three different types of core linguistic information sources.

2.2.1.3 Designing Distinction in Modeling Sentence Processing

Modeling human sentence processing is an attempt to characterize and account for the properties of sentence processing available empirical evidence provides. Obviously, it is a truism that the access of words is the beginning of sentence processing. Yet, it does not imply that the processing operations proceed simply and unidirectionally unfolding from word to comprehension or production. Actually, in the last several decades, a number of models have been proposed for sentence processing. Besides the properties mentioned above, there is the diverse range in proposals for modeling human sentence processing (see, Flitch, 2005, for further discussion in detail). However, in more general terms, one major distinction between the diversities is the designing scheme characterized in the kinds of models (Perfetti, 1999; Pickering, 1999).

Basically, the designing distinction is noted at two different levels: one concerns the level of the core linguistic information represented, and the other relates to the level of the processing operations (Trueswell et al., 1994). At the representational level, there are two alternative accounts, depending on whether the different types of linguistic information are recruited simultaneously in parallel, or serially in hierarchical order as a sentence is being processed (Heim, 2005; Pickering, 1999). At the processing level as well, there are two alternative accounts, depending on whether people can construct only one processing component or process only one at a time, or whether people can construct different processing components or processes at the same time when they are engaged in the language processing operations (Boland & Cutler, 1996; Perfetti, 1999).

One approach to this designing issue has been to assume that, at the representational level, different types of information resources are accessed and incorporated mutually; at the processing level, language is processed simultaneously. According to this view, there are no clearly distinct stages, with syntactic information first and semantic information afterwards, or with phonological processing completed before lexical processing starts. Multiple representations can be constructed at one time. Parallel processing operations can be also available at the same time. Models with this characterization have been called parallel models.

By contrast, the alternative approach, opposing to parallel models, has been to maintain that, at the representational level, only one source of information is represented at a time. At the processing level, solely one processing operation is selected and processed at once. This account claims that linguistic information is sequentially represented and each processing operation takes place serially. There is no interaction among different types of information, and every processing operation is individually autonomous within that particular processing domain. Models with this property have been known as serial models. There has been an ongoing debate about whether the core information is accessed and processed simultaneously or serially, or whether the individual processing is created interactively or autonomously (Boland & Cutler, 1996; Pickering, 1999; Crocker, 2005; Heim, 2005).

However, regarding the issue of the designing distinction at the representational level, such debate has been reframed due to the increasing amount of research findings from neurophysiological and neuroimaging on-line studies. In these studies, recent progress on methods for directly looking at brain activity associated with human cognitive functioning has proved that three types of the core linguistic information (phonological, semantic and syntactic information) are all involved in sentence processing (Friederici, 2002, 2005; Hagoort, 2008). Research using ERPs, further, has made it possible to uncover different aspects of the scalp-recorded electrical activity during language processing, using various types of language related tasks. The electrophysiological data of ERPs have indicated that distinct types of linguistic information are retrieved separately at high speed and they are orchestrated at different phases of processing (see, Friederici, 1995, 1999, 2005). As a result, at the representational level, the current models of human sentence processing (Friederici, 2002; Dominey et al, 2003; Hagoort, 2003b; Grodzinsky & Friederici, 2006) have assumed that linguistic information, each source of which is independently represented, is retrieved serially by making reference to each linguistic level of representation such as phonological, syntactic, and semantic level (see, Jackendoff, 1999, for further discussion on the issue of linguistic information at the representational level from linguistic perspectives). At the processing level, on the other hand, the independence of different processing phases, in each of which each processing operation is not necessarily unitary but can be multidimensional, is presumed as preserved. Therefore, more recently, the main debate of designing distinction in modeling sentence processing has moved on to the issue of how individual processing operations can be characterized and modeled from the issue of how different sources of linguistic information can be represented.

2.2.1.4 Neurophysiological Evidence for Modeling Sentence Processing
Recent development of neurophysiological on-line measures has allowed us to monitor the temporal structure of language processing by registering the brain activity as language is processed over time. The advent of advanced neurophysiological studies using such on-line measures has provided information about the temporal aspect of subcomponent processes underlying language processing.

Of these on-line measuring techniques available, the electroencephalography (EEG) and magnetoencephalography (MEG) studies of language have been known as the most notable methods within the domain of language processing (Kutas & Van Pattern, 1994). The EEG is the technique to measure the modulations of electrical activity at the scalp in response to a particular stimulus event. The MEG is the measure to examine the neuronal magnetic field that is generated by the neural electrical activity. EEG recordings give the millisecond timing of the electrical activity of the brain associated with human sentence processing. The average EEG responses adjusted to a particular stimulus are called the event related brain potential (ERP), in which each EEG response is averaged together as a set of particular stimulus events. By contrast, MEG recordings measure the magnetic field of the brain, although the measurement of the MEG is conducted in much the same way as EEG recordings. The averaged MEG responses to a particular stimulus are referred to as the magnetic event related field (MERF) or the evoked magnetic field (EMF), in which a number of individual MEG responses are averaged together to a set of particular stimulus events. Both electric and magnetic scarp recordings of the ERP and the MEG provide temporal views of the underlying brain activity correlated with human sentence processing over short periods of time. ERP and MERF/EMF measures are suited for tracking the neural changes that coincide with rapid phasic changes in the behavioral state (see, Davidson et al., 2000)

In fact, a fair amount of research using the ERP and the MEG has been devoted to clarifying the temporal profiles (the relative timing and sequence) of underlying processing operations responsible for language comprehension and production. As a result, two of these neurophysiological approaches have given and described fairly well characterized lists of specific ERP and MERF/EMF components sensitive to language processing (Kuriki & Murase, 1989; Kutas & Hillyard, 1980a; Näätänen et al., 1997; Neville et al., 1991; Osterhout & Holcomb, 1992; Poeppel et al., 1996). Using a variety of different tasks relevant to language processing, their research has showed that a number of ERP and MERF/EMF components change systematically with different aspects of processing. Their neurophysiological data has found temporally dissimilar components of the ERP and MERF/EMF responses.

Of these language-related ERP and MERF/EMF components, the following components have been known to be the major neurophysiological markers as the language-relevant components that reflect fundamental language processes concerning human sentence processing: the mismatch negativity (MMN); M100; N150; N320; N350; N400; P600; the left anterior negativity (LAN); the early left anterior negativity (ELAN); and the Closure Positive Shift (CPS). However, their precise components have been partly distinguished between the visual and the auditory modality of processing. Additionally, the exact temporal profile in detail of each component varies according to the methodological and analytic differences among studies.

In the auditory modality of processing, the mismatch negativity (MMN), a negative component peaking at 100 – 250 ms after the stimulus onset, has been noted as an ERP component to be provoked earlier after the onset of the stimulus presentation. The MMN, which has been found mainly in phonological and syllabic discrimination tasks at the sublexical level of processing, reflects the earliest retrieval of phonological information (Näätänen et al., 1997; Näätänen, 2001; Pulvermüller et al., 2004). This MMN, which has been viewed as an early ERP component sensitive to the match or mismatch at the phonological level, is sometimes referred to as the phonological mismatch negativity (PMMN) (Connoly & Phillips, 1994). An MERF/EMF component with a similar time course to the MMN is the M100. The M100 has also been known to be sensitive to the retrieval of phonological information in phonological and syllabic discrimination tasks at the sublexical level (Kuriki & Murase, 1989; Poeppel et al., 1996). The MMN and the M100 components are generally specific for the auditory modality of processing.

In the visual modality of processing, a negative ERP component peaking at 130 – 170 ms (N150) has been elicited as an index of visual word form recognition, which marks the initial processing of lexical materials to distinguish words and word-like stimuli from other visual non-linguistic stimuli (Bentin et al., 1999; Cohen et al., 2000; Lieu & Perfetti, 2003). In the visual modality, in contrast to the auditory modality, the phonological access has been identified to start later at about 250 ms after the onset of the critical stimulus presentation, peaking at 320 ms at the phonetic level (N320) and at 350 ms at the lexical level (N350) (Bentin et al., 1999). The late timing of the phonological access is caused by separate access operations that differ in temporal order between the orthographic and the phonological retrieval. Usually, the phonological retrieval is preceded by the orthographic retrieval in visual processing after the analysis of orthographic word patters has finished (Bentin et al., 1999). The N150, the N320 and the N350 have been recorded mainly for the visual modality of processing. At the level of lexical access, an MEG response component peaking at 300 – 400 ms (M350) has been elicited with a similar temporal profile to N350 (Pylkkänen, et al., 2002). Like N350, M350 has also been observed usually in response to the stimuli presented in the visual modality.

In both the auditory and the visual modality, a negative ERP component peaking at 350 – 400 ms (N400) has been noted as an established ERP component, which is sensitive to the processing of semantic information (Kutas & Hillyard, 1980a, 1980b). In language processing, the N400 has been broadly observed at the level of semantics in response to meaningful stimuli of word, phrase, sentence and discourse in both semantically incongruous and congruous contexts (Brown & Hagoort, 1993; Fischler et al., 1983; Friederici et al., 1993; Kutas & Hillyard, 1980a, 1980b, 1983, 1984; Van Berkum et al., 1999; Van Petten, 1993) (see, Friederici, 2005; Hagoort, 2008; Kutas & Federmeier, 2000; Kutas et al., 2006, for extensive overviews). Another established ERP component is a positive ERP component peaking at around 600 ms (P600), which has been found to be related to the processing of syntactic information (Osterhout & Holcomb,

1992; Osterhout & Mobey, 1995). The P600 has been reported to occur at the level of syntax by reacting to syntactic violations, thematic role violations and syntactically grammatical but unusual constructions (Hahne & Friederici, 2002; Kuperberg et al., 2003; Osterhout & Holcomb, 1992; Osterhout & Mobley, 1995). The P600 has also been extensively observed for both the auditory and the visual modality of language processing.

In addition, there have been other syntax-related ERP components reported: a negative ERP component occurring at 300 – 500 ms with a peak at around 400 ms after the stimulus onset (LAN, the left anterior negativity) (Coulson et al., 1998), and another negative ERP component occurring at 150 – 200 ms with a peak at around 180 ms after the stimulus onset (ELAN, the early left anterior negativity) (Friederici et al., 1993; Friederici et al., 1996; Neville et al., 1991). The LAN has been mostly elicited by syntactic violations of the subject-verb disagreement and the verb's argument structure (Friederici et al., 1993; Friederici et al., 1996; Hagoort et al., 2003; Rösler et al., 1993). The ELAN has been mainly evoked by syntactic violations of the phrase structure and the word-category constraints. The LAN and the N400 have been usually observed within the same temporal range (300 – 500 ms). However, they are different in their distribution over the scalp: the LAN is usually distributed over the anterior part of both hemispheres, and it is sometimes larger over the left than the right hemisphere; the N400 is broadly distributed over the posterior part of both hemispheres, although it is needed to note that the scalp distribution over the particular part such as the frontal or the posterior part does not always mean that the particular neurophysiological component is generated in that particular part of the brain (see, Davis et al., 2003; Kutas & Van Pattern, 1994; Kutas et al., 2006). In contrast, the LAN and the ELAN are distributed over the same part of the scalp, but they are different in that the ELAN is temporally followed by the LAN. The LAN has been observed for both the auditory and the visual modality of language processing, while the ELAN has been found exclusively for the auditory modality.

Furthermore, another distinct, positive going ERP wave component, which reflects prosodic phrasing (i.e., intonational phrasing) has been observed for both the auditory and the visual modality of processing. This ERP component has been noted to take place immediately after the point when a prosodic phrase boundary (an intonational phrase boundary in the auditory stimulus and hence a punctuative boundary in the visual stimulus) is perceived (Steinhauer et al., 1999; Steinhauer & Friederici, 2001). The ERP component is labeled as the Closure Positive Shift (CPS), because it begins to respond shortly after the conclusion (i.e., the closure) of each intonational phrase (Van Petten & Bloom, 1999).

Consequently, by tracing out the temporal order of neural activity reflected in electric and magnetic scarp recordings, a series of neurophysiological research using the ERP and the MEG has provided a body of evidence pertaining to human language processing. Different, distinct time and timing of language-relevant ERP and MERF/EMF components suggest that qualitatively different, separate underlying neural processing operations are associated with human language processing. In addition, the evidence that ERP and MERF/EMF components become apparent shortly after the appearance of the particular stimulus event appears to strongly support the view of models on sentence processing that emphasize the immediate and on-line characterization of processing. Further, the research has identified the fact that specific brain responses to different linguistic features are reflected in distinct ERP and MERF/EMF components. This fact suggests that different types of linguistic information are differently subserved in temporally different stages of processing operations. All such evidence leads to the assumption that there exists a series of processing stages unfolding over time in human language processing. Here, the question will arise again, at the level of individual processing operations, whether people process language serially or multidimensionally through the stages of sentence processing. In the next section, the present study will go back to the designing issue in modeling human sentence processing again. Now, this study will consider the issue of modeling the relationship among individual processing operations, in line with the predictions from neurophysiological evidence.

2.2.1.5 Neurophysiological Models of Sentence Processing
In the neurophysiological studies of language, a large number of research using the ERP and the MEG has been undertaken over the last several decades to investigate a temporal profile of human language processing. Observing the temporal pattern of the brain activity during language processing, the research has demonstrated that distinct types of ERP and MERF/EMF components are involved in that processing, both of which have predicted that there exists the relatively different timing of cognitive operations in human language processing. Further, the existence of these distinct ERP and MERF/EMF components has suggested that human language processing is subserved by the distinct levels of cognitive operations such as in access, representation and processing.

Accordingly, recent research findings from the ERP and the MEG studies have implicated that phonological, semantic and syntactic information (in addition, orthographical information in case of the visual modality) are accessed, represented, and processed differently at distinct levels or/and stages of language processing (Friederici, 2002; Hahne and Friederici, 2002; Hagoort, 2003b; Hoeks et al., 2004; Friederici, 2005; Palolahti et al, 2005; Silva-Pereyra et al, 2005; Hagoort, 2008). In line with these research findings, recent accounts of human language processing have assumed a cognitive mechanism that consists of separate processing levels or/and stages of phonological (respectively orthographical and phonological in case of the visual modality), semantic, and syntactic information. Based on this mechanism, current models of language processing have been arguing for the issue of how people implement and carry out the processing of such linguistic information in the overall sentence processing design.

Recent neurophysiological studies available on language processing have indicated that there have been two general accounts of framing how people exploit linguistic information in the overall design of sentence processing (Friederici, 2002; Hagoort, 2003b; Heim, 2005). One account is to assume that linguistic information is serially processed. On this account, in particular, syntax is autonomous in nature and syntactic information is processed at the early stage of processing prior to the processing of semantic information. This account has been characterized as serial or syntax-first models. The other account is to postulate that different types of linguistic information are processed in parallel at different levels or/and stages of processing. On this account, syntax and semantics interaction starts at the early stage of processing. Syntactic and semantic information are incrementally used for the interpretation of sentence, as soon as the relevant pieces of linguistic information are available. This account has been referred to as parallel, interactive or immediacy models. Both accounts predict that each linguistic information interacts to be integrated at any stage of processing from language perception to understanding; however, the former account predicts interaction at a later stage, while the latter predicts early interaction.

In one version of the former account, Friederici (1995, 1999) has proposed a model of auditory sentence processing with its particular focus on auditory sentence comprehension in terms of the temporal structure of language processing. In her model, Friederici postulates distinct processing phases of sentence comprehension that unroll over time in order. Based on the temporal dissociations of the neurophysiological correlates of language processing, Friederici suggests that on-line processing of auditory sentence comprehension is subdivided into different phases of processing operations (in her term, processes), which are compatible with the temporal structure of the processing steps of the language input.

Friederici (2002) has extended her earlier model (1995, 1999), considering relevant evidence from neuroimaging studies as well as the temporal analysis of the language-related ERP components. Figure 2.1 illustrates a schematic view of her current model (2002). The boxes represent the functional processes, the ellipses indicate the underlying neural correlate, and the phases show the temporal structure of the ERP components. Abbreviations are used as follows in the figure: BA, Brodmann's area; ELAN, early left-anterior negativity; IFG, inferior frontal gyrus; LAN, left-anterior negativity; MTG, middle temporal gyrus; MTL, middle temporal lobe; N400, negativity at approximately 400ms; P345, positivity at approximately 345ms; P600, positivity at approximately 600ms.

In her current model (2002), Friederici posits that lexical access is the basic mechanism of human sentence processing. Lexical entries of words (i.e., morpho-syntactic properties of words) have relevant information necessary to structure the language input and to assign thematic roles. Thus, the basic syntactic structure is primarily determined by the morpho-syntactic properties of words, by which words are combined into phrases and eventually sentences.

Friederici's model has assumed that there are different processing systems for phonological, structural and lexical-semantic information, on the basis of the time course of language comprehension processes revealed by ERP studies. Furthermore, Friederici has stated that these different subprocesses are coordinated over time during the overall process of sentence processing.

First, in her model, after going through the perceptive phase of linguistic input, language processing moves into the phase of the phonological processing operation for the segmental phonetic extraction and the phonological sequencing of linguistic information. Then, the processing goes onto the processing operation, in the same phase, for the lexical form

Chapter 2 Why Phrasal Segmentation? 49

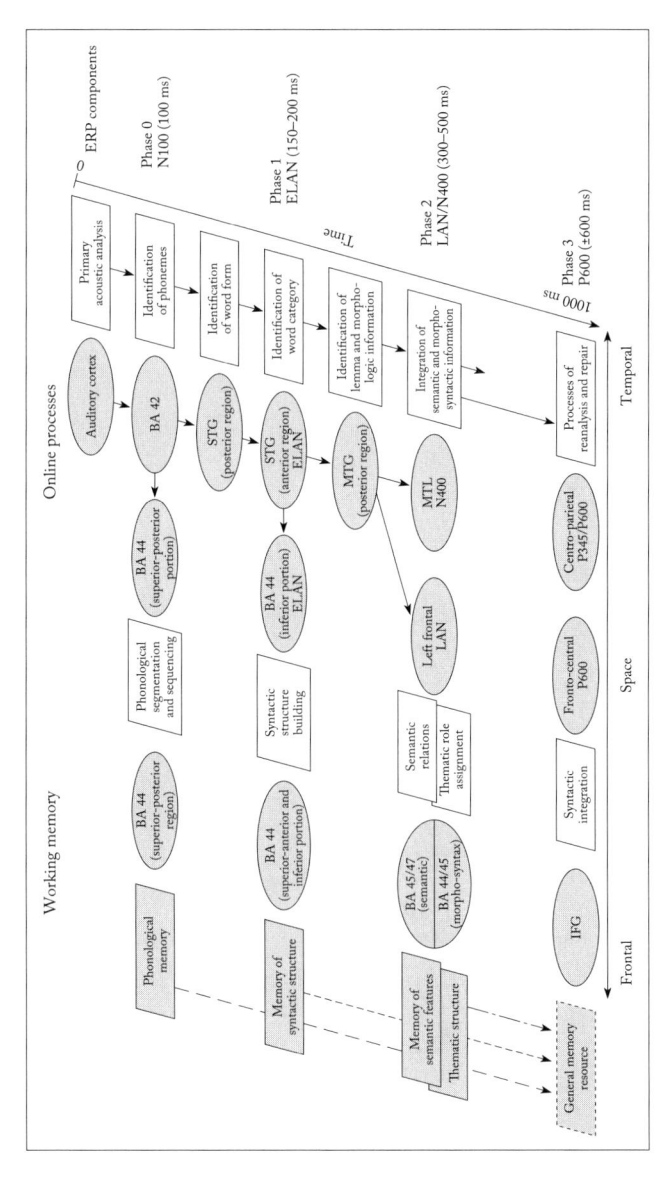

Figure 2.1. Neurocognitive model of auditory sentence comprehension. From "Towards a Neural Basis of Auditory Sentence Processing," by A. D. Friederici, 2002, *TRENDS in Cognitive Sciences*, 6, p. 79. Copyright 2002 by Elsevier Science Ltd.

identification. Friederici refers to the phase of the series of processing operations as Phase 0. Phase 0 is mostly for the processing operations at the sublexical and the lexical level. Next, in Phase 1, the access to word category information starts to build up an incoming sequence of words into a syntactic phrase structure. Phase 1 provides the basis of basic syntactic structure for thematic role assignments in the following phase. Phase 1, therefore, is for the early structure building operation for subsequent thematic role assignments. In parallel with the early structure building in Phase 1, the access to lexical-semantic information becomes active as well. Then, in Phase 2, both the lexical-semantic and the morpho-syntactic information of words are coordinated for thematic role assignments. Finally, in Phase 3, the late interaction and integration take place between syntactic and semantic factors. Thus, in terms of the functional relationship among the phases and the processing operations, Friederici's model has basically postulated the seriality and independence of one another in its architecture, suggesting that the brain reacts in accordance with the grammar.

By contrast, in a version of parallel models, Hagoort (2003b, 2005a) has provided a model of sentence processing, especially focusing on on-line comprehension of a sentence. Hagoort has developed his model called the Unification Model on the basis of functionally dissociated ERP components of language processing. His model predicts that different components of processing operations will take place incrementally in parallel at semantic, syntactic and phonological level of processing. In this model, as soon as semantic, syntactic or phonological information is available, it is accessed simultaneously at different levels of processing. Each type of linguistic information is immediately integrated and used for the purpose of sentence interpretation. This processing mechanism has been referred to as the immediacy assumption (Hagoort & van Berkum, 2007).

Figure 2.2 shows the instance of how syntactic frames are retrieved and linked together on the basis of the incoming word form information in the

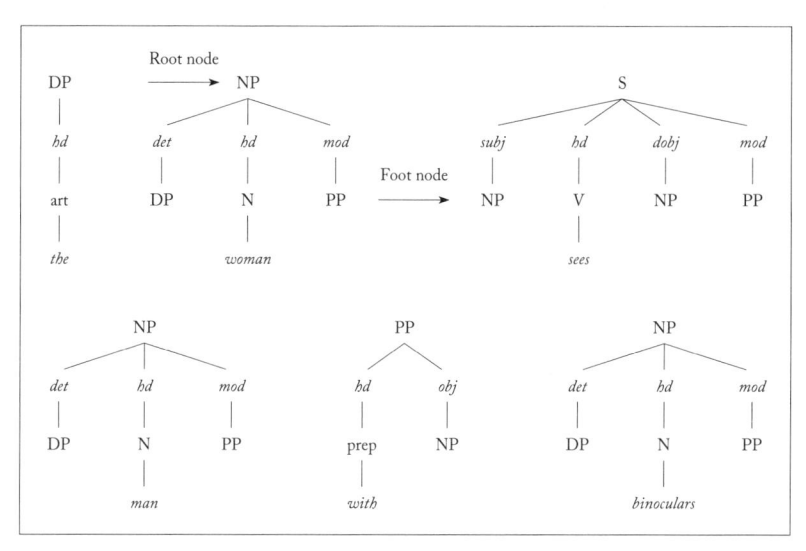

Figure 2.2. Syntactic frames in the mental lexicon and their linking operation. From "On Broca, brain, and binding: a new framework," by P. Hagoort, 2005a, *TRENDS in Cognitive Sciences*, 9, p. 418. Copyright 2005 by Elsevier Science Ltd.

input, for the sentence '*The woman sees the man with binoculars.*' Structure-building operations referred to as the unification will take place incrementally by linking the root node to an available foot node of the same category. By the unification operation that links up lexical items with identical root and foot nodes, constituent structures spanning a whole sentence are formed. Abbreviations are used as follows in the figure: DP, Determiner Phrase; NP, Noun Phrase; S, Sentence; PP, Prepositional Phrase; art, article; hd, head; det, determiner; mod, modifier; subj, subject; dobj, direct object.

Recently, Hagoort and his colleagues have presented further evidence for his proposal from ERP studies in support of parallel processing operations across different information types (Van den Brink & Hagoort, 2004; Müller

& Hagoort, 2006; Van den Brink et al., 2006). They have also provided evidence against the claim of serial models that in lexical processing the access to the semantic properties of words precedes the access to the syntactic properties of words, suggesting that one processing operation at one level does not seem to wait until another processing operation ends at another level (Müller & Hagoort, 2006; Hagoort, 2008).

In Hagoort's model, the crucial triggers are the syntactic properties of words called lemma, which enable on-line assignment of structure to an incoming string of written or spoken words (see, Hagoort et al., 1999). In the on-line comprehension process, lexical items (i.e., words) are retrieved sequentially, driven by the time course of the input. In the mental lexicon, each lexical item is associated with a syntactic frame, which specifies the possible structural environment of the particular lexical item (Figure 2.2). Hence, the lemma information (i.e., lexical-syntactic information) is the crucial input for the computation of sentence structure, where lexical items are combined and integrated into larger structures such as phrases and a sentence at the syntactic level.

Additionally, Hagoort claims that such combinatorial integration operations into larger structures hold true for the semantic and the phonological levels as well as the syntactic level, incrementally in the order that is imposed by the input. He also argues that the language system has a tripartite architecture with levels of phonology, syntax and semantics.

Figure 2.3 shows the tripartite architecture of the language system. The example gives three different tiers of structures for the sentence, 'This little star's beside the big star': (a) Phonological structure, (b) Syntactic structure, and (c) Semantic/conceptual structure. Besides these three tiered structures, (d) Spatial structure is added at the bottom, showing an approximate spatial structure of the reference objects.

As the figure illustrates, on the one hand, the basic linguistic information is independently retrieved from the mental lexicon within each particular

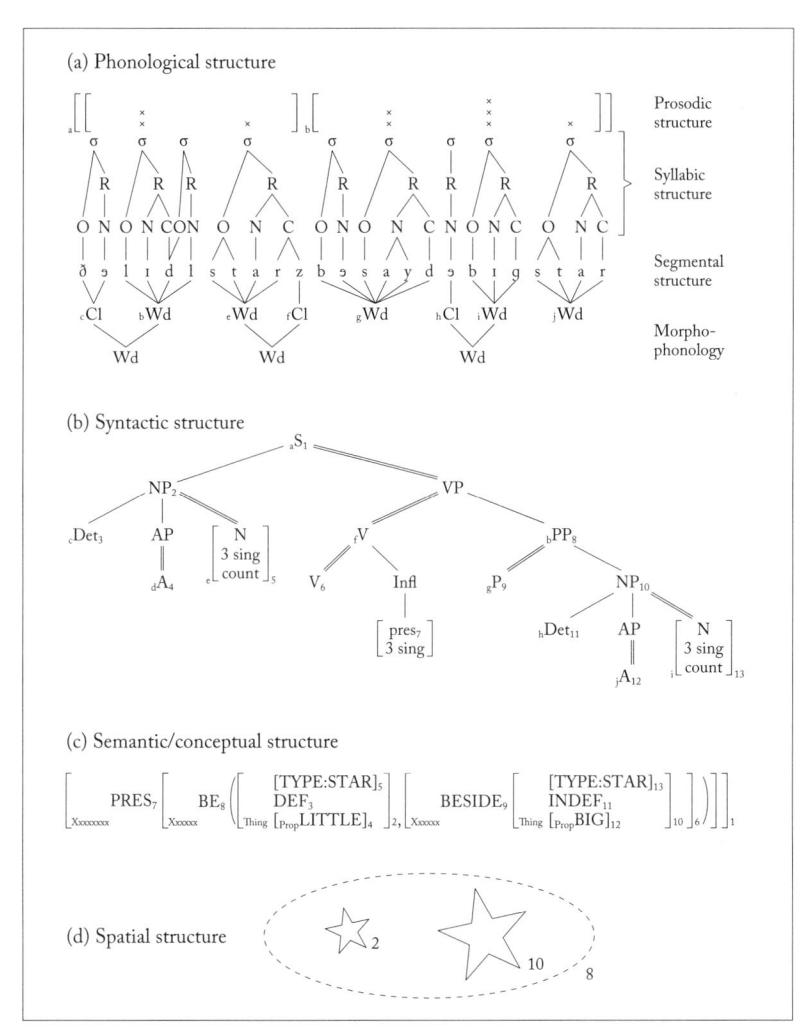

Figure 2.3. Tripartite architecture of language system. From "The representational structures of the language faculty and their interactions," by R. Jackendoff, 1999. In C. M. Brown & P. Hagoort (Eds.), *The Neurocognition of Language*, p. 50. Copyright 1999 by Oxford University Press.

level and it is immediately used to be processed in parallel into larger structures. On the other hand, for the purpose of language interpretation, the relevant pieces of basic linguistic information are assembled and combined concurrently and interactively across the different levels to some extent by the integration operation termed the unification. Thus, Hagoort's model has provided support for the mechanism of sentence processing that allows for the immediate parallel use of the basic linguistic information (phonology, syntax, semantics).

This section has reviewed two alternative views on the model of sentence processing from different neurophysiological perspectives, both of which have mainly focused on on-line processing of sentence comprehension in line with predictions of serial and parallel processing models. To date, regarding the design issue of modeling on-line sentence processing, the least agreement has been found between the two neurophysiological views (see, Kutas et al., 2006, for further discussion). In practice, no direct evidence that successfully supports the superiority of one view over the other between two competing views has been proved. Nevertheless, despite the design argument in modeling, the two views have been two of the most influential neurophysiological views on modeling on-line sentence processing that would provide the overall sentence processing architecture in the light of temporal structure of sentence processing. Indeed, both views have been well supported by a fair amount of neurophysiological research using a variety of experimental paradigms. At the moment, following the predictions obtained from the two different competing views, it would be a valid position to support the processing view that language-related processing operations within any given area will likely draw on at least some phonological, syntactic or semantic information. Their predictions suggest that there is a systematic relation between individual language-related behaviors and processing operations of language-relevant information, whose individual relation is assumed to be instantiated differently in the human brain. Even so, the processing operation of phrasal segmentation and its related neural correlates have not been adequately attested and characterized so far in designing the overall mechanism of sentence processing. To conclude, the exact relationship between the behavior of phrasal segmentation and its relevant brain fact remains subject to further investigation, at present.

As for the issue of the interaction and integration across different sources of the linguistic information, this section has temporarily put it on hold. However, this study will take up and argue the issue of the interaction and integration in the following chapter, in consideration of the place of the mental operation of phrasal segmentation within the overall design of sentence processing. In the next section, this study will go back to the issue of phrasal segmentation and call for the research for the detection of the brain information necessary to understand the on-line processing function of phrasal segmentation.

2.2.2 Premises of the Research of Phrasal Segmentation

As argued so far, this study assumes that a model of sentence processing must be based on an understanding of how words are put together to build interpretations: interpretations of sentences are compositionally built up from words, and then clustered into properly organized constituents. In keeping with this assumption, in the previous sections, this study has discussed relevant issues concerning the approach to understanding the human sentence processing, especially focusing on the issues on modeling sentence comprehension. The discussion provides insights into how the model of sentence processing needs to specify the levels of linguistic information needed and the processing steps required for accessing the relevant pieces of such information and for implementing the necessary computational operations in the overall design of the human sentence processing. The insights help to explain how different sources of linguistic information are recruited and exploited in mapping the string of words onto meaning, and to clarify how different operations of sentence processing are executed in the human brain.

Now, relying on groundings provided by these insights on sentence processing, the present study will consider the issue of phrasal segmentation in the overall design of sentence processing. With regard to the human sentence processing, different language processing functions are considered to reflect different exploitations of different sources of linguistic information in the human brain. This consideration postulates that any different function of language processing has to be instantiated as any different brain fact. In the previous section (Section 2.1), this study has shown that phrasal segmentation is intuitively and empirically verifiable processing function of language. This means that phrasal segmentation is also basically a branch of language processing. Hence, it is reasonable to posit that phrasal segmentation is one of the processing operations associated with the human language processing, recruiting the core sources of linguistic information, at least either or some of phonological, semantic and syntactic information. The assumption is, therefore, that phrasal segmentation is specified as one of the language-related functions within the framework of the neural mechanism of language and hence of the processing mechanism of language. Now, following these considerations, this study will call for the research of phrasal segmentation.

Finally in conclusion, this section will present the premises of the research as provided below for the ensuing fMRI experiments of phrasal segmentation.

(1) Phrasal segmentation is a part of the language processing operations that support the human sentence processing.
(2) Phrasal segmentation is instantiated as any brain fact in the human brain. Therefore, the language function of phrasal segmentation is

attributed to the particular brain function revealed by neural activations within any given area distributed in the brain.

(3) By identifying the involvement of the core linguistic information and the network of brain regions engaged in phrasal segmentation, the processing operation of phrasal segmentation is optimally defined within the framework of the human sentence processing.

Thus, the present focus of the study is on real-time processing properties of phrasal segmentation and, more specifically, what is taking place in the brain while executing phrasal segmentation when humans understand a sentence.

2.3 Summary

In the present chapter, this study has discussed the related issues to understand the behavior of phrasal segmentation, presenting the evidence from the intuitions of language and the research findings of previous behavioral studies. Next, this study has examined the relevant issues to understand the human sentence processing and reviewed the fundamental views on the approach to modeling the overall mechanism of sentence processing. Finally, the study has presented the premises of the study of phrasal segmentation on the basis of the insights obtained from the review of the human sentence processing. In the next chapter, this study will consider the behavior of phrasal segmentation and its functional relationship to the brain and verify the study for the following fMRI experiments.

Chapter 3

Human Language Processing in the Brain

In the previous chapter, this study has argued that language processing is functionally separable by tracing the neural activations that support its individual processing operations. The properties of each processing operation are characterized by differential involvement of the core linguistic information (phonological, syntactic and semantic information) in the brain. This perspective is referred to as the functional view of language in the brain: a particular language function is attributed to a particular brain function. It is now the basic premise of the neurophysiological study on language. Given this perspective, different aspects of language functions and their relevant processing operations are reflected in different brain functions in humans by differential exploitations of the core linguistic information. The functional view supports the idea that on-line language processing is subserved by different processing components and operations in the brain. Following this idea, the research to identify the network of regions of the brain and the functional relationship to the particular language-relevant tasks has been undertaken for the last few decades.

The recent prominence of functional brain imaging, in particular, has made it possible to actually examine how brain functions support the human language processing by attributing a particular brain function to a particular brain region. Using techniques to access changes in brain circulation and metabolism associated with changes in brain cellular activity, functional brain imaging has enabled researchers to quest for an understanding of the functional organization of the normal human brain, where brain circulation changes selectively with neural activity (Raichle, 2006). Thereby, the study of language has given the researchers the potential to look into the functional neuroanatomy of the normal human brain as it perceives, understands, and produces language.

In the present chapter, this study will focus on the issue of the functional relationship between the language-related human behaviors and the place of language processing in the brain. First, this study will mention the basic features and principles of functional brain imaging techniques, as a preliminary introduction of the approach to the functional neuroimaging study of language. Next, this study will present neuroanatomical evidence on the human sentence processing on the basis of modern neuroanatomical and neuroimaging research findings, which will eventually provide an overview for an understanding of how language is processed in the brain. Then, this study will offer current views on the functional relationship between language and the brain. That review incidentally will help to give neuroanatomical grounding of the present study, speculating about the functional role of phrasal segmentation in the overall mechanism of sentence processing. Finally, this study will give the verification of the ensuing fMRI experiments of phrasal segmentation, considering possible directions of the research for brain imaging to solve the issue of phrasal segmentation.

3.1 Human Language Processing

In the last few decades, the neuroimaging study of language has produced a large amount of evidence using a wide range of language-related tasks. This section will make a survey of the major evidence of the human language processing in the brain. However, before taking up doing that survey, the section will briefly outline basic features and principles of functional brain imaging, particularly focusing on techniques using functional magnetic resonance imaging (fMRI). The present section will characterize the impact of the functional brain imaging study on our understanding of language.

3.1.1 Functional Brain Imaging: its Techniques

The advent of methods for imaging brain structures and functions has made it possible to measure various aspects of ongoing neural activities arising from the brain at work. With that, it is now attainable to directly correlate cognitive operations of language with functions of the brain and to depict the functional neuroanatomy of language and the relevant cognitive operations. Thus, functional brain imaging techniques enable us to provide sources of information on the neural correlates of the human language processing. This section will look at several basic features and principles concerning functional brain imaging techniques.

Currently, several techniques have become available in the study of functional brain imaging of language. Those techniques can be classified into two major groups, based on either the electrical or magnetic components of neural activity (EEG (electroencephalography) and MEG (magnetoencephalography), or on the effects of changes in brain activity on blood flow (fMRI, PET (positron emission tomography), and OT (optical topography)). Among others, fMRI, PET, and OT have been most widely used as less invasive devices to investigate brain regions that correlate with behavioral performance of language. These functional brain imaging techniques can provide good spatial resolution, which is a major advantage of the techniques. However, their temporal resolution is relatively poor in comparison with other neurophysiological techniques such as EEG and MEG (Section 2.2.1.4). Nevertheless, they can be very useful as the tools for the mapping of neuronal activity to seek to capture structural and functional information about real-time language processing in the brain, in that they potentially greatly enhance our powers to observe on-line behavioral performance of language.

For the inquiry of the functional relationship between mental operations and brain functions of language, brain imaging techniques require to rest on any physiological information provided by the signal changes of neuronal activity. fMRI measures changes in blood oxygenation in proportion to neuronal activation over events, tracking the signal change called a blood-oxygenation-level-independent (BOLD) response (Kwong et al., 1992; Ogawa et al., 1992). PET records changes in blood flow by using radiopharmaceutical ($H_2^{15}O$) as a radioactive tracer, causing gamma emissions provoked by the positron emitting ^{15}O isotope (Raichle, 2003, 2006). OT estimates changes in blood oxygenation in a comparable manner with the BOLD response in fMRI (Strangman et al., 2002), measuring changes in reflected wavelengths by infrared light.

fMRI and PET can offer information about functional activation covering over relatively large areas of the entire brain, whereas OT is mostly limited to recording from superficial cortical areas 2 – 3 cm below the scalp (Scerif et al., 2006). Usually, fMRI has more accurate spatial resolution than PET, typically on the order of 2 – 4 mm in plane. In contrast, the spatial resolution of PET is about 5 – 10 mm. fMRI is therefore advantageous over other brain imaging techniques when assessing changes in the functioning of small or deep cortical and subcortical structures in the brain at a high resolution. Also, fMRI has superior temporal resolution compared to PET. Thus, fMRI, PET, and OT differ in terms of relative spatial and temporal resolution, depth of recording, relative invasiveness, and ease of use with experiment and experimentation. In view of these facts, this study will choose fMRI as the measuring device used for the study to investigate the neural substrates of phrasal segmentation during sentence processing. In the following, this section will outline the basic assumption underlying the functional brain imaging technique using fMRI, and then the present section will introduce current approaches to experimental design and analysis used for fMRI experiments.

fMRI is the device that records changes in blood flow and indirectly measures neural activity, utilizing the neurophysiological fact that the amount of blood flow and hence the content of oxygen in blood flow increases at the site of an increase in neural activity. The brain activity-associated changes in blood flow cause changes in the amount of oxygen carried by the hemoglobin, which consequently lead to changes in the magnetic susceptibility of hemoglobin and ultimately to changes in the degree of the magnetic field at the site with increased neural activity. Those changes in magnetic field, which are called the BOLD effect, could be detected with fMRI, indexing functional brain activation. The basic premise of fMRI is that regional changes in neural activity are reflected by magnetic difference between oxygenated and deoxygenated blood (Ogawa & Lee, 1990; Ogawa et al., 1992). Thus, the underlying principle used in fMRI is based on hemodynamic responses corresponding to neural activity. Observing the modulation of BOLD response resulting from the evoked neural activity caused by a certain cognitive task, fMRI permits us to detect and map functional activity of the normal human brain.

In an fMRI experiment, the person inside the scanner performs a series of cognitive tasks while fMRI image data are collected. In the majority of fMRI experiments, two main stimulus presentation schemes have been used to acquire fMRI data: one is a block design, and the other is an event-related design. Figure 3.1 depicts these two types of stimulus presentation paradigm. In the figure, the curved line denotes the patterns of hemodynamic responses. Abbreviations are used as follows: T, trial (activation); C, control (rest).

In the block design, a block of stimuli is presented sequentially within a condition, alternating between blocks of one condition and blocks of another.

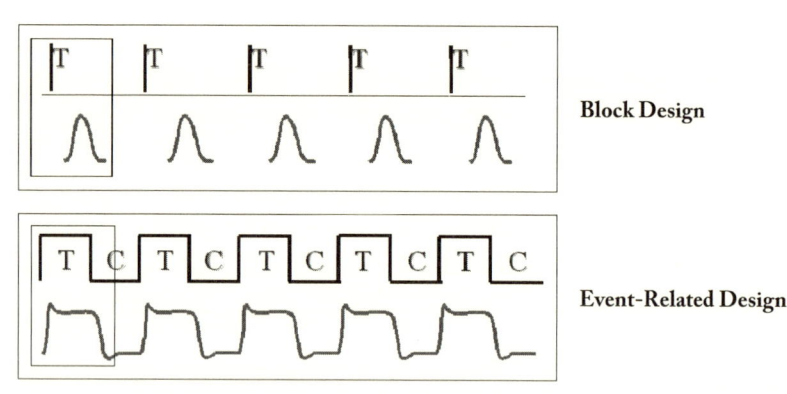

Figure 3.1. Stimulus presentation paradigm. From "Study design in fMRI: Basic principles," by E. Jr. Amaro & G. J. Baker, 2006, *Brain and Cognition*, 60, p. 224. Copyright 2006 by Elsevier Inc.

That design allows for the stability of the hemodynamic response, producing relatively large BOLD signal change (Buxton et al., 1998; Glover, 1999) and the robustness of results (Brockway, 2000; Loubinoux et al., 2001). Adopting a subtraction comparison strategy using classical *t*-test analyses, the block design provides increased statistical power (Friston et al., 1999).

In contrast, in the event-related design, various types of trials are presented in a randomly intermixed manner as a series of trial events. That design makes it possible to individually acquire the hemodynamic response to each single stimulus. Thereby, the event-related design allows for analyses related to individual responses to trials, providing the means to analyze and categorize neural correlates of behavioral responses (Buchanan et al., 2000; Williams et al., 2001). The event-related design has the ability to detect transient variations in hemodynamic responses, allowing the temporal characterization of BOLD signal changes (Buxton et al., 2004; Rosen et al., 1998). Thus, the event-related design can offer advantages over the block design to measure brain activation over events, although the statistical power is relatively lesser compared to the block design. However, regarding which experimental design is more suitable for a particular experiment, the researcher has to decide which to choose as a general principle on the basis of a hypothesis that will be formulated and tested in that experiment.

In the vast majority of fMRI experiments, the images while the subject is performing certain behavioral tasks that differ in at least two conditions are acquired for analysis. Then, to infer differences in processing between these different conditions, brain activation levels in one condition are statistically compared and analyzed relative to those of another. Thereupon, brain regions that would correlate with particular behavioral performance are investigated and identified. The logic of that analysis, which is called the subtraction logic, assumes that difference in a condition between different cognitive tasks reflects difference in behavioral performance and hence brain activation between these tasks. The subtraction logic forms the basis for all fMRI experiments (Culham, 2006). Thus, in fMRI experiments, the researcher needs to choose the best critical condition for comparison that will subtract out all activation other than the processing of interest.

Usually in analysis, statistical tests are conducted to determine whether the difference in condition exists and is unlikely to occur by chance. For statistical comparison, there are two main approaches: the voxelwise approach and the ROI (region of interest) approach (Culham, 2006). In the voxelwise approach, the researcher conducts a statistical comparison between at least two conditions of interest on a voxel-by-voxel basis. No prior assumptions are needed concerning which specific brain areas will be differentially activated. Based on statistical evaluation, a list of areas in which significant activation differences were observed can be created. In the ROI approach, the researcher makes a novel inference with a central focus on the role of previously described brain regions. ROIs are mostly defined on the basis of anatomical criteria. For example, in language study, regions of the left inferior frontal lobe and the left temporal lobe may be identified and selected on the basis of the anatomical slice data. Generally, ROIs are well established areas defined by their functional responses. In the ROI approach, regions are first identified based on prior studies that have reported reliable activation. Then, activation in these ROIs is evaluated independently in an experiment designed to test a new hypothesis. After the ROI has been identified in each subject, the activation time courses are extracted and analyzed statistically to determine whether significant differences exist in the comparison for the new experimental task.

Thus, a recent exponential growth in the functional brain imaging techniques provides us a means to investigate the functional activity of the human brain associated with language processing. fMRI is one of such techniques to allow us to detect brain regions of higher local activity correlating with the particular cognitive tasks of language. The present section has overviewed the basic features and principles of current functional neuroimaging techniques, as the preliminary for the preceding brief description of the findings of neuroanatomical and neuroimaging study of the brain, and further for the study of phrasal segmentation using fMRI. The next section will look at the anatomical relationship between the brain and language, with the particular focus on the issue of the mapping of language in the brain, relying on evidence from the modern neuroanatomical study, and from the recent brain imaging study using the functional brain imaging techniques the present section has reviewed.

3.1.2 Mapping of Language in the Brain

The underlying assumption of the brain imaging study is that all behaviors have some neural correlate in the brain. It is also the assumption much commonly shared and supported by most cognitive neuroscientists. Much of the neuroanatomical and the brain imaging work on language over the past several decades have been influenced by this assumption. The present section will consider evidence for a direct link between language and the brain from neuroanatomical and baring imaging studies in the context of the mapping of language functions in the human brain.

The issue of whether different functions of language are located in different regions of the brain or different language functions are distributed throughout the whole brain has been a subject of controversy for many years in the study of the language and brain relationship (see, Mesulam, 1990, 1998, for example). In the vast majority of people, the observation that language functions are predominantly lateralized to the left hemisphere of the brain has been well known and established even for the left-handed people. The major historical source of evidence for the observation can be traced back to the report in the late 19th century by Paul Broca (1861) and Karl Wernicke (1874) on the basis of their clinical case studies and postmortem dissection of patients with focal brain damage and aphasia. Later after their report, Lichtheim (1885) formulated the neurological model of language processing and showed the location of the main language centers in the brain, drawing on the work of Broca's and Wernicke's and his own clinical observation of aphasic symptoms. His model attributed language production to the left inferior frontal lobe or so-called Broca's area, which covers approximately regions labeled BA (Brodmann's areas) 44 and BA 45, and language comprehension to the left superior temporal lobe or so-called Wernicke's area in the proximity of the auditory association area surrounding the primary auditory cortex. In addition, neural structures such as the supra-marginal gyrus, the angular gyrus, and the arcuate fasciculus, which is a subcortical fiber tract connecting both frontal and temporal language regions, were included as portions of language-related neural substrates in his model. Lichtheim suggested that language is processed in specialized language centers, both of which are known as the perisylvian language areas along the sylvian fissure of the left hemisphere now, along the way of the arcuate fasciculus. His model, postulating the functional localization between language and the brain, became a major reference among neurologists for a long time and greatly influenced subsequent arguments that intend to link language and the brain.

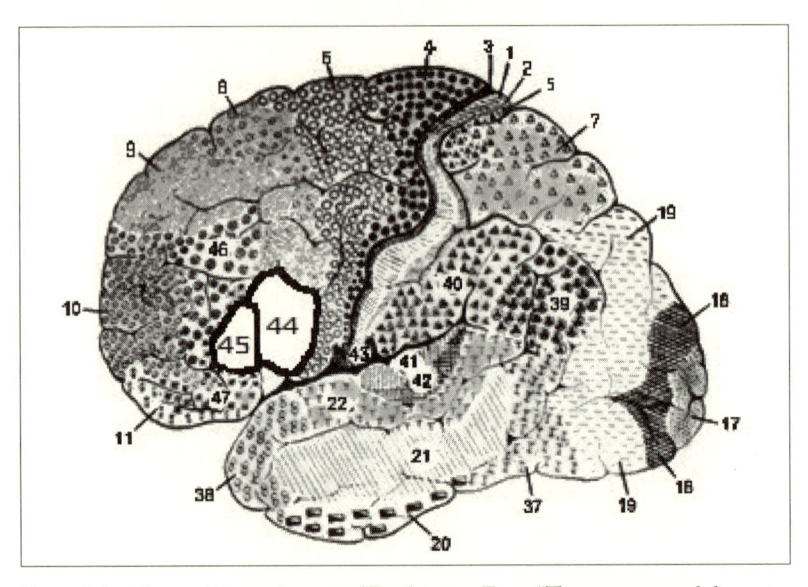

Figure 3.2. Cytoarchitectonic map of Brodmann. From "The structure and dynamics of normal language processing: Insights from neuroimaging," by S. Heim, 2005, *Acta Neurobiologiae Experimentalis*, 65, p. 96. Copyright 2005 by Nencki Institute of Experimental Biology and Polish Neuroscience Society.

Figure 3.2 shows the lateral view of the left hemisphere of the human brain based on the original cytoarchitectonic map of Brodmann (1909). In the figure, the language areas in BA 44 and BA 45, which are called Broca's area, are highlighted.

In the past few decades, the development of functional brain imaging techniques has considerably enhanced the power to observe the on-line human language processing in the brain, in particular to investigate the language and brain relationship in the brain. These techniques have allowed us to study the normal functions of the healthy human brain associated with language processing. Within recent years, using such techniques, a number of studies have indicated that language processing is likely to involve distributed neural networks evoking transient connections between localized regions that are functionally more specialized for particular components of processing at work (Binder et al., 2003; Catani et al., 2004; Giraud & Price, 2001; Just et al., 1996; Mayer et al., 2003; Stowe et al., 2004; Price, Indefrey et al. 1999; Price et al., 1999; Vandenberghe et al., 2002). Their findings have shown that language-related brain functions are not only restricted to the traditional perisylvian language areas but also connected to other areas of both hemispheres of the brain, while they acknowledge that the main language areas predominantly spread along the sylvian fissure over the left hemisphere of the brain (see, Figure 3.4).

Figure 3.3 illustrates the example of the distribution of language related neural activities in the brain, whose findings were based on PET studies of auditory language processing (Démonet et al., 2005). The findings in the figure support the view that language is processed in the distributed neural networks of the brain. In Figure 3.3.A, the rapid acoustic transition task elicited activity in both hemispheres, although more increased activity was identified in the left-side regions. In Figure 3.3.B and C, the contrast between the phoneme detection and the tone discrimination task found increased activity: the activation increased in different regions according to the level of difficulty of each task. In Figure 3.3.D, increased activation was found in the contrast between the phoneme detection and the semantic categorization task. In Figure 3.3.E, different activations were found in the detection task between intelligible speech samples and unintelligible speech-like stimuli. In Figure 3.3.F and G, different patterns of activation were detected in the contrast in the semantic decision task between words and sounds. In Figure 3.3.H, activation spreading over both hemispheres was

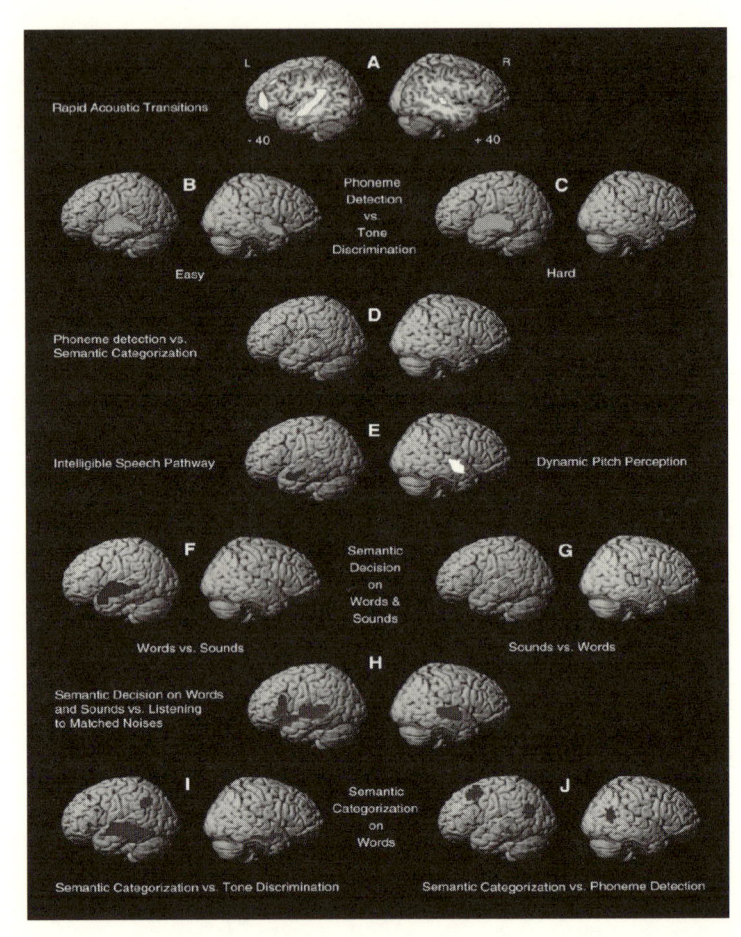

Figure 3.3. Distribution of language-related neural activity. From "Renewal of the neurophysiology of language: functional neuroimaging," by J-F. Démonet, G. Thierry & D. Cardebat, 2005, *Physiological Reviews*, 85, p. 65. Copyright 2005 by the American Physiological Society.

found in the contrast between the semantic decision task and the matched noise listening task. In Figure 3.3.I and J, different patterns of activation were observed in the semantic categorization task on words, respectively in comparison to the tone discrimination and the phoneme detection task. Thus, the findings show that, while language-related brain functions center around the traditional perisylvian language areas, distributed neural networks are involved with different degrees of specialization in language processing.

The present section has observed the evidence that language is processed in distributed areas of the brain beyond the traditional language areas. In addition to this observation, current research using functional neuroimaging techniques have contributed to the localization of which brain regions are involved in any particular aspect of language processing (i.e., particular processing operation) within these distributed language-relevant neural networks in the brain. The following section will look at the issue of language specificity in language processing, providing evidence from recent studies of functional brain imaging in support of the view that distinct areas support different aspects of language processing within language-related neural networks in the brain.

3.1.3 Language Specificity in the Brain

According to a number of review articles and papers (Caplan, 2004; Friederici, 2002; Hagoort, 2005b; Stowe et al., 2005), it has been pointed out that different computational resources of the brain would be required for different operations of language processing. In recent years, that indication has been widely confirmed by the identification of brain regions responsible for particular aspects of processing operations of language. That identification suggests that different areas and networks support different aspects of language processing. In the present section, we will consider the role of the language-relevant brain areas that support the neural basis of language processing.

As argued in the previous section, a large body of recent work of functional neuroimaging has given indication that a particular function of language processing is most likely to be served by a distributed network of areas rather than by one area alone. Additionally, that work has suggested that the local areas of the brain appear to support more than one particular function regarding language processing. For instance, the left superior temporal lobe and the left middle lobe are both involved in different language-related tasks, as indicated in Figure 3.3. More recently, a number of neuroimaging studies of language employing different research paradigms have presented findings that there seem to be functionally defined subregions that are responsible for different functions and operations of language processing: for example, speech listening and production task (Buchsbaum et al., 2001; Hickok et al., 2003; Okada et al., 2003); word categorization task (Chee et al., 2000; Grossman et al., 2002).

Figure 3.4 depicts the anatomical structures of the human brain: Figure 3.4.a shows the lateral view of the left hemisphere of the human brain; Figure 3.4.b shows the medial sagittal view of the right hemisphere of the human brain. In that figure, gray-colored and labeled local areas and subregions are areas and subregions that have been pointed out to be the main anatomical regions involved in language processing. Numbers indicate Brodmann's areas (BA) separated by dotted lines.

In the temporal area, the superior temporal cortex including primary and associative auditory cortex in both hemispheres has been considered to be the main neural substrates associated with human voice (Belin et al. 2000; Belin et al., 2002) and speech sound (Binder et al., 2000; Matthew & Johnsrude, 2003; Vouloumanos et al., 2001) processing. The posterior part of the middle temporal gyrus (i.e., Wernicke's area) in the left hemisphere, close to the superior temporal lobe, has been reported to be involved in the access to word meaning (Fiebach et al., 2002; Fiez et al., 1999) and word meaning category (Bookheimer et al., 2000; Thompson-Schill et al., 1999).

In the left basal occopito-temporal cortex, the fusiform and inferior temporal gyri, which are known as the visual word form area (VWFA), have been predicted to be responsible for the recognition of written word (Cohen & Dehaene, 2004; Cohen et al., 2000; McCandliss et al., 2003), although the role and the functional specificity of that area are currently under lively debate (Price & Devlin, 2003, 2004).

In the left frontal area, the left inferior frontal lobe has been pointed out to be responsible for a variety of language-related processing operations involved in phonological, semantic and syntactic processing of language. The left inferior frontal gyrus (BA 44/45) has been known for the area being involved in syntactic tasks (Friederici, 2004; Hagoort, 2003b; Kaan & Swaab, 2002). The superior posterior portion of the left inferior frontal gyrus (BA 44) has been reported to be involved in phonological tasks such

a. Lateral view of the left hemisphere of the human brain.

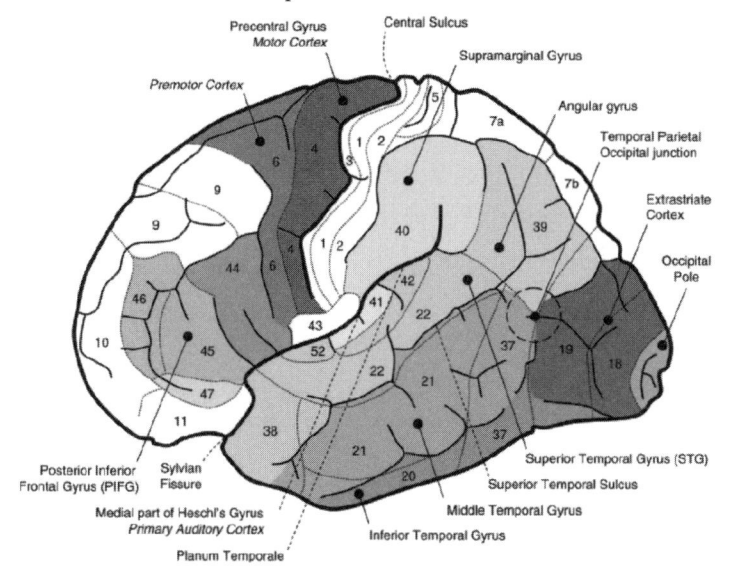

b. **Medial sagittal view of the right hemisphere of the human brain.**

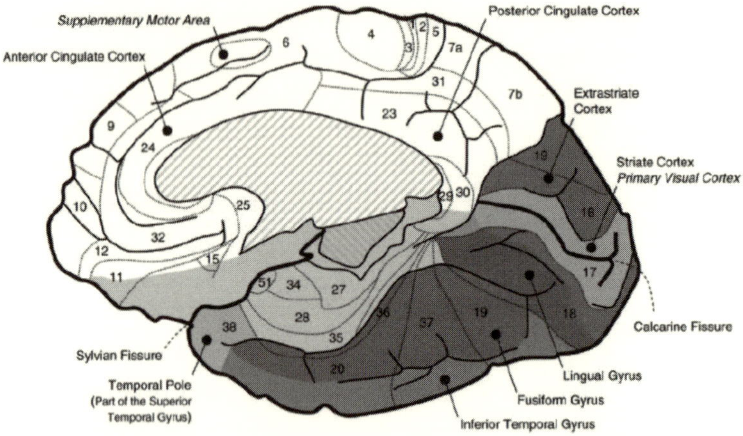

Figure 3.4. Main brain regions involved in human language processing. From "Renewal of the neurophysiology of language: functional neuroimaging," by J-F. Démonet, G. Thierry and D. Cardebat, 2005, *Physiological Reviews*, 85, p. 63. Copyright 2005 by the American Physiological Society.

as phoneme monitoring, phoneme discrimination and phoneme sequencing tasks (Burton, 2000; Fiez & Peterson, 1998; Poldrack et al., 1999). The ventral portion of the left inferior frontal gyrus (BA 47) has been observed as region specialized for accessing and manipulating semantic information (Bokde et al., 2001; Dapretto & Bookheimer, 1999; Ni et al., 2000; Rodd et al., 2005; Ruschemeyer et al., 2006).

In the right hemisphere, the right superior temporal region and its proximity have been identified as regions that support the processing of prosodic information (i.e., suprasegmental information such as accentuation and intonational phrases (Friederici & Alter, 2004; Mayer et al., 2003)).

As shown in the present section, a number of functional brain imaging studies support the view that there are functionally defined subregions that are responsible for different functions and operations of language processing. Distinct areas form the neural basis of different aspects of language processing within language-related neural networks in the brain. As a result, consistent activation patterns associated with particular language processing functions and operations have been investigated and the functional role of each identified cluster has been discussed in relation to functional specialization of regional activations within the processing networks of language.

3.2 Functional Relationship between Language and the Brain

As pointed out in the previous chapter, current neurophysiological findings using EEG and MEG have explored in detail that there are various stages of language processing, fractionating their stages from speech perception, to word recognition, morphological analysis, syntactic parsing and sentence interpretation. These findings have also found that different types of linguistic information are differently recruited in different stages of language processing. These facts suggest that individual processing operations, which reflect different functions of language behaviors, could be mapped in different areas in the brain in connection with individual functions of language processing. The present section will provide the evidence for the functional relationship between language and the brain.

Recent findings of functional brain imaging have presented evidence to confirm the functional relationship between language and the brain. These findings have shown that different aspects of language and language-related functions are widely distributed in the brain. Such language and language-related functions are subserved in the distributed brain networks. Different types of processing operations are involved in these functions, recruiting different sources of linguistic information (i.e., phonological, semantic, and syntactic information).

Figure 3.5 indicates such brain facts to prove the functional relationship between language and the brain (Vigneau et al., 2006). The mapping in the figure provides the perspective on how brain functions support the human language processing by attributing a particular brain function to a particular brain region. The figure shows the mass of the clusters of activation involved in language processing in the left hemisphere of the brain. Each mass of the activation is plotted and labeled according to the processing category of information engaged in language processing: phonological, semantic, and syntactic processing domain. Clusters of different categories that were not spatially distinct are circled with dashed line. Abbreviations are used as follows in the figure: RolS, Rolandic sulcus; RolOp, Rolandic operculum;

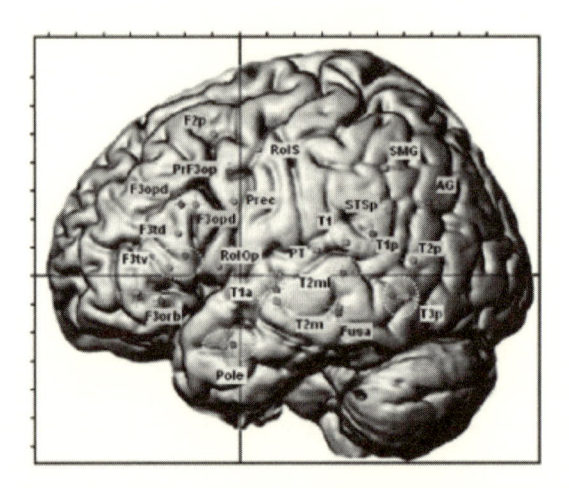

Figure 3.5. Mass of the clusters of language processing in the left hemisphere of the brain. From "Meta-analyzing left hemisphere language areas: phonology, semantics, and sentence processing," by M. Vigneau, V. Beaucousin, P. Y. Hervé, H. Duffan, F. Crivello, O. Houdé, B. Mazoyer, and N. Tzourio-Mazoyer, 2006, *NeuroImage*, 30, p. 1418. Copyright 2006 by Elsevier Inc.

F3t, pars triangularis of the left inferior frontal gyrus; F3op, pars opercularis of left inferior frontal gyrus; F3orb, pars orbitalis of left inferior frontal gyrus; SMG, supramarginal gyrus; PT, planum temporale; T1, superior temporal gyrus; T2, middle temporal gyrus; T3, inferior temporal gyrus; Prec, precentral gyrus; F2, middle frontal gyrus; PrF3op, precentral gyrus/F3op junction; STS, superior temporal sulcus; AG, angular gyrus; Fusa, anterior fusiform gyrus; a, anterior; p, posterior; l, lateral; m, middle; d, dorsal; v, ventral. The mass of the clusters plotted in the figure serves as the marker of language-related neural activities distributed in the left hemisphere of the brain. The figure helps to define the functional mapping of cortical activations devoted to each category of processing (i.e., phonological, semantic, and syntactic processing).

Table 3.1 shows the anatomical label and the stereotactic coordinate of each center of the clusters activated in each category of processing domain in the left frontal and the left temporal lobes presented in Figure 3.5. The number in parentheses denotes the number of activation peaks of each center of activations.

The analysis in Figure 3.5 and Table 3.1 shows that a large number of language-related regional activations are located in the distributed areas in the left frontal and temporal lobes (i.e., the main language processing areas of the brain). Additionally, these distributed regional activations are classified into three domains of processing (i.e., phonological, semantic, and syntactic processing) according to the category of information devoted to each processing operation. The analysis indicates that any particular functional role can be assigned to each of language-related regional activations, relying on each category of processing domain. Therefore, the analysis of the data presented in Figure 3.5 and Table 3.1 provides support for the view of functional specialization between language and the brain.

The analysis in Figure 3.5 and Table 3.1 also shows that individual processing operations, which reflect different functions of language

Table 3.1. Anatomical Locations of Activations Involved in Language Processing

	Phonological	x	y	z	SD (x,y,z)	Semantic	x	y	z	SD (x,y,z)	Syntactic	x	y	z	SD (x,y,z)
Frontal	RolS (21)	-47	-6	44	10.7	PrF3op (27)	-42	4	36	11.4	F2p (14)	-37	10	48	12.3
	Prec (36)	-48	2	26	9.6	F3opd (41)	-44	21	24	11.1	F3opd (15)	-49	16	24	11.2
	F3td (38)	-44	23	15	11.6	F3tv (38)	-43	20	4	16.0	F3tv (30)	-44	26	2	14.9
	RolOp (18)	-48	8	3	14.2	F3orb (39)	-37	31	-9	14.0					
	F3orb/F2 (12)	-33	37	-6	19.0										
Total peaks	(125)					(145)					(59)				
Temporal and parietal	SMG (10)	-42	-52	37	16.4	AG (27)	-45	-68	26	14.1					
	T1 (35)	-50	-38	12	12.4	T1p (15)	-55	-48	15	12.1	STSp (27)	-50	-54	22	11.6
	PT (23)	-60	-27	9	8.4										
	T1a (27)	-56	-12	-3	14.7	T1a (30)	-56	-13	-5	11.6	T1a (16)	-57	-13	-8	10.9
	T3p (17)	-50	-60	-7	14.5	T3p (38)	-46	-55	-7	11.1	T2p (16)	-40	-63	5	15.1
	T2m (10)	-51	-35	-11	12.5	T2ml (21)	-59	-37	1	8.0	T2ml (25)	-57	-40	2	12.0
						Fusa (30)	-38	-35	-13	13.6					
						Pole (16)	-41	3	-24	19.5	Pole (18)	-47	6	-24	15.7
Total peaks	(122)					(177)					(102)				

Note. From "Meta-analyzing left hemisphere language areas: Phonology, semantics, and sentence processing," by M. Vigneau, V. Beaucousin, P. Y. Hervé, H. Duffan, F. Crivello, O. Houdé, B. Mazoyer, and N. Tzourio-Mazoyer, 2006, *NeuroImage*, 30, p. 1419. Copyright 2006 by Elsevier Inc.

behaviors, are mapped in the brain in connection with their individual functions of processing. The analysis offers the validity for the functional brain imaging study of phrasal segmentation, in the sense that a particular language function is attributed to a particular brain function in the brain. Thus, the mental operation of phrasal segmentation also can be defined by the functional relationship between language and the brain. In the next section, the present study will take up the issue of the interaction and integration of processed information and discuss the place of phrasal segmentation within the processing framework of sentence comprehension.

3.3 Sentence Comprehension and Phrasal Segmentation

As the present study has argued, sentence comprehension is the cognitive operation that depends on three different sources of linguistic information (i.e., phonological, semantic, and syntactic information). It is a task that processes and integrates such linguistic information from a speech flow or a string of characters in a particular way in order for the meaning of a sentence to be obtained. Although it is well accepted that phonological, semantic and syntactic information respectively contribute to sentence comprehension, the issue of how and when each category of processed information becomes integrated together still remains to be unsettled (Section 2.2.1.5). This section will take up the issue of the interaction and integration again in consideration of the place of the mental operation of phrasal segmentation within the overall design of sentence comprehension.

In recent years, a number of researchers have reported the studies using the ERP (event-related brain potential) related to sentence comprehension (Friederici, 2002; Hagoort, 2003b; Hahne & Friederici, 2002; Hoeks et al., 2004; Palolahti et al, 2005; Silva-Pereyra et al, 2005). Following the time course of ERP effects on phonological, semantic and syntactic processing, the researchers have indicated that interactive and integrative phases of processing are involved in sentence comprehension. Friederici and her colleague (Friederici, 2002; Friederici & Kotz, 2003) have proposed that sentence comprehension can be subdivided into the following different processing phases: phonological segmentation and sequencing, initial syntactic structure building, semantic integration, morpho-syntactic integration, and late integration phases. Their study suggests that each category of linguistic information is independently integrated. Only at a later phase of processing, syntactic and semantic information interact for integration in reanalysis and repair. In their prediction, first, phonological (i.e., segmental) information is processed in the dorsal portion of the left

IFG (inferior frontal gyrus) (BA 44). Next, the lexical access starts in the left STG (superior temporal gyrus) (BA 22). Then, local phrase structures are built based on the word category information in the anterior ventral portion of the left IFG (BA 44/45) in the syntactic domain. After structural information is provided, semantic relations and thematic roles are assigned in the posterior ventral portion of the left IFG (BA 45/47) in the semantic domain. Finally, syntactic and semantic information interact for integration in reanalysis and repair in the left BG (basal ganglia) and the posterior portion of the left STG. Also in auditory sentence comprehension, prosodic (i.e., suprasegmental) information is processed in the right temporal and frontal (opercular) cortices. Following their prediction, the place of the mental operation of phrasal segmentation is in the processing operation of local phrase structure building in the syntactic processing domain. If so, phrasal segmentation is assumed to take place by recruiting the anterior ventral portion of the left IFG (BA 44/45) in the syntactic processing domain.

With respect to the issue of the interaction and integration in sentence comprehension, Hagoort (2003b, 2005a, 2008) has argued that processed information is immediately integrated for the purpose of interpretation as soon as it becomes available. He insists that all available linguistic information is used in parallel in order that sentence comprehension is extended incrementally over time. He proposes three different parallel processing domains: phonological, syntactic, semantic domain. In the phonological domain, lexical items are integrated into intonational phrases based on the phonological information marked by tone, pausing, lengthening or segmental variation. In the syntactic domain, each lexical item in the lexicon has a syntactic frame (i.e., lexical-syntactic information). The syntactic frame specifies the possible structural environment of the particular lexical item. Phrase configuration is formed based on the syntactic frame of each lexical item. In the semantic domain, the word meaning is combined and integrated into the meaning of larger structures (i.e., phrases, clauses and a sentence). During on-line sentence comprehension, each domain of processing operates concurrently and interacts with each other. For instance, the syntactic linking operation between words can be guided by the semantic information of each word (i.e., lexical-semantic information) (Hagoort, 2003b). In his proposal, lexical-syntactic information is retrieved in the posterior portion of the left STG. Lexical-semantic information is accessed in the left MTG (middle temporal gyrus) and the left ITG (inferior temporal gurus). In the phonological domain, phonological information is integrated in the dorsal portion of the left IFG (inferior frontal gyrus) (BA44) and the ventral portion of the left premotor cortex (BA6). In the syntactic domain, constituent structures are formed in the posterior dorsal portion of the left IFG (BA 44/45). In the semantic domain, the individual word meaning is integrated into the meaning of phrases, clauses and a sentence in the anterior ventral portion of the left IFG (BA 45/47). Following his perspective, the place of the mental operation of phrasal segmentation falls into the syntactic domain. However, the interaction can trigger possible involvement of other processing domains. Therefore, the left IFG is hypothesized to mainly support phrasal segmentation, though the involvement of each region will differ depending on the extent of the interaction.

This section has argued the place of the mental processing of phrasal segmentation from two different perspectives of sentence comprehension. From serial processing view, the anterior ventral portion of the left IFG (BA 44/45) in the syntactic processing domain will be involved in phrasal segmentation. From parallel processing view, the left IFG will be differently recruited in phrasal segmentation depending on the processing interaction. In the next section, this study will take up and argue the research issues before conducting the fMRI experiments of phrasal segmentation to confirm the discussion in the present section.

3.4 Rationale for the fMRI Experiments of Phrasal Segmentation

The present chapter has argued that a particular language function is attributed to a particular brain function in the brain, and it has discussed that phrasal segmentation is a processing operation that is supported by a particular brain function. However, the issue of what type of linguistic information is needed or what processing domain is involved in the exact processing of phrasal segmentation still remains to be unresolved, let alone the issue of what brain regions support the mental processing of phrasal segmentation. Relying on two different proposals of sentence comprehension, this study has predicted the place of the mental operation of phrasal segmentation differently in the brain. To confirm the predictions, this study will conduct the fMRI experiments of phrasal segmentation. Before doing them, this section will take up the research issues involved in the fMRI experiments of phrasal segmentation.

It has been commonly acknowledged that what the sentence conveys is far more than simply adding together the meanings of the individual words (Cutler & Clifton, 1999). Still, so far, no studies have been available, in particular, for explicitly observing and investigating the way of how phrasal units are mentally formed from individual words in a sentence. To clarify this question, the present study seeks to investigate the cortical mechanisms underlying phrasal segmentation and identify the functional specialization of phrasal segmentation in the brain during the on-line sentence comprehension. Here this study focuses on the investigation of the mental operation of phrasal segmentation during Japanese sentence comprehension. First, this study investigates the neural substrates of phrasal segmentation in the course of the visual comprehension of Japanese sentences (the visual experiment). Then, this study examines the neural substrates of phrasal segmentation in the course of the auditory comprehension of Japanese sentences (the auditory experiment). Finally, it will argue the neural basis of phrasal segmentation, comparing the results from two different fMRI experiments.

In the visual experiment, Japanese Kana sentences are introduced as the stimuli. In the visual sentence comprehension, the way of the visual Japanese Kana sentence comprehension is strikingly different from the way of typical Western language's visual sentence comprehension perspective, in which spaces between words are regularly placed and there is no need to identify each individual word and phrase and discover its meaning from a string of characters. In Japanese, each Kana character corresponds to a phonological segmentation unit called the 'mora' (see, Kubozono, 1998a, 1998b, for 'mora'). First, the reader establishes the phonological connection to each Kana character. Next, the reader groups each character into individual words and phrases. Then, the reader parses and integrates them into the sentence meaning to obtain an interpretation of the sentence. Thus, the visual Kana sentence stimuli share the same phonological information as the auditory Japanese sentence stimuli. Resultingly, Kana sentence stimuli make it possible to control the resource of phonological information used between two different modalities of fMRI experiments.

Furthermore, in the auditory experiment, prosodic information is added. Therefore, this study makes the investigation possible into the modality effect on phrasal segmentation, especially, the issue of whether prosodic information is involved in phrasal segmentation or not. In the visual condition, the stimulus sentences do not carry prosodic information; however, in the auditory condition, the stimulus sentences carry it. When taken together, this experimental design will allow the verification of the modality independent effect of phrasal segmentation as well as its modality specific effect during the on-line sentence comprehension.

Thus, Japanese sentence stimuli merit the task materials to control the confounding factors such as the word identification and the inconsistency between auditory and visual processing as noted above. This study will design and conduct the experiment of phrasal segmentation in visual Kana and auditory processing of Japanese as presented in the conditions like the sentence (7a) and (7b). The condition like in the sentence (7a) is referred to as the non-segmented condition, where no space or no pronounced pause is placed, and the condition like in the sentence (7b) as the segmented condition, where a space or a distinct pause is left. In the both conditions,

Non-segmented sentence stimulus:
(7) a.　おばがおじにでんごんをつたえた
　　　　(o-ba-ga-o-zi-ni-de-N-go-N-o-tu-ta-e-ta)
　　　　(aunt-Nom uncle-Dat message-Acc delivered)
　　　　(My aunt delivered the message to my uncle.)

Segmented sentence stimulus:
　　　b.　おとこが　かべに　らくがきを　かいた
　　　　(o-to-ko-ga　ka-be-ni　ra-ku-ga-ki-o　ka-i-ta)
　　　　(man-Nom　wall-Loc　graffiti-Acc　wrote)
　　　　(The man wrote graffiti on the wall.)

readers or hearers need to identify the words, but their difficulty in the word identification is considered to be similar between the two conditions in the experiments. This study seeks to identify the brain function and its relevant neural activities of phrasal segmentation by subtracting the result of cognitive operations in the segmented condition from the result in the non-segmented condition. By doing so, this study attests the validity of the explanation of phrasal segmentation provided by the predictions from serial and parallel perspectives of sentence comprehension.

　　In addition, the language areas in the left IFG, which the present study predicts most likely to be relevant to phrasal segmentation, have been also viewed as the areas of working memory associated with the short-term retention and manipulation of linguistic information (Badre & Wagner, 2007; Chein et al., 2002; Fletcher & Henson, 2001). Hence, this study introduces the control task to subtract the brain activations of working memory from those of phrasal segmentation. In the visual experiment, the subjects are asked to count the instances of the Kana 'い' in each sentence and judge whether the total was odd or even. In the auditory experiment, the subjects are asked to judge whether each stimulus contains the same sound unit ('mora') as the penult or not. These control tasks were chosen on the basis of the behavioral data (the accuracy rate and the response time) obtained from the pilot study.

Using fMRI technique, the present study will specify and compare the neural activations during Japanese sentence comprehension between non-segmented and segmented conditions for the localization of sources concerning phrasal segmentation. When the sentence comprehension task is performed, this study postulates that the mental operation of phrasal segmentation is more involved in the non-segmented condition than in the segmented condition.

3.5 Summary

The present chapter has discussed the issue of the functional relationship between language and the brain and verified the validity of the functional brain imaging study of phrasal segmentation. First, the chapter has thought over the basic features and principles of functional brain imaging techniques as the preliminary step for the discussion of the functional relationship between language and the brain, introducing recent approaches to functional neuroimaging studies. Secondly, the chapter has examined neuroanatomical evidence on the human language processing by tracing back to the modern neuroanatomical study and reviewing the current neuroimaging study of language for an understanding of how language is processed in the brain.

Thirdly, the chapter has looked into the current evidence to prove the functional relationship between language and the brain. Then, the chapter has taken up and argued the interaction and integration of processed linguistic information, in consideration of the place of the mental operation of phrasal segmentation within the overall design of sentence comprehension. Finally, the chapter has argued the research issues of the fMRI experiment and claimed the validity of the experiments to explore the mental operation of phrasal segmentation.

    The following chapters will present the fMRI experiments of phrasal segmentation, using Japanese visual and auditory sentence stimuli. Then, this study will validate the evidence of the functional neural activities supporting phrasal segmentation. Finally, it will also argue the predictions from two different proposals of sentence comprehension, comparing their predictions with the results of the experiments in consideration of the functional specialization of phrasal segmentation in the brain.

Chapter 4

Search for Phrasal Segmentation: Visual fMRI Study

The present chapter will show the visual experiment of phrasal experiment using event-related fMRI and the findings obtained from the experiment. This experiment aims to investigate the neural activations regarding phrasal segmentation during the visual comprehension of Japanese Kana sentences, comparing the neural activation between the segmented and the non-segmented condition. When the sentence comprehension task is performed, the effect of phrasal segmentation is presupposed to be more strongly instantiated in the brain in the non-segmented condition than in the segmented condition. Following this presupposition, the neural activity was measured by fMRI and the neural sources of phrasal segmentation were estimated.

In the previous chapter, this study predicted the place of the mental processing of phrasal segmentation from two different perspectives of sentence comprehension. From serial processing view, the anterior ventral portion of the left IFG (BA 44/45) in the syntactic processing domain was predicted to be involved in phrasal segmentation. From parallel processing view, the left IFG was considered to be differently recruited in phrasal segmentation depending on the interaction of processing. This chapter will closely investigate and discuss the validity of these predictions on the basis of the findings from the visual experiment of phrasal segmentation.

4.1 fMRI Experiment

The following sections will present the research methods of the visual experiment of phrasal segmentation using fMRI.

4.1.1 Participants

Nineteen healthy right-handed volunteers (thirteen males and six females, aged 20 to 25 years) participated in this experiment as subjects. All subjects were native speakers of Japanese. They had normal vision and none had a history of neurological or psychiatric illness. Handedness was evaluated using the Edinburgh Handedness Inventory (Oldfield, 1971). Written informed consent was obtained from all the subjects according to the guidelines approved by Tohoku University and the Helsinki Declaration of Human Rights, 1975.

4.1.2 Stimuli and Task

The experimental stimuli consisted of 180 short Japanese Kana simple sentences: 120 sentences were for a comprehension task and 60 sentences were for a control task. Figure 4.1 illustrates the examples of sentence stimuli used in the present study. Each sentence stimulus was made up of 15 mora units. The sentences used in the study are all canonical Japanese sentences with canonical word orders (see, Gunji, 2002; Masuoka & Takubo, 1992, for the categorization of typical sentence patterns in Japanese). The sentence patterns were based on and adopted from the unmarked basic patterns listed in Basic Grammar of Japanese (Masuoka & Takubo, 1992). Words used in each sentence were selected from Word List by Semantic Principles (National Institute for Japanese Language, 2004). Their word familiarity was checked and controlled at the familiar level (the level between

5 and 7 on a 7-point scale) and their word frequency also at the frequent level (the most frequent level on a 3-point scale) using the database developed by Amano and Kondo (2003). To eliminate the facilitative effect of semantic processing caused by repetitive word presentation, every content word such as noun, verb, adverb, and adjective was used only once across all the stimuli. Half of the presented sentences were segmented (Seg) and the other half were not segmented (Non-seg).

The sentences presented in the comprehension task included both semantically congruent (Congruent) and incongruent (Incongruent) sentences: 60 semantically congruent and 60 incongruent sentences. The sentences presented in the control task (Cont) also included both semantically congruent and incongruent sentences: 30 semantically congruent and 30 incongruent sentences. Each sentence in each task was pseudo-randomly ordered. The sentences in each task were divided into 4 blocks respectively: 30 sentences in each comprehension block and 15 sentences in each control block. Then each comprehension and control block was combined in alternation as a series of 8 blocked tasks for an fMRI session. The presented sentence stimuli were classified into the six categories as follows: Non-seg

a. Congruent Sentences:

Non-seg Correct:
おばがおじにでんごんをつたえた
(o-ba-ga-o-zi-ni-de-N-go-N-o-tu-ta-e-ta)
(aunt-Nom uncle-Dat message-Acc delivered)
(My aunt delivered the message to my uncle.)

Seg Correct:
おとこが　かべに　らくがきを　かいた
(o-to-ko-ga　ka-be-ni　ra-ku-ga-ki-o　ka-i-ta)
(man-Nom　wall-Loc　graffiti-Acc　wrote)
(The man wrote graffiti on the wall.)

> **b. Incongruent Sentences:**
>
> **Non-seg Incorrect:**
> さるがいすにきゅうりょうをはらった
> (sa-ru-ga-i-su-ni-kyu-ryo-o-ha-ra-Q-ta)
> (monkey-Nom chair-Dat salary-Acc paid)
> (The monkey paid the chair its salary.)
>
> **Seg Incorrect:**
> いりぐちで　とが　そでに　はさまった
> (i-ri-gu-ti-de　to-ga　so-de-ni　ha-sa-ma-Q-ta)
> (entrance-Loc door-Nom sleeve-Loc　squeezed)
> (The sleeve squeezed the door at the entrance.)

c. Control Sentences:

> **Non-seg Cont:**
> しゃいんがかいしゃにでんわをかけた
> (sja-i-n-ga-ka-i-sja-ni-de-N-wa-o-ka-ke-ta)
> (staff-Nom company-Dat phone call-Acc made)
> (The staff made a phone call to the company.)
>
> **Seg Cont:**
> けいさつが　かいぞくに　つかまった
> (ke-e-sa-tu-ga　ka-i-zo-ku-ni　tu-ka-ma-Q-ta)
> (police-Nom　pirate by-Agent　were caught)
> (The police were caught by the pirate.)

Figure 4.1. Examples of sentence stimuli presented in the visual experiment.

Congruent, Seg Congruent, Non-seg Incongruent, Seg Incongruent, Non-seg Cont, and Seg Cont.

Figure 4.1 shows the examples of sentence stimuli in the visual experiment. In the segmented conditions, each Kana sentence is segmented into minimal meaningful, syntactic phrasal units called '*seibun* (immediate constituent)' (see, Masuoka, 1997). The underlined Kana indicates the target Kana to be identified in the control stimuli.

4.1.3 Procedure

In each block in an event-related task session, following an initial resting period (15 seconds), during which a fixation cross (10 seconds) and a task instruction (5 seconds) were displayed, each stimulus was presented at the center of the visual field for 2.5 seconds during a period of 5 seconds trial (Appendix B). The duration of a stimulus being presented was decided based on a preparatory study: in 2.5 seconds each participant was able to read through each stimulus without rereading it. During an interval between stimulus deliveries, a fixation cross was displayed. To control the effect of the onset timing, each stimulus delivery was pseudo-randomly changed at three different levels, 0 second, 0.5 second and 1 second of delay from the onset respectively across trials. For each stimulus trial, the response time was recorded and calculated from the onset of each stimulus delivery, using two compatible response buttons. The stimulus delivery and the response time recording were conducted under the control of a Windows computer running Presentation (Neurobehavioral Systems, Albany, CA). Each stimulus was visually presented on a back-projected screen attached to the head-coil of the fMRI scanner.

Each participant performed a comprehension and a control task alternately during each blocked presentation of Japanese Kana sentences. In the comprehension task, each participant judged whether each stimulus is semantically congruent or not, pressing the left button with the index finger if the sentence was semantically congruent, and the right button with the middle finger if the sentence was semantically incongruent. In the control task, each participant counted the instances of the mora /i/ in each sentence and judged whether the total was odd or even, pressing the left button with the index finger if the total was odd, or pressing the right button with the middle finger if the total was even. The control task was designed to control the effect of the use of working memory resources in the brain, which would assist in the temporary retention and manipulation of verbal information (see, Curtis & D'Esposito, 2006, for further discussion of working memory). By subtracting the activated regions in the control task from those in the comprehension task, this study posited that the activated regions involved in sentence processing could be specified without under the influence of working memory. The order of the comprehension and the control task was also interchanged to counterbalance the effect of the task order presented across participants: 10 subjects worked on a series of tasks in which a comprehension task precedes a control task; 9 subjects conducted the same tasks in which a comprehension task follows a control task. Just before performing the fMRI session, each participant was engaged in a brief practice session using the laptop computer in order to become familiarized with the task involved in the study. The practice session included 10 trials, which were conducted using the similar stimuli presented in each task in the study.

Figure 4.2 sketches the experimental task design adopted in the study. Stimuli A and B were respectively randomized. Then they were divided up into each block: 30 stimuli in each comprehension block and 15 stimuli in each control block. Each of comprehension and control task blocks was alternatively presented eight times in total throughout the whole experimental session. In Figure 4.2, the task design, stimulus delivery timing, and stimulus type of fMRI experiment are shown. "A" refers to the comprehension task block, "B" refers to the control task block, and "C" refers to the rest and instruction. In the section 1, the sequence of the experiment is presented. In the section 2, the stimulus delivery timing in each trial is illustrated. In the section 3, each stimulus type is described and the total number of stimuli presented in each category throughout the whole experimental session is shown in the parenthesis.

1. Task design: an event-related design

Task block: A: Comprehension block (30 stimuli)
B: Control block (15 stimuli)

A (30 stimuli) B (15stimuli) A (30 stimuli) B (15 stimuli)

Dummy

C C C C

Each Task block was alternatively presented eight times.
C: Rest and Instruction (15 seconds)

2. Trial & stimulus:

Stimulus (sentence)
━━ (2.5 seconds)
Trial (5 seconds)

3. Stimulus type (the total number of stimuli presented in the experimental session):

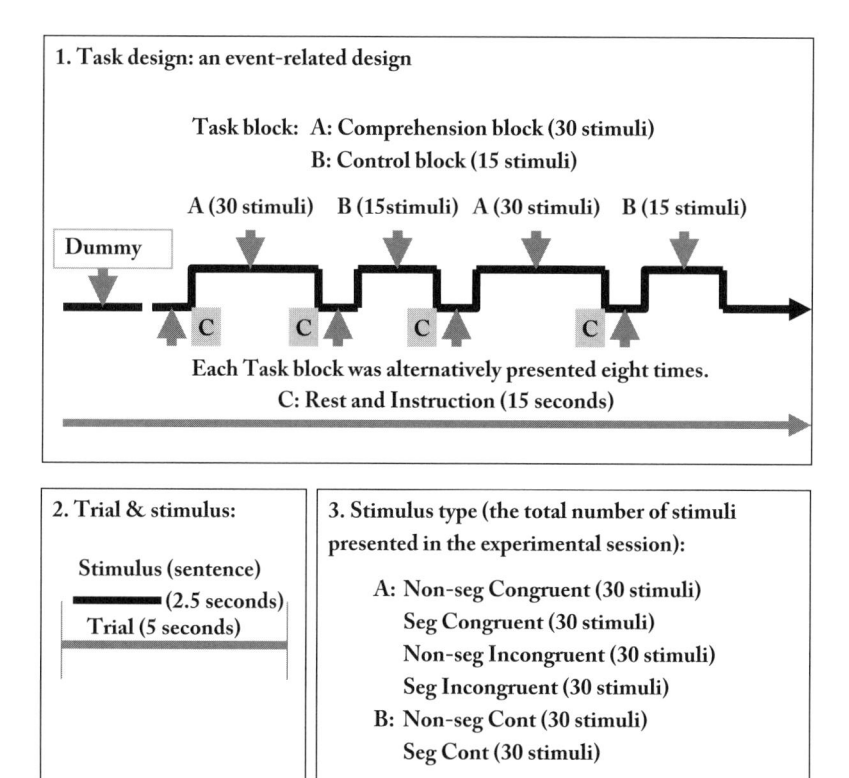

A: Non-seg Congruent (30 stimuli)
Seg Congruent (30 stimuli)
Non-seg Incongruent (30 stimuli)
Seg Incongruent (30 stimuli)
B: Non-seg Cont (30 stimuli)
Seg Cont (30 stimuli)

Figure 4.2. Experimental task design in the visual experiment.

4.1.4   fMRI Data Acquisition and Preprocessing

The visual fMRI experiment of phrasal segmentation was administered on a 1.5-tesla (1.5T) Siemens Symphony scanner system (Siemens, Erlangen, Germany) at Tohoku University. Functional images were acquired using gradient echo planner image sequences with the following parameters: repetition time (TR) = 3,000 ms, echo time (TE) = 60 ms, flip angle = 90°, slice thickness = 3 mm, slice gap = 0.99 mm, field of view (FOV) = 192 mm,

64 × 64 matrix, and 3 × 3 × 3.99 mm voxels of resolution. Thirty-three 3-mm-thick transaxial images covering the entire brain were obtained continuously every 3 seconds (TR) using an echo planar imaging (EPI) sequence during functional measurements. Excluding the initial seven dummy scans used to stabilize the T1 saturation effect from the analysis, 370 volumes were acquired for each participant in each fMRI session. During the fMRI session, the participant's head was secured using a foam rubber pad to minimize artifacts due to movement. T1-weighted structural images were also acquired for each participant to serve as a reference for anatomical correlations: slice thickness = 1.25 mm, FOV = 256 mm, 175 × 256 matrix, TR = 1,900 ms, and TE = 3.93 ms. For the sake of anatomical localization of hemodynamic activation effects, fMRI maps were superimposed on a mean image of the normalized T1-weighted anatomical images of all the participants.

The following preprocessing procedures were conducted using Statistical Parametric Mapping (SPM2) software (Wellcome Department of Cognitive Neurology, London, UK) and MATLAB (Mathworks, Natick, MA, USA): adjustment of acquisition timing across slices, correction for head motion, coregistration to the anatomical image, spatial normalization to the standard brain, and smoothing with an isotropic Gaussian kernel of 10 mm full width at half-maximum (FWHM).

4.1.5 fMRI Data Analysis

From the fMRI data obtained, the data of three participants (two males and one female) were excluded: the data of one male participant whose head motion was excessive (more than 3 mm), and the data of one male and one female participants whose task performance were at the statistically insufficient level (less than 70 % correct response at least one stimulus category). Hence, the data obtained from sixteen subjects were used for the data analysis.

In the data analysis, a voxel-by-voxel multiple regression analysis of the predicted signal change to the preprocessed images was applied for each session for each participant. The analysis adopted a standard event-related convolution model using the hemodynamic response function provided by SPM2. The model of the hemodynamic response function was tailored to the following six categories: Non-seg Congruent, Seg Incongruent, Non-seg Incongruent, Seg Incongruent, Non-seg Cont, and Seg Cont. To detect the differential neural activation during sentence comprehension, the subtraction analyses were performed in the following contrasts: (Seg Congruent + Non-seg Congruent) – (Seg Cont + Non-seg Cont), Non-seg Congruent – Non-seg Cont, Seg Congruent – Seg Cont, and Seg Incongruent – Seg Cont. Statistical inference on these subtractions of parameter estimates was then computed using a between-subject (random effects) model using one-sample t-tests. Contrasts of each subtraction were averaged and inclusively masked with Seg Congruent + Non-seg Congruent, Non-seg Congruent, Seg Congruent, and Seg Incongruent respectively.

To identify the cortical activations reflecting phrasal segmentation during sentence comprehension, a conventional two-step approach was performed for event-related fMRI data. First, the cortical activations involved in sentence comprehension were identified by the following subtraction: (Seg Congruent + Non-seg Congruent) – (Seg Cont + Non-seg Cont) masked with (Seg Congruent + Non-seg Congruent). The statistical threshold was set to $p < 0.001$ for height, corrected to $p < 0.05$ for multiple comparisons using the cluster size ($p < 0.05$ for height for the mask). Then, for each of the local maxima, to examine the effect of phrasal segmentation and compare its effect with the effect of other processing operation (the effect of semantic violations) during sentence comprehension, the region of interest (ROI) analyses were performed in the following contrasts: the Non-seg Congruent – Non-seg Cont masked with Non-seg Congruent and Seg Congruent – Seg Cont masked with Seg Congruent contrast (hereinafter called Non-seg Congruent – Seg Congruent); and the Seg Incongruent – Seg Cont masked with Seg Incongruent and Seg Congruent – Seg Cont masked with Seg Congruent contrast (hereinafter called Seg Incongruent – Seg Congruent). The ROI analyses were conducted at a region-level threshold: the statistical threshold was set to $p < 0.001$ for height, corrected to $p < 0.05$ for multiple comparisons using the cluster size ($p < 0.05$ for height for the mask).

In choosing the contrast in advance, the contrast including the Non-seg Incongruent condition was excluded from the data analysis, lest confounding factors should intrude into the results caused by the interaction between phrasal segmentation and incongruent sentence processing (semantic violations). For the same reason, in choosing the contrast of sentence comprehension, the Seg Congruent and Non-seg Congruent condition were selected as the baseline contrast reflecting the sentence comprehension task, in order that confounding factors of incongruent sentence processing (i.e., semantic violations) should be excluded from the baseline contrast for statistical comparison.

4.2 Results

The following section will present the results of the present experiment. First, the results of the behavioral data (the response time and the accuracy) are shown. Then, the results of the fMRI data are presented.

4.2.1 Behavioral Data

Table 4.1 reports the results of the behavioral performance for 16 participants in the visual experiment: the mean accuracy rate (%) and the mean response time (ms) across all the stimulus categories in the experiment.

The behavioral results were computed and analyzed by using SPSS 16.0 (SPSS Inc., Chicago, Ill). In the mean accuracy rate, the results suggest that the participants were correctly performing the tasks, although the mean accuracy rate was slightly lower in Non-seg Congruent condition than in other stimulus conditions. In the mean response time, the results indicate that the perceptual decisions were faster in the comprehension task than in the control task.

Table 4.1. Behavioral Results

Task	Accuracy rate (%)	SD	Response time (ms)	SD
Comprehension				
Non-seg Congruent	84.17	9.85	3166.94	330.75
Seg Congruent	95.21	4.55	2768.62	392.22
Non-seg Incongruent	92.92	4.01	3090.73	388.23
Seg Incongruent	94.58	4.85	2971.97	353.99
Control				
Non-seg Cont	86.25	6.65	3340.17	288.09
Seg Cont	87.29	8.00	3362.77	258.02

Note. In the response time, the duration of stimulus delivery (2500 ms) is included.

In the mean accuracy rate, the main effect of stimulus category was found. One-way ANOVA with stimulus category as a factor and the mean accuracy rate as the dependent measure revealed a significant effect of stimulus category: $F(5, 90) = 8.098$, $p < 0.001$. The post hoc multiple comparisons (the Scheffe post hoc analysis) confirmed that there was a statistically significant difference in the mean accuracy rate between Non-seg Congruent and Seg Congruent condition ($p = 0.001$) and between Non-seg Congruent and Seg Incongruent condition ($p = 0.003$) in the comprehension task. The difference between Non-seg Congruent and Non-seg Incongruent condition was weakly significant ($p = 0.023$). However, the difference in the accuracy rate between Seg Congruent and Seg

Incongruent condition was not statistically significant. In the control task, there was no significant difference between Non-seg Cont and Seg Cont condition. Between the comprehension and the control task, a weakly significant difference was found between Seg Congruent and Non-seg Cont ($p = 0.018$), and between Seg Incongruent and Non-seg Cont ($p = 0.036$).

In the mean response time, the main effect of stimulus category was also found. One-way ANOVA with stimulus category as a factor and the mean response time as the dependent measure revealed a significant effect of stimulus category: $F(5, 90) = 7.130$, $p < 0.001$. However, the post hoc multiple comparisons (the Scheffe post hoc analysis) showed that no significant difference was found across the stimulus categories in the comprehension task and the control task respectively. There was a significant difference only between Seg Congruent and Non-seg Cont condition and between Seg Congruent and Seg Cont condition ($p < 0.001$ respectively).

4.2.2 fMRI Result

The main goal of the present study is to examine the neural activation for phrasal segmentation during sentence comprehension. In this experiment, the fMRI data analyses were performed in two steps to determine the neural activation involved in phrasal segmentation. First, the analysis was conducted to identify the areas related to sentence comprehension. Then, a priori regions of interest (ROIs) were defined for the left IFG, STG and STS (superior temporal sulcus), based on the results obtained from the first analysis. These regions were used to precisely identify the anatomical locations of activations associated with phrasal segmentation.

Figure 4.3 shows the brain activations when the participants were engaged in the sentence comprehension task: the Seg Congruent and Non-seg Congruent condition. Statistical threshold was set to $p < 0.001$ for height, then, corrected to $p < 0.05$ for multiple comparisons using the cluster size ($p < 0.05$ for height for the mask). A direct comparison of the (Seg

Congruent + Non-seg Congruent) – (Seg Cont + Non-seg Cont) condition masked with (Seg Congruent + Non-seg Congruent) revealed significant activation in the left inferior frontal lobe (BA 44, 45, and 47), basal ganglia, superior temporal lobe (temporal pole) (BA 38), and middle temporal lobe (BA 21 and 22).

Contrast: (Seg Congruent + Non-seg Congruent) – (Seg Cont + Non-seg Cont) (masked with (Seg Congruent + Non-seg Congruent))

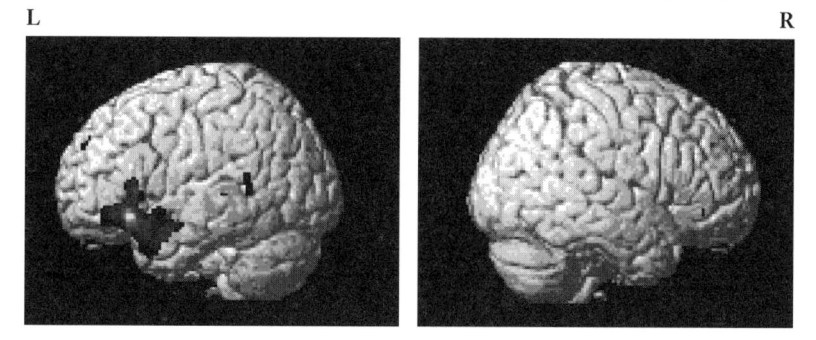

L   R

Figure 4.3. Cortical areas showing greater brain activation during the congruent sentence comprehension task: Seg Congruent and Non-seg Congruent condition.

The results proved that significantly greater activations were spreading in part of the so-called traditional language areas and their proximity in the left hemisphere of the brain. The left inferior frontal lobe and the anterior temporal pole of the left superior temporal lobe responded strongly to the sentence comprehension task. The small portion of the left middle temporal lobe also showed strong response to the same task. These results were compatible with the previous findings that language is processed in the distributed areas of the brain, mainly whose areas are spreading around the left hemisphere of the brain, as pointed out in the foregoing chapter. In the present experiment, the brain activations obtained from the sentence comprehension task were set as the baseline activations used to precisely identify the anatomical locations of activations associated with phrasal segmentation. In the following, each category of the fMRI results is analyzed in comparison with these baseline activations.

Table 4.2. Cortical Activations during Sentence Comprehension

Structure	Talairach coordinate (mm)			t value
	x	y	z	
Left IFG				
Pars triangularis	-52,	22,	6	5.66
Pars orbitalis	-48,	24,	-18	7.01
Pars orbitalis	-46,	28,	-10	6.30
Left STG				
	-64,	-48,	10	4.25
Left MTG				
	-54,	12,	-30	6.80
	-56,	-4,	-18	7.98
Left basal ganglia				
	-16,	12,	0	4.58

Secondary, in order to investigate the effect of phrasal segmentation, the local maxima of cortical activations were computed within the sentence comprehension areas, which were identified as the brain areas related to sentence comprehension as a result of the first analysis. Table 4.2 shows the peak maxima of cortical activations during sentence comprehension.

Table 4.2 shows Talairach coordinates and t values of their peak activations while the participants were comprehending sentences. The

Talairach coordinates and the *t* values of the peak activations were respectively obtained from the direct comparison of the (Seg Congruent + Non-seg Congruent) – (Seg Cont + Non-seg Cont) condition masked with (Seg Congruent + Non-seg Congruent).

As a result of the analysis, statistically significant cortical activations were revealed in the following areas: (a) the pars triangularis (BA 45) and the pars orbitalis (BA 47) of the left IFG; (b) the middle portion (BA 22) of the left STG; (c) the middle portion (BA 21) of the left MTG; and (d) the left basal ganglia. Within these areas, seven activated local maxima were found. Three peaks were located in the left IFG: (-52, 22, 6), (-48, 24, -18), (-46, 28, -10) ; one peak was in the left STG: (-64, -48, 10); two peaks were in the left MTG: (-56, -4, -18) and (-54, 12, -30), and one peak was in the left basal ganglia: (-16, 12, 0) (Talairach coordinates) (Talairach & Tournoux, 1988) (see, Table 4.2, for the statistic values (*t* values)). Thus, in total, seven peaks were identified as the local maxima of significant cortical activations during the visual comprehension task of congruent sentences.

Then, these seven peaks of the local maxima were selected for the regions of interest (ROIs) analysis, and their intensity of cortical activations were computed for comparison to precisely identify the anatomical locations of activations associated with phrasal segmentation.

Table 4.3 presents the Talairach coordinates as a result of the statistical comparisons of the activation peaks for the Non-seg Congruent – Seg Congruent contrast (*t*-values threshold was set at $p < 0.001$, corrected for multiple comparisons using the cluster size ($p < 0.05$)). '*' indicates significant effect of phrasal segmentation (Non-seg Congruent – Seg Congruent), $p < 0.05$.

Table 4.3 shows the results of the ROI analysis: significant activations and their anatomical locations were identified during phrasal segmentation, in two peaks out of seven peaks of the local maxima found in the cortical activations of sentence comprehension. First, to test the effect of phrasal

Table 4.3. Significant Activation during Phrasal Segmentation

Contrast	Non-seg Congruent > Seg Congruent			
	Talairach coordinate (mm)			
Structure	x	y	z	t value
Left IFG				
Pars orbitalis	-48	24	-18	2.21*
	-46	28	-10	2.65*

segmentation, the mean signal changes were calculated for these anatomical locations (i.e., ROIs) in the following condition: the Non-seg Congruent – Seg Congruent condition. Then, the statistical comparisons were conducted on the ROIs for that condition. In addition, other comparisons were made with other contrasts in this experiment to test other possible factors involved in phrasal segmentation.

As a result of the analysis, significantly greater volume of cortical activations was found in the following anatomical locations: (-48, 24, -18) and (-46, 28, -10), two greater activations in the pars orbitalis (BA 47) of the left IFG (Non-seg Congruent > Seg Congruent). Thus, during the sentence comprehension task, the Non-seg Congruent condition produced significantly greater activations in two of the local maxima in the left IFG (BA 47) than Seg Congruent condition. The result proved that the effect of phrasal segmentation was identified in the pars orbitalis (BA 47) of the left IFG.

Further, to specify the effect and the cortical organization of phrasal segmentation, other comparisons were made with other contrasts in this experiment. In consequence, from the comparison between Seg Incongruent and Seg Congruent conditions, significantly greater activations were revealed in the left IFG (BA 45/47) and the left STG (BA 22): in three of the local maxima, Seg Incongruent condition caused significantly greater activations than Seg Correct condition.

Table 4.4 shows the result of the comparison: significant activations and their anatomical locations between phrasal segmentation and incongruent sentence processing (semantic violations). The table presents and compares the activation peaks for the Non-seg Congruent − Seg Congruent and the Seg Incongruent − Seg Congruent contrast (t-values threshold was set at $p < 0.001$, corrected for multiple comparisons using the cluster size ($p < 0.05$)). '*' indicates significant effect of phrasal segmentation (Non-seg Congruent - Seg Congruent), $p < 0.05$. '**' indicates significant effect of the semantic violations in sentence comprehension (Seg Incongruent − Seg Congruent), $p < 0.05$. In Table 4.4, the statistical comparison between both of the activation patters of the local maxima suggests that the processing operation of phrasal segmentation is differently characterized from that of semantic violations. One of the significant activations out of four peaks in the local maxima was overlapping between phrasal segmentation and

Table 4.4. Significant Activations in Phrasal Segmentation and Semantic Violations

Structure	Comparison	
Talairach coordinate (mm)	Non-seg Congruent > Seg Congruent	Seg Incongruent > Seg Congruent
(x y z)	(t value)	(t value)
Left IFG		
Pars triangularis		
(-52, 22, 6)	0.45	5.42**
Pars orbitalis		
(-48, 24, -18)	2.21*	1.88
(-46, 28, -10)	2.65*	3.72**
Left STG		
(-64, -48, 10)	0.68	2.55**

semantic violations. However, in phrasal segmentation, two greater activations were centering in the pars orbitalis (BA 47) of the left IFG, while in semantic violations, three greater activations were spreading around the different areas of the left hemisphere of the brain, in the left IFG (BA 45/47) and in the left STG (BA 22).

Thus, the present experiment identified the effect of and the cortical regions involved in phrasal segmentation: the strong effect of phrasal segmentation was observed in the left IFG (BA 47).

To further confirm the effect of phrasal segmentation, the transaxial section images and the means of parameter estimates of signal intensity are presented for each of the significantly greater activations in the following.

First, Figures 4.4.a and 4.4.b provide the transaxial section images and the means of parameter estimates of signal intensity, showing significantly greater activation in Non-seg Congruent condition than in Seg Congruent condition.

The results of the statistical comparison confirmed the effect of phrasal segmentation during sentence comprehension. As a consequence of the statistical comparison, two peaks greatly activated in the pars orbitalis (BA 47) of the left IFG: (-48, 24, -18) and (-46, 28, -10) (paired t-test, $p < 0.05$).

Each of the transaxial section images shows the greater activations in the pars orbitalis (BA 47) of the left IFG (Figures 4.4.a and 4.4.b). The graph shows activation profile at the peak of each activated areas: the mean of the parameter estimates (arbitrary unit) and its standard error (error bar) are shown for Seg Congruent and Non-seg Congruent conditions respectively.

Next, Figures 4.5.a, 4.5.b, 4.5.c and 4.5.d show the transaxial section images and the mean signal intensity of cortical areas that activated more greatly in Seg Incongruent condition than in Seg Congruent condition. The results indicate the effect of semantic violations during sentence

Chapter 4 Search for Phrasal Segmentation 105

a. Left inferior frontal gyrus (pars orbitalis) (-48, 24, -18) ($t = 2.21, p < 0.05$)

Signal Intensity (%)

Seg Congruent < Non-seg Congruent

b. Left inferior frontal gyrus (pars orbitalis) (-46, 28, -10) ($t = 2.65, p < 0.05$)

Signal Intensity (%)

Seg Congruent < Non-seg Congruent

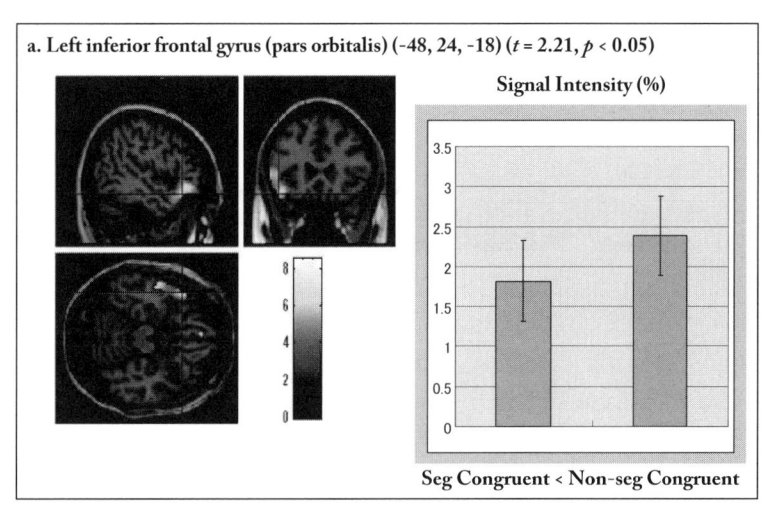

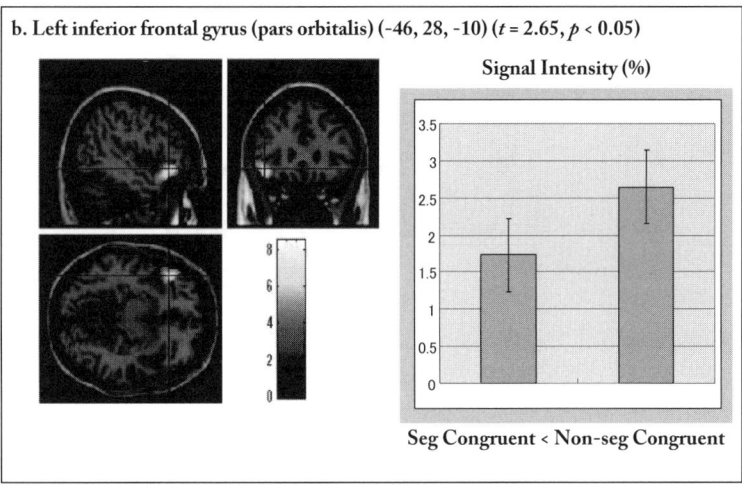

Figure 4.4. Cortical areas activated greatly in Non-seg Congruent condition.

a. Left inferior frontal gyrus (pars orbitalis) (-48, 24, -18) ($t = 1.88$, $p = 0.08$ n.s.)

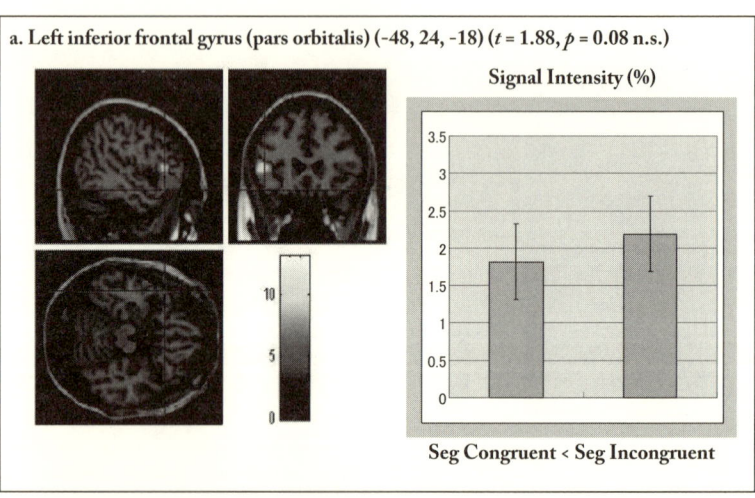

Seg Congruent < Seg Incongruent

b. Left inferior frontal gyrus (pars orbitalis) (-46, 28, -10) ($t = 3.72$, $p < 0.05$)

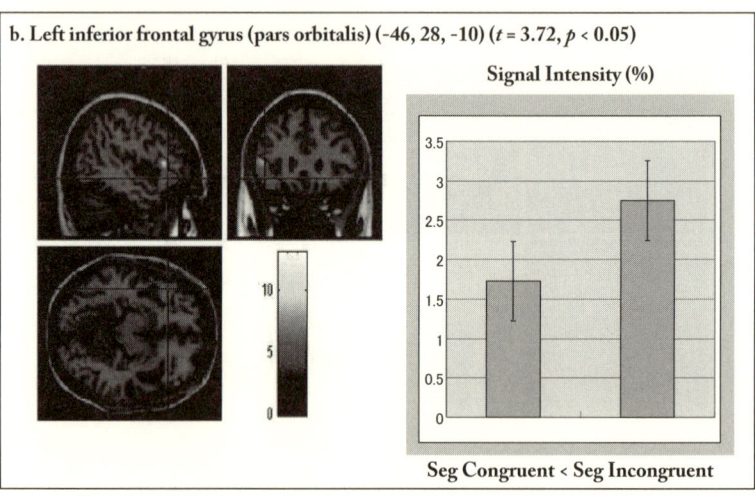

Seg Congruent < Seg Incongruent

Chapter 4 Search for Phrasal Segmentation 107

c. Left inferior frontal gyrus (pars triangularis) (-52, 22, 6) ($t = 5.25$, $p < 0.05$)

Signal Intensity (%)

Seg Congruent < Seg Incongruent

d. Left superior temporal gyrus (-64, -48, 10) ($t = 2.55$, $p < 0.05$)

Signal Intensity (%)

Seg Congruent < Seg Incongruent

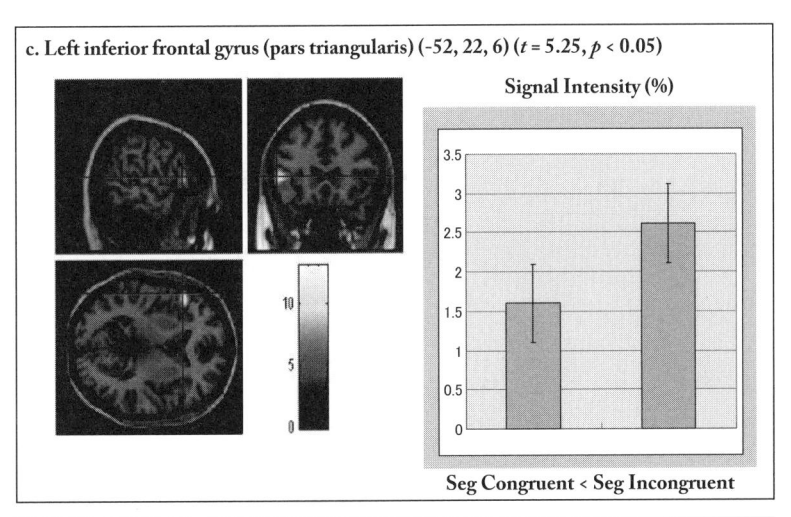

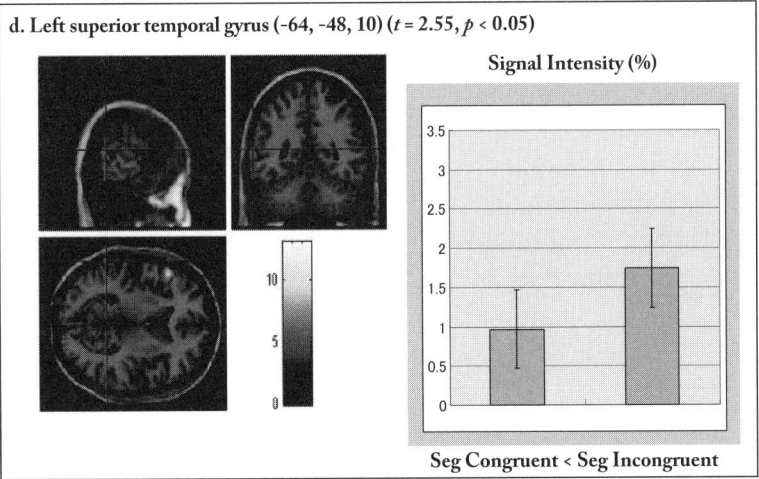

Figure 4.5. Cortical areas activated greatly in Seg Incongruent condition.

comprehension. In the comparison between Seg Incongruent and Seg Congruent conditions, three peaks showed significantly greater activations in the pars triangularis (BA 45) and the pars orbitalis (BA 47) of the left IFG, and the middle portion (BA 22) of the left STG: (-52, 22, 6) (BA 45); (-46, 28, -10) (BA 47); and (-64, -48, 10) (BA 22) (paired *t*-test, $p < 0.05$). In addition, one peak weakly greatly activated in the pars orbitalis (BA 47) of the left IFG: (-48, 24, -18) (BA 47) (paired *t*-test, $p = 0.08$, statistically nonsignificant).

Each of the transaxial sections shows the activations respectively in the pars orbitalis (BA 47) of the left IFG (Figures 4.5.a and 4.5.b), the pars triangularis (BA 45) of the left IFG (Figure 4.5.c), and the middle portion of the left STG (Figure 4.5.d).

The graph shows activation profile at the peak of each of the activated areas. "n.s." denotes statistically nonsignificant.

To sum it up, the statistical comparison between phrasal segmentation and semantic violations revealed the following results. The left inferior frontal gyrus (the left IFG) showed a statistically significant increase in activation in both of the contrasts Non-seg Congruent − Seg Congruent and Seg Incongruent − Seg Congruent (paired *t*-test, $p < 0.05$) (Table 4.4).

However, the regions that showed significant increase in activation were not the same between the two contrasts. Two locations in the left IFG were significantly activated in the Non-seg Congruent − Seg Congruent contrast: (-46, 28, -10) and (-48, 24, -18) in the pars orbitalis (BA47) of the left IFG (paired *t*-test, $p < 0.05$) (Figure 4.4.a and 4.4.b).

The same two locations were also activated in the Seg Incongruent − Seg Congruent contrast, but increase in activation was relatively weak in one location (-48, 24, -18) (paired *t*-test, $p = 0.08$), compared to the activation in the other (-46, 28, -10) ($p < 0.05$) (Figure 4.5.a and 4.5.b). In addition, the further statistical comparisons observed other significant activations in other locations in the Seg Incongruent − Seg Congruent. Two other locations were significantly activated in the Seg Incongruent − Seg Congruent contrast: (-52, 22, 6) in the pars triangularis of the left IFG (BA 45) and (-64, -48, 10) in the middle portion (BA 22) of the left STG (paired t-test, $p < 0.05$) (Figure 4.5.c and 4.5.d). In the same areas, significant activations were not detected in the Non-seg Congruent − Seg Congruent contrast. Thus, these comparisons suggest that phrasal segmentation and semantic violations were recruiting different neural substrates of the language areas in the left hemisphere.

In conclusion, the results presented above indicate that the processing operation of phrasal segmentation is supported by different network of regions of the brain from that of semantic violations. The statistical comparisons of the mean signal intensity confirmed that the processing operations of phrasal segmentation and semantic violations are subserved by different neural network and neural substrates of the brain, hence different brain function of language processing. The results found that the left IFG (pars orbitalis) (BA 47) was the cortical regions specific to phrasal segmentation.

4.3 Discussion

The present experiment has identified cortical regions involved in phrasal segmentation (the pars orbitalis of the left IFG (BA 47)) and found the significant increase of activations in these particular regions. This section will discuss and specify the functional role of the activated regions during the processing of phrasal segmentation.

As a result of the fMRI data analysis, this experiment found statistically significant activations specific to phrasal segmentation and semantic violations within the language areas in the left hemisphere of the brain. The statistical comparison between these processing operations found that the overlapped pattern of increased activation existed in one local maximum in the left pars orbitalis of the left IFG (BA47) (Figure 4.4.a and 4.4.b; Figure 4.5.a and 4.5.b). Therefore, this result was further compared with other results to test whether the peak activations in the left IFG is task-specific and stimulus-dependent, thus particular activations attributed to the processing operation of phrasal segmentation. Further comparison revealed that different pattern of the brain activations was found in semantic violations: (1) activation in the left inferior frontal gyrus (the left IFG) (the left pars triangularis (BA 45) (Figure 4.5.c) and the left pars orbitalis (BA47) (Figure 4.5.b)); (2) activation in the left superior temporal gyrus (the left STG) (the middle region, BA22) (Figure 4.5.d). The results demonstrated that one of the peak activations was overlapping, although two other peak activations were specific to semantic violations. Thus, the results confirmed that one of the peak activations in the pars orbitalis (BA 47) of the left IFG were specific to phrasal segmentation. They indicate that the processing operations of phrasal segmentation and semantic violations are supported by different neural network and neural substrates of the brain, thus by functionally different role of the brain.

The following subsections will further discuss and verify the issue of the brain function of phrasal segmentation, in comparison with the brain function of semantic violations. First, this section will take up and argue the results of cortical activation in phrasal segmentation. Then, this section will look into the results of cortical activation in semantic violations. Eventually, the following sections will argue the issue of the place of the mental processing of phrasal segmentation within the overall framework of sentence comprehension, in light of two different perspectives of sentence comprehension (i.e., serial vs. parallel processing model).

4.3.1 Cortical Area Involved in Phrasal Segmentation

In the Non-seg Congruent – Seg Congruent contrast, increased activation specific to phrasal segmentation was found in the left IFG (the pars orbitalis

(BA47)). The left IFG has been well known as part of the language areas in the left hemisphere of the brain. Activation in and in proximity of the left IFG has been most repeatedly reported to be implicated in supporting language processing (Caplan et al., 1999; Embick et al., 2000; Fiebach et al.; 2004; Inui et al., 1998; Kuperberg et. al., 2000; Moro et al., 2001; Ni et al., 2000; Poldrack et al., 1999). The cortical region specific to phrasal segmentation also falls within the same cortical region.

Recently, a number of studies have indicated that the left IFG plays a central role in human language processing (e.g., Caplan, 2004; Friederici, 2002; Hagoort, 2005b; Stowe et al., 2005). They point out that each local region of the left IFG has been considered to differently subserve the processing operations of language. Therefore, within that particular region, it has been stated that a fair amount of variability exists in the cortical organization of language processing (Bookheimer, 2002; Friederici, 2002; Price, 2000).

In this experiment, the activation loci specific to phrasal segmentation were observed in the left pars orbitalis (BA 47), one of whose activations was overlapping with one of the activation loci of semantic violations identified by the Seg Incongruent and Seg Congruent contrast. Considering the issue of the variability in the cortical organization of the left IFG, it is unlikely that the overlapping activation directly leads to the result that the processing of phrasal segmentation and semantic violations are mutually the similar processing associates. Rather, the overlapping is not an implausible result when focused on the fact that the brain allocates its finite processing resources to the accomplishment of an infinite range of behaviors (Raichle, 2006).

In the Non-seg Congruent − Seg Congruent contrast, significantly great activations was identified in the left IFG (the left pars orbitalis) (Figures 4.4.a and 4.4.b). These activations are seen as the index to stand for the effect of phrasal segmentation. In the Seg Incongruent − Seg Congruent contrast, the same region was activated. It is suggested that this given area was also involved in the processing of sentences including semantic violations (Figures 4.5.a and 4.5.b). The present results of involvement of the left pars orbitalis in phrasal segmentation and semantic violations support the views that sentence comprehension, in response to different processing tasks, is subserved by partially overlapped brain resources within the common cortical regions. Thus, it will be concluded that the left pars orbitalis is the sensitive brain regions to the different processing operations of phrasal segmentation and semantic violations.

The functional significance of increased activation in the left IFG (the left pars orbitalis) has well accorded with the results shown in previous findings. They have indicated that the left pars orbitalis plays a specific role for semantic processing in sentence comprehension (Dapretto & Bookheimer, 1999; Dronkers et al., 2004; Hagoort et al., 2004; Homae et al., 2002). The left pars orbitalis has been viewed as the operating region that is responsible for semantic integration from words into phrases and further into a sentence by selecting, comparing and integrating semantic information, based on the syntactic structures given during sentence comprehension (Dapretto & Bookheimer, 1999; Hagoort et al., 2004; Homae et al., 2002). Thus, the results that the left pars orbitalis subserves the processing operation of phrasal segmentation and its enhanced cortical activation suggest that phrasal segmentation is the processing operation of semantic information that would lead the individual word meaning to the integration into the phrasal meaning and eventually the sentence meaning.

This processing view is further supported by the fact that in the present experiment, the sentence comprehension task including the processing operation of phrasal segmentation was supported by the neural resources including the brain regions sensitive to both syntactic and semantic processing in the left IFG: BA 44/45 for syntactic processing; BA 47 for semantic processing (Figure 4.3; Figures 4.4.a and 4.4.b). However, in this experiment, the neural substrates that support semantic processing were more greatly activated in the Non-segmented Congruent condition than in the Segmented Congruent condition. The enhanced cortical activation of phrasal segmentation was particularly found in the left pars orbitalis (BA 47) as a result of the experiment. Therefore, the present results are consistent with the indications from previous studies that lexico-semantic information (i.e., the word meaning) is integrated on the basis of syntactic information (i.e., syntactic structures) (Homae et al., 2002, 2003).

The present results are also compatible with the predictions of parallel processing in sentence comprehension. In this experiment, the stimulus conditions were designed to reflect the phrase-by-phrase processing of sentences: non-segmented vs. segmented conditions. Thus, the results support the view that the sentence meaning is assigned phrase-by-phrase, not sentence-by-sentence in the course of sentence comprehension (Hagoort, 2003b, 2005a, 2008). The phrase-by-phrase processing of semantic information during phrasal segmentation clearly corresponds to the predictions from parallel processing view of sentence comprehension. Hence, in the course of phrasal segmentation, the following processing mechanism will be presupposed, relying on the predictions from the parallel processing view. In the syntactic domain, constituent structures are formed in the posterior dorsal portion of the left IFG (BA 44/45). In the semantic domain, the individual word meaning is integrated into the meaning of phrases, clauses and a sentence in the anterior ventral portion of the left IFG (BA 45/47). In this experiment, the results suggest that the semantic domain was greatly activated in the Non-segmented Congruent condition (i.e., the experimental condition).

The location of the activation peak this experiment specified was quite close to the location Hagoort and the colleagues (2004) identified in their study of semantic violations in sentence comprehension. However, there is a difference between their study and this experiment in the experimental procedures. Their study was intended to indirectly elicit the processing of semantic integration, employing the semantic violation task to stimulate the interpretation load during sentence comprehension, instead of explicitly observing semantic integration from individual words within a sentence. In contrast, this experiment was designed to directly observe semantic integration by phrasal segmentation, focusing on the processing of integration from individual words to a sentence, and compare its neural activation with that of semantic violations. The current results showed that the same locations in the left pars orbitalis ((-48, 24, -18) and (-46, 28, -10)) were activated between both the semantic violation and the phrasal segmentation task (Table 4.4). The activation of this region reached a similar level of intensity in the two tasks. These results were also consistent with the results observed in the previous ERP and fMRI imaging studies, which pointed out that the effect of semantic integration during sentence comprehension is not only concerned with semantic violations but also related to the semantic integration of a word into its sentential context in congruent sentences (Hagoort, 2005a; Hahne & Friederici, 2002). The comparison of cortical activation with the two different conditions provides evidence in favor of the hypothesis that there are certain cortical regions that are specialized for semantic integration from the word into the sentence in the semantic domain of sentence comprehension. It follows from the findings obtained from this experiment that both of the processing operations concerning phrasal segmentation and semantic violations appear to be involved in the process that underlies the capacity to understand a sentence, subserving semantic integration differently during sentence comprehension. Therefore, the processing operation of phrasal segmentation is considered to be situated in one of the processing operations in the semantic domain of processing, in consistent with the proposal of parallel processing.

In conclusion, phrasal segmentation is viewed as the processing operation that serves to link individual word meaning into phrase and sentence meaning. This experiment has determined the neural correlates of phrasal segmentation in the left pars orbitalis (BA 47). The results specified the effect of phrasal segmentation in the brain and also found the effect of semantic integration to build up each individual word's meaning into larger units of meaning at the phrase level during visual sentence comprehension in the brain. Without relying on the violation paradigm, the present fMRI experiment attested the functional specialization of phrasal segmentation in the semantic domain of the brain for the first time so far as known during processing of normally structured, meaningful sentences, by factoring out the task effect of semantic violations on sentence stimuli.

To assess the validity of the present results, the following subsection will argue the issue of the difference of the functional role in the network of regions of the brain between phrasal segmentation and semantic violations. Finally, this chapter will verify the argument that phrasal segmentation and semantic violations are supported by different neural substrates in the brain, claiming that phrasal segmentation is subserved by specific functional role in the brain.

4.3.2 Cortical Area Involved in Semantic Violations

The results of the present visual fMRI experiment showed that the cortical activations and their activation patterns were not the same between phrasal segmentation and semantic violations. In the middle portion of the left IFG (the proximity between the left pars triangularis and the left pars orbitalis), another different significant increase in activation was observed in the Seg Incongruent – Seg Congruent contrast (Figure 4.5.c). However, the same increase in activation was not found in the Non-seg Congruent – Seg Congruent contrast. This fact suggests that semantic violations are not reflected in the same processing operations of the brain by phrasal segmentation. Therefore, it is assumed that there exist the cortical areas exclusively specific to semantic violations.

The similar result in increased activation in the left IFG was also detected in the previous studies of semantic violations (Hagoort et al., 2004; Hagoort, 2005a). For instance, Hagoort (2005a) explained the result for sentences containing ambiguous words, suggesting that these sentences require a higher semantic unification load because stronger contextual selection is needed to achieve a coherent interpretation. The same region has been also most commonly reported in the studies of semantic violations (Ni et al., 2000; Ruschemeyer et al., 2006) and semantic judgment that contains ambiguous words (Bokde et al., 2001; Dapretto & Bookheimer, 1999; Rodd et al., 2005). These studies have indicated that the proximity between the left pars triangularis and the left pars orbitalis showed increased involvement in the processing of information that involves semantically ambiguous or anomalous words. The observed activations have argued to be involved in the processing operation that semantically mediates implausible word meaning to appropriate one. Consequently, this processing operation is considered to cause difficulties in establishing a sensible relationship between the word and the previous sentence context (Ruschemeyer et al., 2006) or to place a substantial load in computing sentence meanings (Rodd et al., 2005). The results of their studies imply that the left IFG has functional subdivisions on mediating semantically ambiguous word meanings. In this experiment, increased activations in semantic violations are consistent with the previous findings pointing out the effect of semantic violations and semantic judgment that contains ambiguous words. Thus, the grater activations in the proximity between the left pars triangularis and the left pars orbitalis are consistent with the view that the given areas support possible association of semantic processing of lexical mediation, one of the processing operations of semantic violations. As a consequence, in the left IFG, the brain function and the neural substrates of semantic violations are differently instantiated from those of phrasal segmentation.

Further, in the Seg Incongruent – Seg Congruent contrast, another different activation was observed in the middle portion of the left STG (Figure 4.5.d). However, the same activation was not found in the Non-seg Congruent – Seg Congruent contrast. The results of the statistical comparison suggest the possible role of this region involved in semantic violations. The current results found the related areas specific to semantic violations in the left IFG (the proximity between the left pars triangularis and the left pars orbitalis) and the left STG. Observation in previous studies has indicated that the left IFG and the left STG are both involved in the processing operations of semantically ambiguous and anomalous words (see, Van Petten & Luka, 2006, for a review of previous studies).

Van Petten and Luka (2006) have suggested that each of the related regions are differently sensitive to and selectively support the processing operations of semantic violations, showing the evidence of ERP studies that the left temporal lobe is the largest source of the N400 semantic context effect, which is considered to be an index of the ease or difficulty of retrieving stored conceptual knowledge associated with a word. With respect to the involvement of the left STG in semantic violations, they have argued that the region may reflect some aspect of the comprehension of a word per se, rather than strategic processing of word meanings that can be observed in the proximity between the left pars triangularis and the left pars orbitalis. Their view accords with the previous results that there are a certain amount of differences in the cortical organization during the tasks of semantic violations and semantic judgment containing ambiguous and anomalous words. Some of the studies have reported that both the left IFG and the left STG were significantly activated (Dapretto & Bookheimer, 1999; Ni et al., 2000), whereas some other studies have showed significant activation only in the left IFG (Bokde et al., 2001; Hagoort et al., 2004; Rodd et al., 2005) or in the left STG (Friederici et al., 2003). In the present experiment, two of the related regions were significantly activated in the processing of sentences that contained semantically anomalous words. Consequently, the results were consistent with the studies reported by Dapretto & Bookheimer (1999) and Ni et al. (2000), suggesting that semantic violations reflect differences of degree of activation within similar networks of the processing of semantic violations. In this experiment, the cortical activations of semantic violations agree with the results found in previous studies of semantic violations and semantic judgment containing ambiguous and anomalous words.

In conclusion, it might be possible to say the present visual fMRI experiment of phrasal segmentation confirmed that phrasal segmentation and semantic violations are supported by different neural networks in the brain. Two of the different types of language processing are manifested as the different processing operations and neural computations of the brain, requiring the functionally specialized allocation of processing resources. Thus, phrasal segmentation is subserved by specific functional role in the brain. The results of the current visual fMRI experiment validate the proposal of phrasal segmentation that has been argued thus far in this book.

4.4 Summary

In this experiment, significant activations specific to phrasal segmentation were found in the left pars orbitalis (BA 47). This region falls within the cortical region that has been agued to be involved in semantic processing in previous studies of functional neuroimaging. Among others, the related regions to phrasal segmentation were in the regions that have been proposed to be the cortical areas of semantic integration from word meaning to phrasal and sentence meaning. The results suggest that phrasal segmentation is one of the processing operations that lead a sequence of word strings in a sentence into sentence comprehension. In addition, the statistical comparisons of phrasal segmentation with semantic violations have revealed the brain regions specific to semantic violations in the proximity between the left pars triangularis and the left pars orbitalis (BA 44/45/47), and in the left STG (BA 22). The results verified that the processing operation and its cortical activations of phrasal segmentation are different from those of semantic violations. The results were consistent with the functional view of language processing: different computational resources of the brain would be required for different operations of language processing, as argued in the previous chapter. The present results were also compatible with the proposals of parallel processing view of sentence comprehension. Consequently, the visual experiment of phrasal segmentation using fMRI have for the first time identified the cortical areas supporting phrasal segmentation within the language-related cortical regions.

In the next chapter, this study will further investigate the issue of whether the cortical areas of phrasal segmentation is responsible for auditory processing of phrasal segmentation, conducting another fMRI experiment of phrasal segmentation using auditory Japanese sentence stimuli.

Chapter 5

Search for Phrasal Segmentation: Auditory fMRI Study

In the previous chapter, the visual experiment of phrasal segmentation found that the left IFG (pars orbitalis) (BA 47) was the cortical regions specific to phrasal segmentation. The present chapter will conduct the auditory experiment of phrasal segmentation using event-related fMRI. This chapter will further test the effect of phrasal segmentation during the auditory comprehension of Japanese sentences, comparing the neural activations between the segmented and the non-segmented condition. This chapter will examine the localization of sources of phrasal segmentation during auditory sentence comprehension. It will also investigate the influence of stimulus modality on and the involvement of prosodic information in phrasal segmentation, comparing the results with those of the visual experiment of phrasal segmentation. In the auditory experiment, the same experimental design was introduced other than the modality difference in stimulus delivery. Thus, when the sentence comprehension task was performed, the effect of phrasal segmentation was presupposed to be more strongly instantiated in the non-segmented condition than in the segmented condition. Following this presupposition, the neural activity was measured by fMRI and the neural sources of phrasal segmentation were estimated. Therefore, the primary aim of this experiment is to investigate whether the cortical areas of phrasal segmentation exist in both visual and auditory sentence comprehension.

5.1 fMRI Experiment

The following sections will present the research methods of the auditory experiment of phrasal segmentation using fMRI. To test the effect of phrasal segmentation and to investigate whether it would be influenced by the modality difference of the stimuli, the same methods were introduced in the auditory experiment as the methods adopted in the visual experiment, except that the stimulus modality was different between the auditory and the visual experiment.

5.1.1 Participants

Seventeen healthy right-handed volunteers (twelve males and five females, aged 20 to 27 years) participated in the study as subjects. All subjects were native speakers of Japanese. They had normal sense of hearing and none had a history of neurological or psychiatric illness. Handedness was evaluated using the Edinburgh Handedness Inventory (Oldfield, 1971). Written informed consent was obtained from all the subjects according to the guidelines approved by Tohoku University and the Helsinki Declaration of Human Rights, 1975.

5.1.2 Stimuli and Task

The experimental stimuli were 180 short Japanese simple sentences: 120 sentences were for a comprehension task and 60 sentences were for a control task. Each sentence was made up of 15 mora units. Sentences are all canonical Japanese sentences with canonical word orders (Gunji, 2002; Masuoka & Takubo, 1992). The sentence patterns were based on and adopted from the unmarked basic patterns listed in Basic Grammar of Japanese (Masuoka & Takubo, 1992). Words used in each sentence were selected from Word List by Semantic Principles (National Institute for Japanese Language, 2004). Their word familiarity was checked and controlled at the familiar level (the level between 5 and 7 on a 7-point scale) and their word frequency also at the frequent level (the most frequent level on a 3-point scale) using the database developed by Amano and Kondo (2003). To eliminate the facilitative effect of semantic processing caused by repetitive word presentation, every content word such as noun, verb, adverb, and adjective was used only once across all the stimuli. Of all the stimuli, half was segmented (Seg) and the other half was not segmented (Non-seg) (see, Figure 5.1, for the visualized examples of stimuli). In the Seg condition, a pause with one mora length was made between phrases in each sentence, while in the Non-seg condition, such a pause was not left between phrases or words.

The sentences presented in the comprehension task included both semantically congruent (Congruent) and incongruent (Incongruent) sentences: 60 semantically congruent and 60 incongruent sentences. The

a. Congruent Sentences:

> **Non-seg Correct:**
> おばがおじにでんごんをつたえた
> (o-ba-ga-o-zi-ni-de-N-go-N-o-tu-ta-e-ta)
> (aunt-Nom uncle-Dat message-Acc delivered)
> (My aunt delivered the message to my uncle.)
>
> **Seg Correct:**
> おとこが　かべに　らくがきを　かいた
> (o-to-ko-ga ka-be-ni ra-ku-ga-ki-o ka-i-ta)
> (man-Nom wall-Loc graffiti-Acc wrote)
> (The man wrote graffiti on the wall.)

b. Incongruent Sentences:

Non-seg Incorrect:
さるがいすにきゅうりょうをはらった
(sa-ru-ga-i-su-ni-kyu-ryo-o-ha-ra-Q-ta)
(monkey-Nom chair-Dat salary-Acc paid)
(The monkey paid the chair its salary.)

Seg Incorrect:
いりぐちで　とが　そでに　はさまった
(i-ri-gu-ti-de to-ga so-de-ni ha-sa-ma-Q-ta)
(entrance-Loc door-Nom sleeve-Loc squeezed)
(The sleeve squeezed the door at the entrance.)

c. Control Sentences:

Non-seg Cont:
しゃいんがかいしゃにでんわをかけた
(sja-i-n-ga-ka-i-sja-ni-de-N-wa-o-ka-ke-ta)
(staff-Nom company-Dat phone call-Acc made)
(The staff made a phone call to the company.)

Seg Cont:
けいさつが　かいぞくに　つかまった
(ke-e-sa-tu-ga ka-i-zo-ku-ni tu-ka-ma-Q-ta)
(police-Nom pirate by-Agent were caught)
(The police were caught by the pirate.)

Figure 5.1. Examples of the visualized image of sentence stimuli presented in the auditory experiment.

sentences presented in the control task (Cont) also included both semantically congruent and incongruent sentences: 30 semantically congruent and 30 incongruent sentences. Each sentence in each task was pseudo-randomly ordered. The sentences in each task were divided into 4 blocks respectively: 30 sentences in each comprehension block and 15 sentences in each control block. Then each comprehension and control block was combined in alternation as a series of 8 blocked tasks for an fMRI session. The presented sentence stimuli were classified into the six categories as follows: Non-seg Congruent, Seg Congruent, Non-seg Incongruent, Seg Incongruent, Non-seg Cont, and Seg Cont.

Figure 5.1 illustrates the examples of sentence stimuli used in the present study. The hyphen denotes the delimiting border between morae. The space indicates the pause between phrases. In the segmented conditions, each sentence is segmented into minimal meaningful, syntactic phrasal units called '*seibun* (immediate constituent)' (see, Masuoka, 1997). The underlined mora denotes the penultimate mora in the control stimuli.

In order to control the phonetic properties in speech, each auditory stimulus was digitally created with the standard Japanese pronunciation and prosody under the control of a Windows computer running the text-to-speech exchange software Raku Speech S (Free's, Fukuoka, Japan). Half of the stimuli were created with the man's voice and the other half with the woman's voice to counterbalance the effect of the voice familiarity between man's and woman's voices. The comprehension and the control task blocks were respectively divided into the man's-voiced and the woman's-voiced blocks. Each voice block was alternately ordered across the blocks. The order of the voice blocks was interchanged to counterbalance the effect of the voice order presented across participants.

5.1.3 Procedure

In each block in a session, following an initial resting period (15 seconds), during which a fixation cross (10 seconds) was presented and then a task instruction (5 seconds) was displayed and aurally presented, each stimulus was aurally presented for 2.5 seconds during a period of 5 seconds trial (Appendix B, for a visualized example of the list of stimulus delivery). The duration of a stimulus being presented was decided based on a preparatory study: in 2.5 seconds each participant was able to listen to each stimulus to the end. During an fMRI session, a fixation cross was displayed on the screen to control the eye movement. To control the effect of the onset timing, each stimulus delivery was pseudo-randomly changed at three different levels, 0 second, 0.5 second and 1 second of delay from the onset respectively across trials. For each stimulus trial, the response time was recorded and calculated from the onset of each stimulus delivery, using two compatible response buttons. The stimulus delivery and the response time recording were conducted under the control of a Windows computer running Presentation (Neurobehavioral Systems, Albany, CA). Each stimulus was aurally presented on a head set held on tightly inside the head-coil of the fMRI scanner.

Each participant performed a comprehension and a control task alternately during each blocked auditory presentation of Japanese sentences. In the comprehension task, each participant judged whether each stimulus is semantically congruent or not, pressing the left button with the index finger if the sentence was semantically congruent, and the right button with the middle finger if the sentence was semantically incongruent. In the control task, each participant judged whether each stimulus contains the same sound unit ('mora') as the penult or not, pressing the left button with the index finger if the same sound unit ('mora') as the penult was included in the stimulus, and the right button with the middle finger if the same one was not included. The control task was designed to control the effect of working memory that would assist in the temporary retention and manipulation of verbal information. By subtracting the activated regions in the control task from those in the comprehension task, this study posited that the activated regions involved in sentence processing could be specified without under the influence of working memory. The order of the comprehension and the control task was also interchanged to counterbalance the effect of the task order presented across participants. Before performing the fMRI session, each participant conducted a brief practice session using the laptop computer in order to become familiarized with the task involved in the study. The practice session included 10 trials that were similar to the stimuli presented in each task in the study.

Figure 5.2 sketches the experimental task design adopted in the study. The present experiment employed the same experimental task design as the visual experiment adopted, in order to compare and argue the results of the two experiments in the same experimental framework. Stimuli A and B

1. Task design: an event-related design

   Task block: A: Comprehension block (30 stimuli)
                B: Control block (15 stimuli)

   A (30 stimuli) B (15 stimuli) A (30 stimuli) B (15 stimuli)

   Dummy

   C   C   C   C

   Each Task block was alternatively presented eight times.
   C: Rest and Instruction (15 seconds)

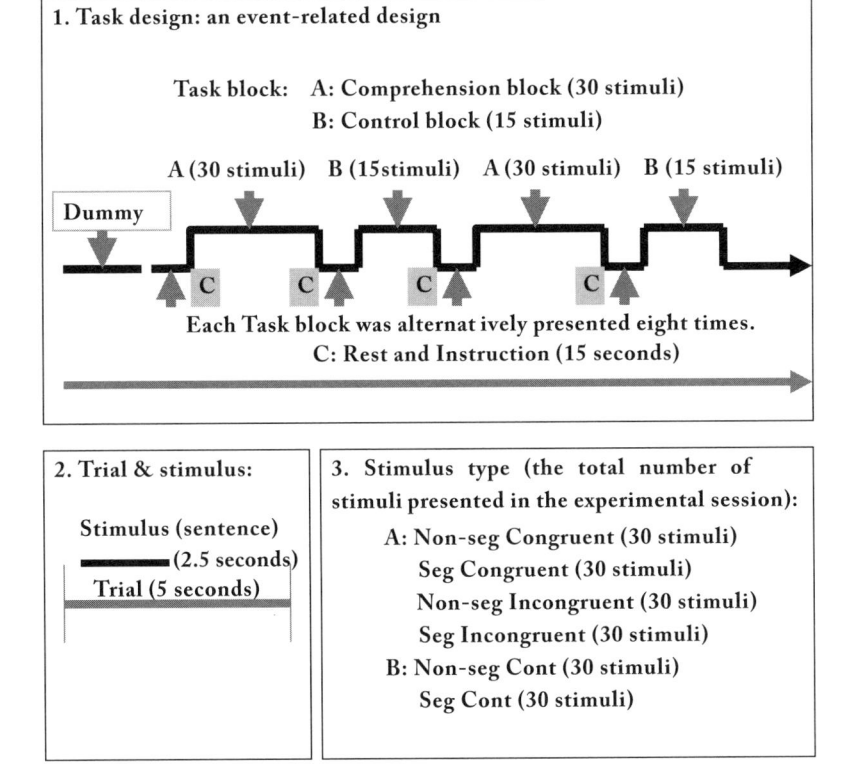

2. Trial & stimulus:

   Stimulus (sentence)
   ──── (2.5 seconds)
   Trial (5 seconds)

3. Stimulus type (the total number of stimuli presented in the experimental session):
   A: Non-seg Congruent (30 stimuli)
      Seg Congruent (30 stimuli)
      Non-seg Incongruent (30 stimuli)
      Seg Incongruent (30 stimuli)
   B: Non-seg Cont (30 stimuli)
      Seg Cont (30 stimuli)

Figure 5.2.   Experimental task design in the auditory experiment.

were respectively randomized. Then they were divided up into each block: 30 stimuli in each comprehension block and 15 stimuli in each control block. Each comprehension and control task block was alternatively presented eight times in total through the experimental session.

In Figure 5.2, the task design, stimulus delivery timing, and stimulus type of fMRI experiment are shown. "A" refers to the comprehension task block, "B" refers to the control task block, and "C" refers to the rest and instruction. In the section 1, the sequence of the experiment is presented. In the section 2, the stimulus delivery timing in each trial is illustrated. In the section 3, each stimulus type is described and the number of each stimulus category in each task block is shown in the parenthesis.

5.1.4 fMRI Data Acquisition and Preprocessing

The auditory experiment of phrasal segmentation using fMRI was conducted in the same manner as the visual experiment of phrasal segmentation using fMRI. The fMRI experiment was administered on a 1.5-tesla (1.5T) Siemens Symphony scanner system (Siemens, Erlangen, Germany) at Tohoku University. Functional images were acquired using gradient echo planner image sequences with the following parameters: repetition time (TR) = 3,000 ms, echo time (TE) = 60 ms, flip angle = 90°, slice thickness = 3 mm, slice gap = 0.99 mm, field of view (FOV) = 192 mm, 64 × 64 matrix, and 3 × 3 × 3.99 mm voxels of resolution. Thirty-three 3-mm-thick transaxial images covering the entire brain were obtained continuously every 3 seconds TR using an echo planar imaging (EPI) sequence during functional measurements. Excluding the initial seven dummy scans used to stabilize the T1 saturation effect from the analysis, 370 volumes were acquired for each participant in each fMRI session. During the fMRI session, the participant's head was secured using a foam rubber pad to minimize artifacts due to movement. T1-weighted structural images were also acquired for each participant to serve as a reference for anatomical correlations: slice thickness = 1.25 mm, FOV = 256 mm, 175 × 256 matrix, TR = 1,900 ms, and TE = 3.93 ms. For the sake of anatomical localization of hemodynamic activation effects, fMRI maps were superimposed on a mean image of the normalized T1-weighted anatomical images of all the participants.

The following preprocessing procedures were conducted using Statistical Parametric Mapping (SPM2) software (Wellcome Department of Cognitive Neurology, London, UK) and MATLAB (Mathworks, Natick, MA, USA): adjustment of acquisition timing across slices, correction for head motion, coregistration to the anatomical image, spatial normalization to the standard brain, and smoothing with an isotropic Gaussian kernel of 10 mm full width at half-maximum (FWHM).

5.1.5 fMRI Data Analysis

To the data analysis, in this experiment, the same procedures adopted in the visual experiment were applied. In doing so, the conditions of both experiments were controlled other than the modality difference in stimulus presentation.

From the fMRI data obtained, the data of three participants (two males and one female) were excluded: the data of one male participant whose head motion was excessive (more than 3 mm), and the data of one male and one female participants whose task performance were at the statistically insufficient level (less than 70 % correct response at least one stimulus category). Hence, the data obtained from fourteen participants were used for the data analysis.

In the data analysis, a voxel-by-voxel multiple regression analysis of the predicted signal change to the preprocessed images was applied for each session for each participant. The analysis adopted a standard event-related convolution model using the hemodynamic response function provided by SPM2. The model of the hemodynamic response function was tailored to the following six categories: Non-seg Congruent, Seg Incongruent, Non-seg Incongruent, Seg Incongruent, Non-seg Cont, and Seg Cont. To detect the differential neural activation during sentence comprehension, the subtraction analyses were performed in the following contrasts: (Seg Congruent + Non-seg Congruent) - (Seg Cont + Non-seg Cont), Non-seg Congruent – Non-seg Cont, Seg Congruent – Seg Cont, and Seg Incongruent – Seg Cont. Statistical inference on these subtractions of parameter estimates was then computed using a between-subject (random effects) model using one-sample t-tests. Contrasts of each subtraction were averaged and inclusively masked with Seg Congruent + Non-seg Congruent, Non-seg Congruent, Seg Congruent, and Seg Incongruent respectively.

To identify the cortical activations reflecting phrasal segmentation during sentence comprehension, a conventional two-step approach was performed for event-related fMRI data. First, the cortical activations involved in sentence comprehension were identified by the following subtraction: (Seg Congruent + Non-seg Congruent) - (Seg Cont + Non-seg Cont) masked with (Seg Congruent + Non-seg Congruent). The statistical threshold was set to $p < 0.001$ for height, corrected to $p < 0.05$ for multiple comparisons using the cluster size ($p < 0.05$ for height for the mask). Then, for each of the local maxima, to examine the effect of phrasal segmentation and compare its effect with the effect of other processing (the effect of semantic violations) during sentence comprehension, the region of interest (ROI) analyses were performed in the following contrasts: the Non-seg Congruent – Non-seg Cont masked with Non-seg Congruent and Seg Congruent – Seg Cont masked with Seg Congruent contrast (hereinafter called Non-seg Congruent – Seg Congruent); and the Seg Incongruent – Seg Cont masked with Seg Incongruent and Seg Congruent – Seg Cont masked with Seg Congruent contrast (hereinafter called Seg Incongruent – Seg Congruent). The ROI analyses were conducted at a region-level threshold: the statistical threshold was set to $p < 0.001$ for height, corrected to $p < 0.05$ for multiple comparisons using the cluster size ($p < 0.05$ for height for the mask).

In choosing the contrast in advance, the contrast including the Non-seg Incongruent condition was excluded from the data analysis, lest confounding factors should intrude into the results caused by the interaction between phrasal segmentation and incongruent sentence processing (semantic violations). For the same reason, in choosing the contrast of sentence comprehension, the Seg Congruent and Non-seg Congruent condition were selected as the baseline contrast reflecting the sentence comprehension task, in order that confounding factors of incongruent sentence processing (i.e., semantic violations) should be excluded from the baseline contrast for statistical comparison.

5.2 Results

The following section will present the results of the experiment. First, the results of the behavioral data (the response time and the accuracy) are shown. Then, the results of the fMRI data are presented.

5.2.1 Behavioral Data

Table 5.1 reports the results of the behavioral performance for 14 participants in the visual experiment: the mean accuracy rate (%) and the mean response time (ms) across all the stimulus categories in the experiment. The behavioral results were computed and analyzed by using SPSS 16.0 (SPSS Inc., Chicago, Ill).

In the mean accuracy rate, the results suggest that the participants were correctly performing the tasks. In the mean response time, the results indicate that the perceptual decisions were faster in the comprehension task than in the control task. These results were consistent with the behavioral results in the visual experiment, although the perceptual decisions were

Table 5.1. Behavioral Results

Task condition	Accuracy rate (%)	SD	Response time (ms)	SD
Comprehension				
Non-seg Congruent	84.28	8.31	3636.66	474.16
Seg Congruent	82.14	9.02	3537.25	410.49
Non-seg Incongruent	87.14	6.11	3621.56	461.82
Seg Incongruent	85.00	5.66	3862.54	428.96
Control				
Non-seg Cont	83.57	5.77	4683.01	487.07
Seg Cont	80.23	7.09	4699.45	459.97

Note. In the response time, the duration of stimulus delivery (2500ms) is included.

slightly faster in the visual experiment than in the auditory experiment (see, Figure 4.1).

In the mean accuracy rate, the main effect of stimulus categories on the mean accuracy rate was statistically significant (one-way analysis of variance (ANOVA), $F(5, 78) = 7.332, p < 0.001$). As a result of the post hoc multiple comparisons (the Scheffe post hoc analysis), there was a statistically significant difference in the mean accuracy rate between Seg Congruent and Non-seg Incongruent conditions ($p < 0.001$) in the comprehension task. There was also a weakly significant difference between Non-seg Congruent and Non-seg Incongruent conditions ($p = 0.013$). However, the difference in the accuracy rate between Non-seg Congruent and Seg Congruent conditions was not statistically significant. In the control task, there was no significant difference between Non-seg Cont and Seg Cont conditions. Between the comprehension and the control tasks, a significant difference was found between Non-seg Incongruent and Non-seg Cont ($p = 0.006$), and between Non-seg Incongruent and Seg Cont ($p < 0.001$).

In the mean response time, the main effect of stimulus categories on the mean response time was statistically significant (one-way ANOVA, F (5, 78) = 19.840, $p < 0.001$). However, the post hoc multiple comparisons (the Scheffe post hoc analysis) showed that no significant difference was found across the conditions in the comprehension task and the control task respectively. There were only significant differences between Seg Congruent and two control conditions, Non-seg Cont and Seg Cont conditions ($p < 0.001$ respectively).

5.2.2 fMRI Result

The main goal of the present study is to examine the neural activation for phrasal segmentation during sentence comprehension. In this experiment, the fMRI data analyses were performed in two steps to determine the neural activation involved in phrasal segmentation. First, the analysis was conducted to identify the areas related to sentence comprehension. Then, a priori regions of interest (ROIs) were defined for the left IFG and STG and the right STG, based on the results obtained from the first analysis. These regions were used to precisely identify the anatomical locations of activations associated with phrasal segmentation.

Figure 5.3 shows the brain activations when the participants were engaged in the sentence comprehension task: the Seg Congruent and Non-seg Congruent condition. Statistical threshold was set to $p < 0.001$ for height, then corrected to $p < 0.05$ for multiple comparisons using the cluster size ($p < 0.05$ for height for the mask).

A direct comparison of the (Seg Congruent + Non-seg Congruent) − (Seg Cont + Non-seg Cont) condition masked with (Seg Congruent + Non-seg Congruent) revealed significant activation in the left inferior frontal lobe (BA 47), superior temporal lobe (temporal pole) (BA 38), and middle temporal lobe (BA 22), and in the right superior temporal lobe (temporal pole) (BA 38) and middle temporal lobe (BA 22), as shown in Figure 5.3.

**Contrast: (Seg Congruent + Non-seg Congruent) − (Seg Cont + Non-seg Cont)
(masked by (Seg Congruent + Non-seg Congruent))**

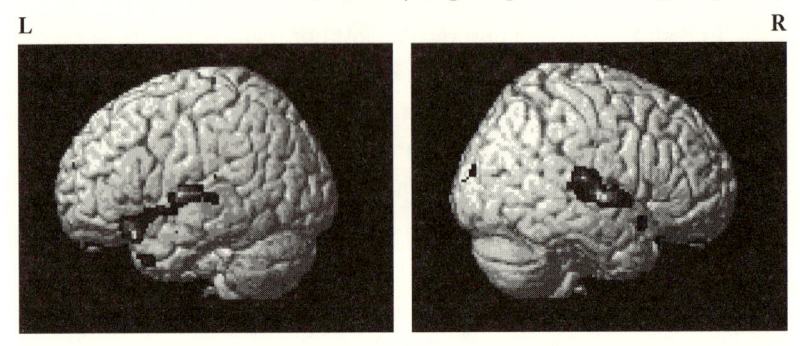

L R

Figure 5.3. Cortical areas showing greater brain activation during the congruent sentence comprehension task: Seg Congruent and Non-seg Congruent condition involved in sentence comprehension.

The results proved that significantly greater activations were found in part of the so-called traditional language areas and the proximity in the left hemisphere of the brain. Also, significantly increased activations were observed in the superior temporal cortex including primary and associative auditory cortex in both hemispheres, areas known as the auditory areas. The left inferior frontal lobe and the anterior temporal pole in the left superior temporal lobe responded strongly to the sentence comprehension task. The results were well consistent with the results of the visual experiment of phrasal segmentation reported in the previous chapter. However, bilateral strong brain response in the auditory areas was not observed in the visual experiment. The latter results were exclusively found in the auditory experiment of phrasal segmentation. As for the bilateral strong brain activations in the auditory areas, previous studies have confirmed the fact that the auditory areas are more likely to be responsive unimodally to human voice (Belin et al., 2000; Belin et al., 2002) and speech sound (Binder et al., 2000; Matthew & Johnsrude, 2003; Vouloumanos et al., 2001). Therefore, in the present experiment as well in the same manner as in the visual experiment, the brain activations during the sentence comprehension task were set as the baseline activations used to precisely identify the anatomical locations of activations associated with phrasal segmentation. In the following, each category of the fMRI results is analyzed in comparison with these baseline activations.

Table 5.2. Cortical Activations during Sentence Comprehension

Structure	Talairach coordinate (mm)			t value
	x	y	z	
Left IFG				
Pars orbitalis	-44,	26,	-16	7.78
Left STG	-48,	22,	-20	9.40
	-62,	-12,	4	7.35
Right STG				
	66,	-22,	12	6.88
	58,	14,	-16	6.34
	58,	-14,	2	7.01

Next, in order to investigate the effect of phrasal segmentation in sentence comprehension, the local maxima of cortical activations were computed within the sentence comprehension areas, which were identified as the brain areas related to sentence comprehension as a result of the first analysis.

Table 5.2 shows the peak maxima of cortical activations during sentence comprehension. Table 5.2 shows Talairach coordinates and t values of their peak activations while comprehending sentences. The Talairach coordinates and the *t* values of the peak activations were respectively obtained from the contrast (Seg Congruent + Non-seg Congruent) − (Seg Cont + Non-seg Cont) masked with (Seg Congruent + Non-seg Congruent).

As a result of the analysis, statistically significant cortical activations were revealed in the following areas: (a) the pars orbitalis (BA 47) of the left IFG; (b) the anterior portion (temporal pole) (BA 38) and the middle portion (BA 22) of the left STG; and (c) the anterior portion (temporal pole) (BA 38) and the middle portion (BA 22 and BA 42) of the right STG. Within these areas, six activated local maxima were found. One peak was located in the left IFG: (-44, 26, -16); two peaks were in the left STG: (-48, 22, -20) and (-62, -12, 4); and three peaks were in the right STG: (66, -22, 12), (58, 14, -16), and (58, -14, 2) (Talairach coordinates) (Talairach & Tournoux, 1988) (see, Table 5.2, for the statistic values (*t* values)). Thus, in total, six peaks were identified as the local maxima of significant cortical activations during the auditory comprehension task of congruent sentences.

Then, these six peaks of the local maxima were selected for the regions of interest (ROIs) analysis, and their intensity of cortical activations were examined for comparison to precisely identify the anatomical locations of activations associated with phrasal segmentation.

Table 5.3 presents the Talairach coordinates as a result of the statistical comparisons of the activation peaks for the Non-seg Congruent − Seg Congruent contrast (*t*-values threshold was set at $p < 0.001$, corrected for multiple comparisons using the cluster size ($p < 0.05$)). '*' indicates significant effect of phrasal segmentation (Non-seg Congruent - Seg Congruent), $p < 0.05$.

Table 5.3 shows the results of the ROI analysis: significant activations and their anatomical locations were identified during phrasal segmentation, in two peaks out of six peaks of the local maxima found in the cortical activations of sentence comprehension. First, to test the effect of phrasal

Table 5.3. Significant Activation during Phrasal Segmentation

Contrast	Non-seg Congruent > Seg Congruent			
	Talairach coordinate (mm)			
Structure	x	y	z	t value
Left IFG				
Pars orbitalis	-44	26	-16	2.06*
Left STG				
Temporal pole	-48	22	-20	2.36*

segmentation, the mean signal changes were calculated for these anatomical locations (i.e., ROIs) in the following condition: the Non-seg Congruent – Seg Congruent condition. Then, the statistical comparisons were conducted on the ROIs for that condition. In addition, other comparisons were made with other contrasts in this experiment to test other possible factors involved in phrasal segmentation.

As a result of the analysis, significantly greater volume of cortical activations was found in the following anatomical locations respectively: (-44, 26, -16) and (-48, 22, -20), one greater activation in the pars orbitalis (BA 47) of the left IFG and another greater activation in the temporal pole (BA 38) of the left STG (Non-seg Congruent > Seg Congruent). Thus, during the sentence comprehension task, the Non-seg Congruent condition produced significantly greater activations in two of the local maxima in the left IFG (BA 47) and the left STG (BA 38) than Seg Congruent condition. The result confirmed that the effect of phrasal segmentation was identified in the pars orbitalis (BA 47) of the left IFG and in the temporal pole (BA 38) of the left STG.

Further, to specify the effect and the cortical organization of phrasal segmentation, other comparisons were made with other contrasts in this experiment. In consequence, from the comparison between Seg Incongruent

Table 5.4. Significant Activations in Phrasal Segmentation and Semantic Violations

Structure	Comparison	
Talairach coordinate (mm)	Non-seg Congruent > Seg Congruent	Seg Incongruent > Seg Congruent
(x y z)	(t value)	(t value)
Left IFG		
Pars orbitalis		
(-44, 26, -16)	2.06*	1.41
Left STG		
(-48, 22, -20)	2.36*	1.33
(-62, -12, 4)	1.50	1.99**

and Seg Congruent conditions, significantly greater activation was revealed in the middle portion of the left STG (BA 22): in one of the local maxima, Seg Incongruent condition caused significantly greater activation than Seg Congruent condition.

Table 5.4 shows the result of the comparison: significant activations and their anatomical locations between phrasal segmentation and incongruent sentence processing (semantic violations). The table presents the Talairach coordinates and the t-values as a result of the statistical comparisons of the activation peaks between the contrasts Non-seg Congruent – Seg Congruent, and Seg Incongruent – Seg Congruent (t-values threshold set at $p < 0.001$, corrected for multiple comparisons using the cluster size ($p < 0.05$)). '*' indicates significant effect of phrasal segmentation (Non-seg Congruent - Seg Congruent), $p < 0.05$. '**' indicates significant effect of semantic violations in sentence comprehension (Seg Incongruent – Seg Congruent), $p < 0.05$.

As shown in Table 5.4, the statistical comparison between both of the activation patters of the local maxima suggests that the processing operation of phrasal segmentation is differently characterized from that of semantic violations. No significant activations were overlapping between phrasal segmentation and semantic violations. Nor were the activated areas overlapping between these conditions. In phrasal segmentation, one greater activation peak was found in the pars orbitalis (BA 47) of the left IFG and another greater activation peak was detected in the temporal pole (BA 38) of the left STG. In semantic violations, one greater activation peak was identified in the left STG (BA 22).

Thus, the present experiment identified the effect of and the cortical regions involved in phrasal segmentation: the strong effect of phrasal segmentation was observed the pars orbitalis (BA 47) of the left IFG and the temporal pole (BA 38) of the left STG. The results found consistently robust, greater activation in the pars orbitalis (BA 47) of the left IFG between the visual and the auditory experiment.

To further confirm the effect of phrasal segmentation, the transaxial section images and the means of parameter estimates of signal intensity are presented for each of the significantly greater activations in the following.

The results of the statistical comparison confirmed the effect of phrasal segmentation during sentence comprehension. As a consequence of the statistical comparison, two peaks greatly activated respectively in the pars orbitalis (BA 47) of the left IFG and the temporal pole (BA 38) of the left STG: (-44, 26, -16) and (-48, 22, -20) (paired t-test, $p < 0.05$).

Each of the transaxial section images shows the greater activations in the pars orbitalis (BA 47) of the left IFG (Figures 5.4.a) and in the anterior portion (temporal pole) (BA 38) of the left STG (5.4.b). The graph shows activation profile at the peak of each activated areas: the mean of the parameter estimates (arbitrary unit) and its standard error (error bar) are shown for Seg Congruent and Non-seg Congruent conditions respectively.

First, Figures 5.4.a and 5.4.b provide the transaxial section images and the means of parameter estimates of signal intensity, showing significantly greater activation in Non-seg Congruent condition than in Seg Congruent

a. Left inferior frontal gyrus (pars orbitalis) (-44, 26, -16) ($t = 2.06, p < 0.05$)

Seg Congruent < Non-seg Congruent

b. Left superior temporal gyrus (temporal pole) (-48, 22, -20) ($t = 2.36, p < 0.05$)

Seg Congruent < Non-seg Congruent

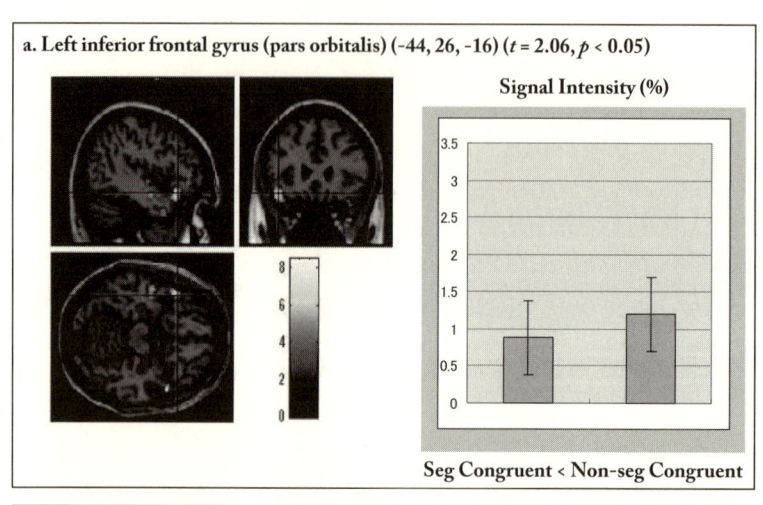

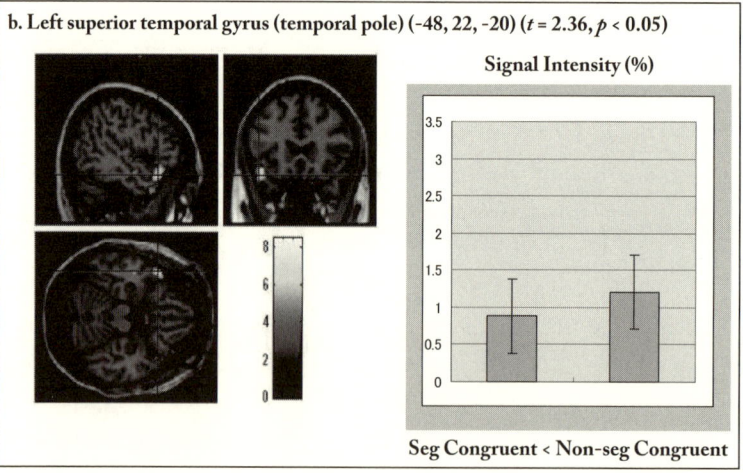

Figure 5.4. Cortical areas activated greatly in Non-seg Congruent condition.

condition.

Next, Figures 5.5.a, 5.5.b, and 5.5.c provide the transaxial section images and the signal intensity of cortical areas that presented greater in Seg Incongruent condition than in Seg Congruent condition. The results indicate the effect of semantic violations during sentence comprehension. In the comparison between Seg Incongruent and Seg Congruent conditions, one peak showed significantly greater activation in the middle portion of the left STG: (-62, -12, 4) (BA 22) (paired t-test, $p < 0.05$). In addition, two peak weakly greatly activated in the pars orbitalis (BA 47) of the left IFG and the anterior portion (temporal pole) (BA 38) of the left STG: (-44, 26, -16) (BA 47) (paired t-test, $p = 0.09$, nonsignificant); and (-48, 22, -20) (BA 38) (paired t-test, $p = 0.10$, nonsignificant).

In Figures 5.5.a, 5.5.b and 5.5.c, each of the transaxial section images shows the activation. The graph shows activation profile at the peak. The graph shows activation profile at the peak of each of the activated areas.

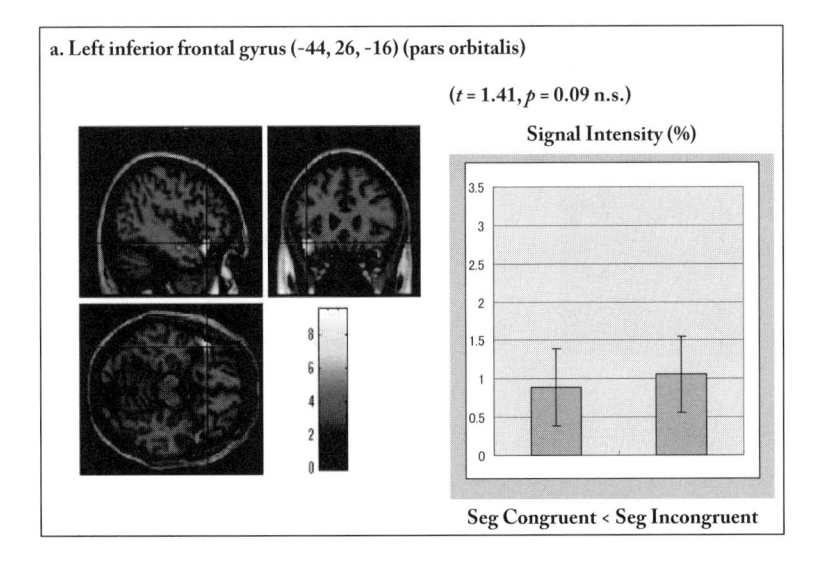

a. Left inferior frontal gyrus (-44, 26, -16) (pars orbitalis)

($t = 1.41$, $p = 0.09$ n.s.)

Signal Intensity (%)

Seg Congruent < Seg Incongruent

b. Left superior temporal gurus (temporal pole) (-48, 22, -20)

($t = 1.33, p = 0.10$ n.s.)

Signal Intensity (%)

Seg Congruent < Seg Incongruent

c. Left superior temporal gyrus (-62, -12, 4) ($t = 1.99, p < 0.05$)

Signal Intensity (%)

Seg Congruent < Seg Incongruent

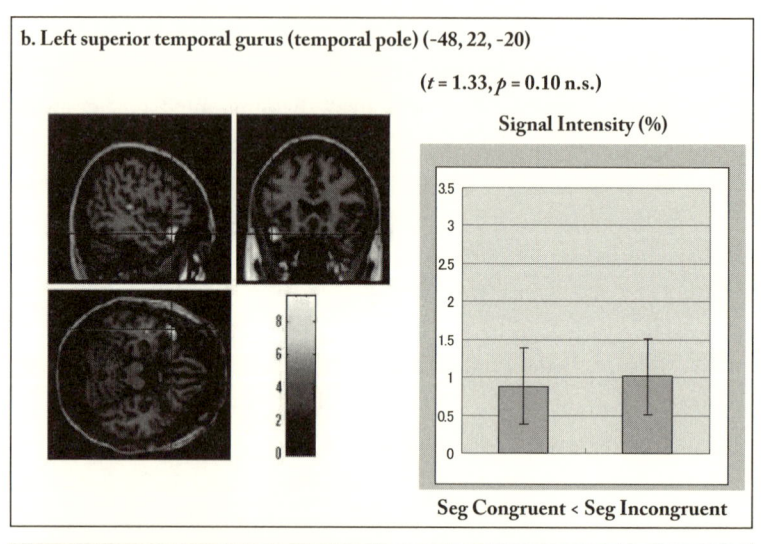

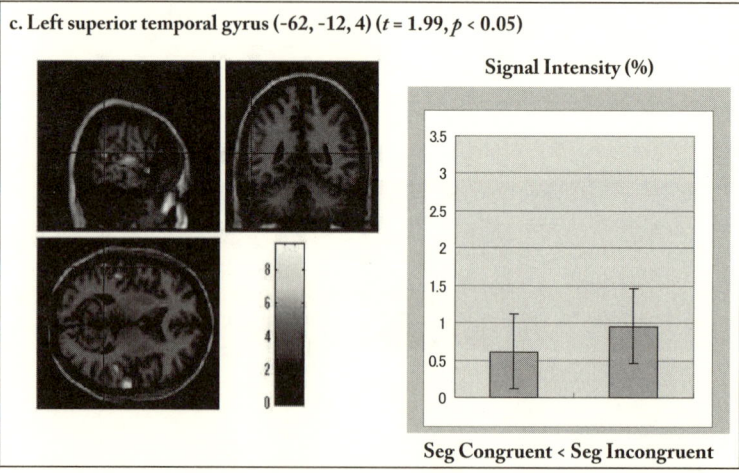

Figure 5.5. Cortical areas activated greatly in Seg Incongruent condition.

"n.s." denotes nonsignificant.

When compared with the activations of semantic violations, the activations of phrasal segmentation were significantly increased in two locations in the pars orbitalis (BA 47) of the left IFG and the anterior portion (temporal pole) (BA 38) of the left STG: (-44, 26, -16) (BA 47) and (-48, 22, -20) (BA 38). In the same locations, the activations of semantic violations weakly enhanced. However, they did not reach the statistically significant level of cortical activation. Therefore, the statistical comparison confirmed that two of the peak activations in the pars orbitalis (BA 47) of the left IFG and the anterior portion (temporal pole) (BA 38) of the left STG were specific to phrasal segmentation. In semantic violations, significant increase in activation was detected in the middle portion (BA 22) of the left STG: (-62, -12, 4) (BA 22). In the same location, no significantly increased activation was found in phrasal segmentation.

To sum it up, the statistical comparison between phrasal segmentation and semantic violations revealed the following results. There were no overlapping or common areas that showed a statistically significant increase in activation in both of the contrasts Non-seg Congruent – Seg Congruent and Seg Incongruent – Seg Congruent (paired t-test, $p < 0.05$) (Table 5.4). Thus, the regions that showed significant increase in activation were not the same between the two contrasts.

The results presented above show that the processing operation of phrasal segmentation is supported by different network of regions of the brain from that of semantic violations. The statistical comparisons of the mean signal intensity proved that the processing operations of phrasal segmentation and semantic violations are subserved by different neural network and neural substrates of the brain, hence different brain function of language processing. Hence, the auditory experiment of phrasal segmentation found that the left IFG (pars orbitalis) (BA 47) and the left STG (temporal pole) (BA 38) were the cortical regions specific to phrasal segmentation.

As for the involvement of prosodic information in phrasal segmentation, no evidence supporting its involvement was found in cortical activations in this experiment: no greater activation of phrasal segmentation was observed in the regions supporting the processing of prosodic information (viz., the right STG and its proximity) (see, Friederici & Alter, 2004; Mayer et al., 2003).

In conclusion, the results suggest that the processing operation of phrasal segmentation is supported by the modality independent brain function, predominately recruiting the language areas in the left hemisphere of the brain.

5.3 Discussion

The auditory experiment found the cortical regions specific to phrasal segmentation, observing the significant increase of activations in the following regions: the pars orbitalis (BA 47) of the left IFG and the anterior portion (temporal pole) (BA 38) of the left STG. In this section, the present study will discuss and verify the brain function of phrasal segmentation, arguing both of the results obtained from the visual and the auditory experiment together.

As a result of the fMRI data analysis, the auditory experiment found statistically significant brain activations associated with phrasal segmentation and semantic violations within the language areas in the left hemisphere of the brain. The statistical comparison between these processing operations confirmed that there was no overlapping pattern of increased activations to be found between phrasal segmentation and semantic violations. In phrasal segmentation, the pars orbitalis (BA 47) of the left IFG (Figure 5.4.a) and the anterior portion (temporal pole) (BA 38) of the left STG (Figure 5.4.b) were significantly greatly activated. In semantic violations, the middle portion (BA22) of the left STG (Figure 5.5.c) was significantly strongly activated. Thus, this experiment identified the different regions of cortical activations specific to phrasal segmentation and semantic violations respectively. The results also proved that the processing operations of phrasal segmentation and semantic violations are supported by different neural network and neural substrates of the brain, thus by functionally different role of the brain.

In the following subsections, this study will further specify the functional role of the activated regions during the processing of phrasal segmentation, in contrast to the functional role of the regions sensitive to semantic violations, comparing the results between the visual and the auditory experiment. By doing so, it will argue the issue of whether the brain function of phrasal segmentation is subserved by the common, modality independent neural correlates of the brain, and hence it will take up the issue of the functional specialization of phrasal segmentation in the brain.

5.3.1 Cortical Area Involved in Phrasal Segmentation

The auditory fMRI experiment of phrasal segmentation found the activation peaks specific to phrasal segmentation in the left hemisphere of the brain: two locations showed significantly increased activations in phrasal segmentation (i.e., the Non-seg Congruent – Seg Congruent contrast). In phrasal segmentation, one activation maximum was significantly greatly activated in the pars orbitalis (BA 47) of the left IFG (Figure 5.4.a). This location of the activation maximum was within the same anatomical region as the locations of the activation maxima found in the visual experiment: (-44, 26, -16) (the pars orbitalis) (BA 47) (Figure 5.4.a) (the auditory experiment); (-48, 24, -18) (the pars orbitalis) (BA 47) (Figure 4.4.a) and (-46, 28, -10) (the pars orbitalis) (BA 47) (Figure 4.4.b) (the visual experiment). These activations are seen as the index to stand for the effect of phrasal segmentation. The results confirmed the prediction from the visual experiment that the left pars orbitalis plays a key role in the processing operation of phrasal segmentation. The results, in addition, proved that this particular region subserves phrasal segmentation bimodally during sentence comprehension, without depending on the perceptive modality of stimuli. In consequence, the pars orbitalis (BA 47) of the left IFG supports the functional specialization of phrasal segmentation in the brain in the course of visual and auditory sentence comprehension.

As for the functional role of the left pars orbitalis (BA 47), a number of previous studies have pointed out that this particular region of the brain plays a specific role for semantic processing in sentence comprehension (Dapretto and Bookheimer, 1999; Dronkers et al., 2004; Hagoort et al., 2004; Homae et al., 2002). They have noted that the left pars orbitalis is viewed as the region responsible for semantic integration. According to their proposals, it serves to integrate the meaning of individual words into the meaning of phrases and further into the whole meaning of a sentence by selecting, comparing and integrating semantic information available in the input, based on the syntactic structures assigned by syntactic information, during sentence comprehension (Dapretto & Bookheimer, 1999; Hagoort et al., 2004; Homae et al., 2002). The results are consistent with their proposals, in that phrasal segmentation is the processing operation that leads the word meaning to the integration into the phrasal meaning and hence the sentence meaning, accompanied with the processing operation of syntactic information.

This processing view is further supported by the fact that in the visual and the auditory experiment, the sentence comprehension task including the processing operation of phrasal segmentation was supported by the brain regions including the areas sensitive to both syntactic and semantic processing in the left IFG: BA 44/45 for syntactic processing; BA 47 for semantic processing (Figure 4.3; Figures 4.4.a and 4.4.b in the visual experiment, Figure 5.3; Figures 5.4.a in the auditory experiment). However, in both of these experiments, the neural substrates supporting semantic processing were more greatly activated in the Non-segmented Congruent condition than in the Segmented Congruent condition. As a result, the enhanced cortical activation of phrasal segmentation was predominantly found in the left pars orbitalis (BA 47) throughout the experiments. Therefore, the present results are consistent with the indications from previous studies that lexico-semantic information (i.e., the word meaning) is integrated on the basis of syntactic information (i.e., syntactic structures) (Homae et al., 2002, 2003).

In the auditory experiment, another significantly activated maximum specific to phrasal segmentation was found in the temporal pole (BA 38) of the left STG. This location of the activation maximum was within the different anatomical region from that of the activation maxima discussed above: (-48, 22, -20) (the temporal pole) (BA 38) (Figure 5.4.b). In the visual experiment, no significant activations were observed from the statistical comparison at the location. However, a closer investigation of the results provided evidence that the activated regions were extending from the left IFG to the left temporal pole (Figure 4.3; Figures 4.4.a and 4.4.b). Therefore, both of the results from two experiments in this study suggest that the temporal pole (BA 38) of the left STG was also involved in phrasal segmentation. As for the functional role of the left anterior temporal pole (i.e., the left anterior temporal cortex), a number of studies have confirmed that this area is involved in composing and binding meaningful components into one message (Chee et al., 1999; StGeorge at al., 1999; Vandenberghe et al. 2002). They have proposed that the left anterior temporal pole has a key role in the composition of sentence meaning, binding together meaningful constituents into one message. Their proposals do not disagree with the present results, in that the left anterior temporal pole can contribute to the composition of sentence meaning in phrasal segmentation as well. Thus, the results found another region associated with phrasal segmentation, the left anterior temporal pole, which was activated when the participants were engaged in sentence comprehension, particularly in the auditory experiment.

5.3.2 Cortical Area Involved in Semantic Violations

The results of the present auditory fMRI experiment showed that the cortical activations and their activation patterns were not the same between phrasal segmentation and semantic violations. In semantic violations, the auditory experiment found one activation maximum that produced significantly greater activation in the middle portion (BA 22) of the left STG (Figure 5.5.c). This location of the activation maximum was within the same anatomical region as the location of the activation maximum found in the visual experiment: (-62, -12, 4) (BA 22) (Figure 5.5.c) (the auditory experiment); (-64, -48, 10) (BA 22) (Figure 4.5.d) (the visual experiment). In the visual experiment, another location of the activation maximum specific to semantic violations was identified in the pars triangularis (BA 45) of the left IFG: (-52, 22, 6) (BA 45) (Figure 4.5.c). However, in the auditory experiment, no similar brain activations were found in this area. Thus, in semantic violations, the locations of the activation maxima were not consistent between the visual and the auditory experiment.

As for the inconsistent results between these experiments, Van Petten and Luka (2006) have indicated that each of the related regions of the left IFG and STG are differently sensitive to and selectively support the processing operations of semantic violations. They have suggested that semantic violations do not recruit one specific area, providing the evidence from ERP studies. With respect to the involvement of the left STG (BA 22) in semantic violations, they have argued that the region may reflect some aspect of the comprehension of a word per se, rather than strategic processing of word meanings that can be observed in the proximity (BA 44/45) between the left pars triangularis and the left pars orbitalis. Their view accords with the results that there are a certain amount of differences in the cortical organization during the tasks of semantic violations (Ni et al., 2000; Ruschemeyer et al., 2006) and semantic judgment containing ambiguous and anomalous words (Bokde et al., 2001; Dapretto & Bookheimer, 1999; Rodd et al., 2005). In fact, some studies have reported that both the left IFG and the left STG were significantly activated (Dapretto & Bookheimer, 1999; Ni et al., 2000), whereas some other studies have showed significant activation only in the left IFG (Bokde et al., 2001; Hagoort et al., 2004; Rodd et al., 2005) or in the left STG (Friederici et al., 2003). In the present experiment, one of the related regions (the left STG) was significantly activated in the processing of sentences that contained semantically anomalous words. The inconsistent results between the visual and the auditory experiment were consistent with the previous findings reported by Dapretto & Bookheimer (1999) and Ni et al. (2000). They suggest that the brain activations involved in semantic violations can be reflected differently in their distributions within similar networks in the brain, depending on the degree of activations produced by the processing operations of semantic violations. Therefore, the different cortical activations of semantic violations, as identified in two of the experiments in the present study, are consistent in their results with the cortical activations found in previous studies of semantic violations and semantic judgment containing ambiguous and anomalous words. In conclusion, regarding the results of semantic violations, two of the bimodal fMRI experiments in this study showed similar patterns of cortical activations that were provided by previous studies of semantic violations as argued in the preceding sections and chapters in this book. Both of the activation patters matched well in their results. Thus, the results of semantic violations during processing of incongruent sentences were consistent bimodally between the visual and the auditory fMRI experiments.

Finally, in the auditory experiment of phrasal segmentation, no overlapping activations were observed between phrasal segmentation and semantic violations. The present fMRI experiment found the activation peaks specific to either phrasal segmentation or semantic violations in the left hemisphere of the brain: two locations showed significantly increased activations in phrasal segmentation (i.e., the Non-seg Congruent – Seg Congruent contrast); one location in semantic violations (i.e., the Seg Incongruent – Seg Congruent contrast). Further, together with the findings obtained from the visual fMRI experiment in this book, two of the present fMRI experiments led to the results that there exist cortical sites encompassing two sensory modalities between the visual and the auditory processing operations of phrasal segmentation and semantic violations respectively during processing of sentence comprehension. Their cortical activations did not overlap between phrasal segmentation and semantic violations. It is claimed that the effect of phrasal segmentation did not interact with the effect of semantic violations: an examination of the cortical activation graphs for the semantic domain of the brain (the left pars orbitalis (BA47)) show that the effect of phrasal segmentation was primarily driven by Non-seg condition (i.e., the Non-seg Congruent – Seg Congruent contrast). It seems that phrasal segmentation is a major factor of the bimodal cortical activations in Non-seg condition. The present findings provide evidence that there is a bimodal network of regions that subserve the functional specialization of phrasal segmentation in the brain

5.4 Summary

This chapter, first, reported on the auditory experiment of phrasal segmentation during Japanese sentence comprehension. The auditory experiment identified activation peaks specific to either phrasal segmentation or to semantic violations in the left hemisphere of the brain. In phrasal segmentation, two of the activation peaks were detected as significantly increased activations: one was in the pars orbitalis (BA 47) of the left IFG and the other was in the temporal pole (BA 38) of the left STG. In semantic violations, one location produced significantly greater activation: it was in the middle portion (BA 22) of the left STG. Two sets of the results in the auditory experiment indicated that there were no overlapping regions activated between phrasal segmentation and semantic violations: the activation pattern of phrasal segmentation was different from the activation pattern of semantic violations. The present results provide further support for our proposal, as indicated by the results from the visual experiment, that phrasal segmentation is supported by a particular network of regions distributed in the left hemisphere of the brain. The findings obtained in the auditory experiment suggest that the processing operation of phrasal segmentation is differently manifested in the brain from those of semantic violations.

Next, together with the results from the visual experiment, the results from the present experiment identified the bimodal brain activations supporting phrasal segmentation in the left pars orbitalis (BA 47). The results suggest that processing behaviors of phrasal segmentation were indeed specifically instantiated in the cortical activations in the brain. Two sets of the results from the visual and the auditory study provide evidence for our claim that there will be a network of regions that subserve the functional specialization of phrasal segmentation in the brain. The present findings identified the place of the mental processing associated with phrasal segmentation in the domain of semantic processing in the left hemisphere of the brain.

In the next chapter, this study will discuss the findings obtained from the visual and the auditory fMRI experiments within the framework of the approaches to modeling human sentence processing in the brain.

Chapter 6

What Happens with Phrasal Segmentation in the Brain, Then?

Thus far, this book successfully achieved the goal to clarify the processing domain and region of phrasal segmentation in the brain. The preceding two chapters provided evidence that the cortical area specific and pertaining to phrasal segmentation exists in the human brain. From the cortical activations, this book was able to trace the processing operations of phrasal segmentation in the brain. The results of the fMRI experiments proved that the cortical activations of phrasal segmentation were characterized by different involvement of the core linguistic information (i.e., phonological, syntactic and semantic information, in particular, in phrasal segmentation, syntactic and semantic information) in the brain. This book achieved the first goal presented in Section 1.5 in Chapter 1. To achieve the second goal of this book, this chapter will revisit and challenge the issue of the relation between phrasal segmentation and the modeling of language processing in the human brain.

First, this chapter will look in depth at our fMRI evidence and see about the characteristics of phrasal segmentation with respect to the effect and the nature of its processing operations during sentence comprehension. Next, the chapter will argue the processing operations of phrasal segmentation within the framework of two competing approaches to human sentence processing, regarding the serial and the parallel processing accounts of sentence comprehension (see, Section 2.2.1.5, for their detailed processing accounts). Then, the chapter will consider the validity of these two approaches to explain the fMRI findings of phrasal segmentation the current study provided. Finally, the chapter will put forward the proposal that phrasal segmentation reflects the parallel architecture of language processing in the brain. The chapter will claim that phrasal segmentation is universally associated with language processing.

6.1 Phrasal Segmentation in the Brain

The following sections will look in depth at the evidence of the processing operations of phrasal segmentation found in the brain and specify the effect and the nature of these processing operations observed in the brain, based on the fMRI findings obtained from this study.

6.1.1 Effect of Phrasal Segmentation in the Brain

From two fMRI experiments, the present results proved that the neural correlates supporting phrasal segmentation are different from those implicated in semantic violations, in that the cortical activations did not overlap in the place and the domain of their peak activations (see, Sections 4.3 & 5.3). The results also well accorded with the proposal of the functional view of language processing: different computational resources of the brain are required for different operations of language processing. Actually, the fMRI results verified that different aspects of language processing are supported by different areas and networks of the brain, from the comparison of cortical activations between phrasal segmentation and semantic violations.

Regarding the processing operations of phrasal segmentation, their activations were supported by the pars orbitalis (BA 47) in the left IFG and the temporal pole (BA 38) in the left STG: the pars orbitalis (BA 47) in the left IFG was activated in the visual and the auditory condition, and the temporal pole (BA 38) was simultaneously activated in the auditory condition. Both regions of the pars orbitalis (BA 47) and the temporal pole (BA 38) are anatomically connected via the ventral pathway (i.e., the inferior-occipito-frontal fasciculus passing through the left IFG and the left lateral temporal lobe), and those two brain regions are reported to yield the semantic effects showing their distributed functional connectivity patterns during on-line language processing (Vigneau et al., 2006; Turken & Dronkers, 2011). In particular, the results showed that the pars orbitalis (BA 47) worked as a particular brain region involved in phrasal segmentation; the activations of the pars orbitalis (BA 47) were observed in both the visual and the auditory conditions. Thus, the effect of phrasal segmentation was found robustly during sentence comprehension, independently of the sensory modality of the input.

In contrast, the processing operations of semantic violations were recruiting the temporo-frontal network of the left hemisphere of the brain, differently between two experiments. In the visual experiment, the pars triangularis (BA 45) of the left IFG and the left STG (BA 22) were responsible for semantic violations, while in the auditory experiment, the left STG (BA 22) was predominantly tied to that particular processing. The results showed that the processing operations of semantic violations were differently instantiated in the cortical activations between the visual and the auditory experiments. In regard to the presentation of sentences with semantic violations, Rogalsky & Hickok (2011) pointed out that there are inconsistencies of cortical activations across studies depending on the sensory modality of the stimuli (the visual stimuli or the auditory stimuli). In fact, in our fMRI experiments, the distribution of activation foci for semantic violations spread over distinct regions: the pars triangularis (BA

45) and the pars orbitalis (BA 47) in the left IFG, and the middle portion of the left STG in the visual stimulus condition; the middle portion of the left STG in the auditory stimulus condition. Such results of semantic violations were consistent with the claim of the bimodal inconsistent distribution of activation foci: the left IFG did not activate during the performance of sentence comprehension with semantic violations in the auditory experiment, while it activated in the visual experiment. Thus, in this study, the difference of the results in semantic violations can be attributed to the difference of the sensory modality of the stimuli, reflecting the different degree of activations within similar networks of the processing of semantic violations (see, Section 5.3.2, for the issue of the inconsistent degree of activations of the processing of semantic violations).

Our fMRI results suggest that the effect of phrasal segmentation is characterized in the processing operations and the functional connectivity differently from the effect of semantic violations. As for the effect of phrasal segmentation, the pars orbitalis (BA 47) showed the modality independent, robust greater activations. The effect of semantic violations, on the other hand, was observed unimodally as visual or auditory effect, spreading over the core areas of language functioning in the brain. For this reason, it would be reasonable to conclude that the present study adequately identified the effect of phrasal segmentation in the brain and also it validly determined the cortical regions involved in phrasal segmentation, by introducing two different modalities of fMRI experiments and by comparing two different cortical activations between phrasal segmentation and semantic violations. Thus, the modality independent involvement of the pars orbitalis (BA 47) of the left IFG in phrasal segmentation provides evidence for the effect of phrasal segmentation, during on-line sentence comprehension, in that particular cortical region of the brain.

Finally, the results in our fMRI experiments lead us to the conclusion that there is a robust effect of phrasal segmentation in our brain when we understand sentences presented either visually or aurally. The results of bimodal cortical activations elicited during processing of phrasal segmentation suggest that phrasal segmentation would be universally associated with language processing during sentence comprehension. The study will go back to the issue of the relation between phrasal segmentation and language processing, in particular, phrasal segmentation and its possible roles in language processing later in this chapter. Before that, the next section will examine the nature of the processing operations of phrasal segmentation in the brain and the characteristics of the neural substrates supporting the processing operations of phrasal segmentation.

6.1.2 Nature of Phrasal Segmentation in the Brain

The preceding section discussed the effect of the functional neural activities obtained from two fMRI experiments in light of the evidence of phrasal segmentation in the brain. The section validated the involvement of the language-relevant brain regions to the processing of phrasal segmentation. The results of the fMRI experiments suggest that the cortical activations invoked by phrasal segmentation are functionally attributed to the activations that reflect any of the universal processing operations involved in the on-line comprehension of normally structured, meaningful sentences (i.e., semantically congruent sentences). These results lead us to propose that on-line phrasal segmentation would be implicated as a critical function of language processing in our normal, ordinary processing of sentence comprehension. Next, this section will look into and argue the nature of the processing operations of phrasal segmentation in the brain, regarding how the particular linguistic sources of information can be accessed and processed (i.e., access and processing of core linguistic information such as phonological, syntactic and semantic information) and how the particular brain activations of phrasal segmentation will be engaged in processing of language during sentence comprehension. This section will further specify the processing operations of phrasal segmentation within the framework of two competing approaches to human sentence processing (i.e., serial vs. parallel processing of sentence comprehension). Finally, the section will evaluate and argue the validity of the predictions from two different proposals of sentence comprehension to explain the cortical activations of phrasal segmentation that our current study provided.

Our fMRI findings identified evidence that the left pars orbitalis (BA 47) bimodally supports the processing operations of phrasal segmentation during on-line sentence comprehension. Those fMRI findings specifically detected the significant effect of phrasal segmentation in the semantic domain of the human brain, the left pars orbitalis (BA 47), in both the visual and the auditory experiments. At the same time, our results confirmed that the parallel activations in the syntactic domain (i.e., pars triangularis (BA 45) & pars opercularis (BA 44) in the left IFG) as well as the semantic domain (i.e., pars orbitalis (BA 47) in the left IFG) of the brain during processing of normally structured, semantically congruent sentences (see, Figure 4.3 and Figure 5.3); however, the activations in the syntactic domain of the brain were not strong enough in statistical comparison to reflect significant level of activations (see, Sections 4.3.1 & 5.3.1, for detailed discussions). These two of our fMRI results lead to the conclusion that our fMRI results found the modality independent effects of phrasal segmentation during sentence comprehension in the particular brain region, specifically in the left pars orbitalis (BA 47), the domain of semantic processing in the brain (see, Sections 4.3.1 & 5.3.1). Furthermore, our results identified the functionally different nature of activations in the left pars triangularis (BA 45) and the left pars opercularis (BA 44), the domain of syntactic processing, in parallel with the activations in the domain of semantic processing in the brain. Thus, our fMRI results showed that different types of linguistic information were accessed and processed differently in the different functional domains of the brain: semantic information was in the semantic domain of the brain, the left pars orbitalis (BA 47) in the left IFG; syntactic information was in the syntactic domain of the brain, the left pars triangularis (BA 45) and the left pars opercularis (BA 44), during processing of normally structured, meaningful sentences in sentence comprehension. Both of these fMRI findings provide support for the claim that semantic and syntactic processing operations of phrasal segmentation are independently in parallel involved in processing of normal, ordinary simple sentences.

On the one hand, our findings justified the specific effect of phrasal segmentation in the semantic domain of the brain. On the other, our findings found the parallel cortical activations in the syntactic domain of the brain along with the cortical activations in the semantic domain. What it comes down to, from both of these results, is that different types of linguistic sources of information subserved the cortical activations differently in their functions in different brain regions in parallel during the processing of normally structured, semantic sentences. Our fMRI data suggest that such parallel processes result in the different degree of specialization in the left IFG for sentence comprehension. The data support our claim of the parallel processing account of linguistic information that syntactic and semantic information are accessed and processed on-line in parallel at different levels in functionally different areas and networks of the brain. Therefore, different linguistic information (syntactic and semantic information in our fMRI study) is viewed to be implicated in the processing operations of phrasal segmentation in parallel at different levels. That claim is consistent with the proposals of parallel processing that different linguistic sources of information are encoded and processed in parallel during on-line sentence comprehension.

So far, the proposals of parallel processing seem to well accord to explain our fMRI evidence, as compared to the proposals of serial processing. Thus, the predictions of serial processing do not seem to properly explain our fMRI data in the study of on-line phrasal segmentation. In the next section, we will go back to the issue of the relation between phrasal segmentation and language processing, in particular, phrasal segmentation and its possible roles in language processing.

6.2　What is Phrasal Segmentation?

This study has argued that the left pars orbitalis (BA 47) has been viewed as the operating region responsible for semantic integration in the semantic domain of processing. It serves to integrate the meaning of individual words into the meaning of phrases and further into the whole meaning of a sentence, using semantic information available in the input, in parallel with the processing of syntactic information to couple words into larger syntactic units such as phrases and sentences, during sentence comprehension. In the processing operations of phrasal segmentation, the left pars orbitalis (BA 47) is responsible for the processing of semantic sources of linguistic information. This study also claimed that such processing operations would take place at different linguistic levels based on different types of linguistic information such as syntactic and phonological information. This study has also identified such processing operations at syntactic level in the syntactic domain of the brain (pars triangularis (BA 45) & pars opercularis (BA 44) in the left IFG). So far, the claim of this study supports the predictions of parallel processing in sentence comprehension.

Further, in our fMRI experiments, the stimulus conditions were designed to reflect the phrase-by-phrase on-line processing of sentences between non-segmented vs. segmented conditions. As a result, this study identified the effect of phrase-by-phrase processing in parallel in syntax and semantics. The effect was stronger in the semantic than in the syntactic domain of the brain. Our study did not find cortical activations that support sentence-by-sentence serial operations from syntax to semantics in the way that the sentence meaning is given only after the syntactic structure was parsed well enough. If phrasal segmentation needs much stronger demands to process the structure of each phrase first of all, we could detect any stronger cortical activation in the syntactic domain; the result was the stronger effect of phrasal segmentation in the semantic domain (see, Friederici, 2002; Friederici & Kotz, 2003; Grodzinsky & Friederici, 2006, for the proposal of serial processing). Our results, thus, support the proposal of parallel processing, in that the structure and the meaning are assigned phrase-by-phrase in each phrase in parallel at syntactic and at semantic level respectively, reflecting the different degree of processing at each level (see, Hagoort, 2003b, 2005a, 2008; Culicover & Jackendoff, 2005, 2006; Jackendoff, 2010, for the proposal of parallel processing).

The parallel cortical activations in the semantic and the syntactic domain will predict the following processing mechanism during phrasal segmentation. In the syntactic domain, constituent structures of each phrase are formed in the posterior dorsal portion of the left IFG (BA 44/45). In the semantic domain, the individual word meaning is combined into the meaning of each phrase in the anterior ventral portion of the left IFG (BA 47). In this study, the results found that the semantic domain was greatly activated in the Non-segmented Congruent condition (i.e., the experimental condition), suggesting that the greater involvement of semantic processing was observed in phrase-by-phrase processing in our fMRI experiments.

In addition, this study provides evidence to support the claim that the semantic effect of phrasal segmentation is viewed as the processing operations that serve to link each individual word meaning into each phrase in parallel at the semantic level. Regarding the role of the left pars orbitalis (BA 47), many studies argued that this specific region is responsible for the processing operations of semantic information, especially important for executive aspects of semantic processing, during processing of language (Bookheimer, 2002). However, so far, the actual involvement of that area in the semantic domain during sentence comprehension remained to be less clear (Gbalieli et al., 1998; Price et al., 1999; Thompson-Schill et al., 1997). Our study has determined the bimodal brain functions of phrasal segmentation at the semantic level in the semantic domain of the brain: the cortical activations in the left pars orbitalis (BA 47). The effect of phrasal segmentation identified in the semantic domain was functionally different from the effect of semantic violations observed spreading over the language areas of the brain. Our study has adequately confirmed the involvement of that particular brain region in our normal, ordinary comprehension of meaningful sentences, without relying on the semantic violation paradigm (see, Hagoort et al., 2004, for the cortical activations of the left pars orbitalis (BA 47), using the semantic violation paradigm in visual sentence comprehension). The present results suggest that the left pars orbitalis (BA 47) serves to link and integrate the meaning of each individual word into the whole meaning of each phrase in the course of sentence comprehension. For this reason, the effect of phrasal segmentation will specify the role of the left pars orbitalis (BA 47), reflecting the processing of normally structured, meaningful sentences.

One major finding of our study is that the cortical activations of the left pars orbitalis (BA 47) were observed during on-line comprehension of meaningful, simple sentences. So far, several findings pointed out that the left pars orbitalis (BA 47) would serve to bind together word meaning to achieve a coherent interpretation of a sentence (Hagoort et al., 2004; Hagoort, 2005a). However, their empirical evidence exclusively relied on the semantic violation paradigm for the activations of the left pars orbitalis (BA 47). As argued earlier, the results of the cortical activations using such violation paradigms were inconsistent in their results of the cortical activations, depending on type of the task and the stimulus modality. Our fMRI experiments factored out the inconsistent results of activations that might be caused by the violation paradigms, and our study finally specified robust greater cortical activations bimodally in the left pars orbitalis (BA

47). At the same time, in parallel, our study found bimodal cortical activations in the syntactic domain of the brain, the left pars triangularis (BA 45) and the left pars opercularis (BA 44). In the same vein, so far, the cortical activations of the syntactic domain (BA 44/45) were also mainly obtained from the studies, based on the syntactic violation paradigms (Rogalsky & Hickok, 2011). To date, no studies were available that explicitly detect the cortical activations in parallel in the semantic and the syntactic domain of the brain without employing any of the violation paradigms. Our fMRI findings claim that our results of phrasal segmentation validly reflect the cortical activations attributed to our normal processing of sentence comprehension.

Therefore, one important implication of our study is that the left pars orbitalis (BA 47) appears to work as a focal point of phrasal segmentation at the semantic level during processing of normally structured, meaningful sentences. At the same time, in parallel with the activity of that region, the left pars triangularis (BA 45) and the left pars opercularis (BA 44) seem to function as focal points of phrasal segmentation at the syntactic level. Those brain regions in the left IFG are viewed to play a crucial role in phrasal segmentation in the comprehension of normally structured, meaningful sentences. Our fMRI findings suggest that phrasal segmentation serves to bind together semantic and syntactic sources of linguistic information at each level in parallel in the input phrase-by-phrase when we understand sentences either visually or aurally.

Further, our study claims that there are processing operations to mediate and organize different sources of linguistic information in parallel into a proper integration of linguistic units such as phrases and sentences. These processing operations will lead us to the understanding of normally structured, meaningful sentences during normal, ordinary sentence processing. Phrasal segmentation is predicted to reflect such processing operations during on-line language processing, in particular in this study, during on-line sentence comprehension. The parallel accounts of sentence processing, further, argue that different types of linguistic sources are combined and integrated on-line in parallel, being mediated and organized at each processing level and across different processing levels. If so, phrasal segmentation will be the processing operations that lead the word meaning to the integration into the phrasal meaning, and further to the whole sentence meaning, together with the processing operations of syntactic information in parallel and interactively from the word level, through the phrase level, to the sentence level. Of course, further studies will be needed in order to evaluate the validity of those predictions our study presented here. Such attempts would surely contribute to consider the role of phrasal segmentation within the framework of approaches to modeling sentence processing properly.

Finally, this section puts forward the proposal that phrasal segmentation reflects the parallel architecture of on-line language processing, being universally involved in sentence processing. In that architecture, during on-line phrasal segmentation, syntactic and semantic information encoded at the word level are modulated and integrated in parallel into larger combinatorial groups of structured units such as phrases and sentences. The processing operations of phrasal segmentation are responsible for coupling each individual word properly into phrases and sentences. In particular, in sentence processing, phrasal segmentation serves as the intervening functions that combine and group individual words into larger linguistic units of phrases and sentences, using syntactic and semantic sources of linguistic information in parallel and concurrently in the input. The modality independent, parallel effect of phrasal segmentation in our study will support the claim that phrasal segmentation is universally associated with the parallel, coordinated recruitment of linguistic information available in the input in the course of sentence comprehension.

One of mainstream assumptions in linguistics is that the structure is built up piece by piece by putting words and phrases together to get larger phrases (see, Culicover, 2009). Phrasal segmentation would be viewed to universally reflect such process to build larger linguistic units from individual words in production and comprehension of language. Speaking to this concern, one possible realization of such universality in phrasal segmentation might be instantiated in the linguistic operation called Merge. Merge is the basic linguistic operation of putting any two linguistic elements together, pairwise, in the Minimalist Program (Chomsky, 1995). The operation of attaching an already merged element of structure is called External Merge. Therefore, any word and phrase can be combined into larger linguistic units with any word or phrase. In the sense of grouping words into larger units, the operation is substantially the same between phrasal segmentation and Merge. In the Minimalist Program, however, Merge is the purely syntactic operation to form larger linguistic units, basically being motivated by syntactic information. On the other hand, phrasal segmentation is the operation motivated by syntactic and semantic information. Following the claim of Merge, the operation to combine words into larger linguistic units could be instantiated in the cortical activations dominantly in the syntactic domain of the brain. However, in reality, in our study, the operation to combine words into larger units was subserved by the parallel activations in the syntactic and the semantic domain of the brain: the left pars triangularis (BA 45) and the left pars opercularis (BA 44) in the syntactic domain; the left pars orbitalis (BA 47) in the semantic domain. One possible explanation of this result is that Merge is the structural process to group words into larger units at the syntactic level; phrasal segmentation reflects the process to combine words structurally and semantically in parallel into larger units. Substantially, the formation operation in Merge can overlap the processing operation of phrasal segmentation at the syntactic level. The process to combine words into larger units is universally observed in human languages as the bootstrapping operation from words to phrases and sentences.

Therefore, phrasal segmentation is predicted to be one of the universal processing operations in human language in production and comprehension of language.

Regarding the co-involvement of syntactic and semantic information to group words into larger units, Culicover & Jackendoff (2005) suggest that the head of each syntactic phrase canonically maps the semantic function to combine words together into syntactic phrases, allowing the possibility that syntactic and semantic structures are to some degree independent in organization. If that is the case, each syntactic and semantic sources of information can be encoded in parallel in the brain in order to combine words into phrases even in the forming operation of Merge as well as phrasal segmentation. Lastly, in conclusion, in accordance with our fMRI results, this study supposes that the parallel processing of syntactic and semantic information is universally responsible for the process to combine words into larger units in language processing. This book insists that phrasal segmentation reflects such process of grouping words in the course of the comprehension of normally structured, meaningful sentences. That grouping process of words is triggered by semantic information as well as syntactic information in parallel in sentence processing. Therefore, the processing operations regarding phrasal segmentation would be universally associated with sentence processing, which is needed to be properly formalized in the overall architecture of sentence processing.

Using the fMRI system, this book specified the contribution of syntactic and semantic information to the processing operations carried out in the brain during phrasal segmentation. Our results predict that phrasal segmentation might instantiate the coordinated recruitment and integration of such different sources of linguistic information in sentence processing, from words, through phrases, to a sentence. Also, further investigations will be needed to explain and specify the overall mechanism of phrasal segmentation during sentence processing in the brain. Such attempts will enable us to insist and construct a suitable account of phrasal segmentation within a proper, valid framework of sentence comprehension.

Finally, this book will address one question to the future study of phrasal segmentation. This book has insisted that phrasal segmentation would involve the interface operations to process and mediate different sources of linguistic information simultaneously in parallel at each linguistic level. However, the present findings did not establish the mechanism of the parallel involvement of how different linguistic information was retrieved and integrated in parallel, being formulated from words to larger linguistic units of phrases and sentences. Particularly, in our fMRI experiments, the neural computations of phonological information remain to be unclear: under the task conditions introduced in this book, our study did not find the involvement of that information in phrasal segmentation. The next question for future investigations of phrasal segmentation is to explore the interface operations that would adjust and mediate phonological, syntactic, and semantic information of individual constituents into larger units, in parallel and recursively in on-line sentence processing. For the architectural considerations on such interface operations of parallel language processing accounts, recently, Culicover & Jackendoff (2005, 2006) and Jackendoff (2010) theoretically developed the framework of the parallel architecture of language (the Parallel Architecture in their term), with a vision of better facilitating the linguistic theory with concerns of language processing, language acquisition, and biological foundations of the language faculty. The Parallel Architecture involves the three-way divisions into generative components of phonology, syntax, and semantics, a crosscutting division into phrasal and morphological departments, interface principles of three different components (Culicover & Jackendoff, 2005). Their considerations are consistent with our claim of phrasal segmentation, in that individual sources of linguistic information in phonology, syntax, and semantics are processed independently at each level in parallel and mediated interactively by interface operations with each other. In their framework, they argue the issue of how the integration of each component of linguistic information will be accomplished, by introducing the interface rules responsible for the mapping among phonology, syntax, and semantics. However, the discussion of how such interface rules work in the brain will need further investigations. Despite such limitations at present, the study of phrasal segmentation, with newly available tools and theories for assessing the fact of the brain, is a step in the right direction for understanding how language is processed and organized in the brain.

6.3 Summary

First, this chapter assessed our fMRI evidence and characterized phrasal segmentation with respect to the effect and the nature of its processing operations during on-line sentence comprehension. Next, the chapter argued the processing operations of phrasal segmentation within the framework of two competing approaches, the serial vs. the parallel accounts of sentence processing. Then, the chapter evaluated the validity of these approaches to explain our fMRI findings of phrasal segmentation. Finally, the chapter claimed that phrasal segmentation reflects the parallel architecture of language processing when grouping words into larger linguistic units, predicting that it is universally associated with our processing of sentences at the syntactic level as well as the semantic level of processing. Lastly, in the next chapter, this book will conclude our study of phrasal segmentation, providing an overview of the present study.

Chapter 7

Conclusion

Finally, this book will conclude our study of phrasal segmentation, reviewing the discussion and the results of the fMRI experiments so far. The chapter will summarize and overview the argument of phrasal segmentation this book has provided in our study.

7.1 Concluding Remarks

A sentence consists of words and phrases. This observation represents the fact that in a sentence, words are structured into phrases, and phrases are organized into a sentence. In sentence comprehension, people have the ability to perceive phrasal units from a string of words in a sentence, deducing their syntactic organization and meaning. The present study was an attempt to aim at the clarification of the perceptive behavior of phrases during sentence comprehension. This mental operation was referred to as phrasal segmentation: a bootstrapping operation from words to phrases and sentences.

During sentence comprehension, people also have the ability to detect and identify the individual words from a string of words in a sentence. This is referred to as word segmentation. Word segmentation and phrasal segmentation have been viewed as the processing operations supporting sentence comprehension. These two of processing issues have been referred to as the segmentation problem, which has been one of the main issues in the studies of human language behaviors.

In particular, regarding the segmentation problem at the word level, a number of researchers have achieved fruitful results in these studies. However, the segmentation problem at the phrase level has been neglected for a long time, other than studies focusing on the issue from the perspectives of prosodic studies. As this study has argued against these approaches, the prosodic solutions of phrasal segmentation (i.e., prosodic bootstrapping) do not work well, especially when dealing with the issues at the syntactic phrase level. That is, a number of discrepancies and inconsistencies between prosodic and syntactic phrases (Chomsky & Halle, 1968).

This study has sought to deal with and clarify the issue of phrasal segmentation, employing the neuropsychological approach to this issue. In the course of the argument, this study has taken up the issues of human language processing, modeling human sentence processing, and neurophysiological findings in order to provide the groundings for this study (viz., the premises and rationale for the study). Eventually, this study sought to investigate and understand the issue of how phrasal segmentation is instantiated in the brain, using functional brain imaging (fMRI) techniques.

Throughout the visual and the auditory experiment, this study found the brain regions responsible for phrasal segmentation in the pars orbitalis (BA 47) of the left IFG. It revealed that these particular regions served as the brain function to integrate the individual words into phrases in the semantic domain of processing during sentence comprehension. At the same time, in parallel, our study found bimodal cortical activations in the syntactic domain of the brain, the left pars triangularis (BA45) and the left pars opercularis

(BA 44). Our fMRI results discovered the involvement of these brain regions in phrasal segmentation in the semantic and the syntactic domain of processing for the first time in the comprehension of normally structured, meaningful sentences. At the same time, our study evaluated the effect of phrasal segmentation, comparing it with the effect of semantic violations. Our study revealed that the effect of phrasal segmentation is different in its nature and characteristics of cortical activations and activation patterns from the effect of semantic violations. Thus, the effect of phrasal segmentation was found robustly during sentence comprehension, independently of the sensory modality of the input.

Therefore, this study will shed new light on neuropsychological studies that aim to bridge the gap between human cognitive behaviors and their underlying neural events through the measurement of changes in brain blood flow, employing functional brain imaging techniques. Actually in this study, functional brain imaging experiments using fMRI gave the opportunity to observe and validate real-time in vivo mental processing associated with phrasal segmentation during sentence comprehension. In doing so, this study sought to identify the neural basis of phrasal segmentation and investigate the functional relationship between language and the brain. In order to achieve the goal, this study schemed and conducted a series of fMRI experiments with two different modalities of phrasal segmentation (the visual and the auditory experiment). It also argued several background issues involved in phrasal segmentation such as the issues of modeling language processing and core linguistic sources in language processing. The discussion helped to understand and consider the issue of phrasal segmentation in the overall framework of sentence comprehension. Thereby, this study further considered possible contributions to theories and models of sentence comprehension.

As a result of the fMRI experiments, this study identified the cortical regions involved in phrasal segmentation in both visual and auditory processing of Japanese sentences during sentence processing. However, the possible role and mechanism of phrasal segmentation still remain to be unclear. In particular, the results found the involvement of the semantic domain of the brain in phrasal segmentation and identified its neural correlates in the left pars orbitalis (BA 47), in parallel with the involvement of the syntactic domain in phrasal segmentation as well in the left pars triangularis (BA 45) and the left pars opercularis (BA 44). However, our study was not able to find the involvement of the phonological domain in phrasal segmentation, nor able to detect the interface operations that would adjust and mediate phonological, syntactic, and semantic information of individual constituents into larger units, in parallel and recursively in on-line sentence processing. Those unresolved issues of phrasal segmentation will require further research.

Using the fMRI system, this book specified the contribution of syntactic and semantic information to the processing operations carried out in the brain during phrasal segmentation. Our results predict that phrasal segmentation might instantiate the coordinated recruitment and integration of such different sources of linguistic information in sentence processing, from words, through phrases, to a sentence. For further close investigation of phrasal segmentation, future research and study will be expected. Such attempts will ensure greater contributions of the study of phrasal segmentation to the development of theories and models of on-line language processing. As this study has been seen, it is a fascinating enterprise to seek to find unknown brain functions that have remained to be identified underlying human language behaviors.

In the following section, this book will summarize our attempt here briefly, with the hope that future research will achieve better understanding of human language behaviors and contribution to the study of language.

7.2 Summary

In Chapter 1, this study has made a statement of the issues and the goals of the study, reviewing the background of the study. Then, this chapter has provided the methodological considerations for the validity of the study, specifying the scope of and the approach to the study. In the final part, it has given the definitions and the explanations of the terms used in a special or a technical sense in this study. Finally, it has presented the outline of each chapter and the overall organization of this work.

In Chapter 2, this study has reviewed the related issues to understand the behavior of phrasal segmentation, presenting the evidence of the linguistic intuitions and the previous research findings. Next, it has looked at the relevant issues to understand the human sentence processing and the fundamental views on the approach to modeling human sentence processing. Finally, it has considered the premises of the study, based on the insights from the review argued here.

In Chapter 3, this study has taken up the issue of the functional relationship between the human language behaviors and the place of language processing in the brain. First, the chapter has argued the basic features and principles of functional brain imaging techniques, as a preliminary for the ensuring fMRI experiments. Next, it has presented neuroanatomical evidence on the human sentence processing from previous research findings. Then, it has shown current views on the functional relationship between language and the brain. Finally, it has presented the rationale for the study of phrasal segmentation.

In Chapter 4, in the visual experiment, significant activations specific to phrasal segmentation were identified in the left pars orbitalis (BA 47). This region falls within the cortical region involved in the semantic domain of processing in previous studies. Among others, the related region to phrasal segmentation was within the region of semantic integration from word meaning to phrase and sentence meaning. The results proved the involvement of the left pars orbitalis (BA 47) in the processing operation that leads a sequence of word strings into sentence comprehension. In addition, the comparison between phrasal segmentation and semantic violations revealed the specific regions sensitive to either phrasal segmentation or semantic violations, with no functional connectivity between two of the sentence comprehension tasks. The results verified the processing operation of phrasal segmentation is different from that of semantic violations. The visual experiment has validly identified the activated cortical regions specific to phrasal segmentation.

In Chapter 5, in the auditory experiment, significant activations specific to phrasal segmentation were identified in the left pars orbitalis (BA 47) and the left temporal pole (BA 38). Both of the regions fall within the cortical regions involved in semantic domain of language processing. The related regions to phrasal segmentation were in the regions responsible for executive functions of semantic information and semantic integration from words to phrases and setnences. The results were consistent with the results of the visual experiment. The results suggested that phrasal segmentation is bimodally associated with processing of normally structured, meaningful sentences. In addition, the comparison between phrasal segmentation and semantic violations revealed the specific regions either of phrasal segmentation or semantic violations, with no functional connectivity between two of the tasks. The results verified that processing operations of phrasal segmentation is differently characterized from those of semantic violations. The auditory experiment identified the brain regions specific to phrasal segmentation and confirmed the bimodal effect of phrasal segmentation in the left pars orbitalis (BA 47) of the IFG. Our fMRI results attested the bimodal effect of phrasal segmentation during on-line sentence comprehension.

In Chapter 6, our fMRI evidence was assessed and the characteristics of phrasal segmentation were examined with respect to the effect and the nature of its processing operations during on-line sentence comprehension. Next, the chapter argued the processing operations of phrasal segmentation within the framework of two competing approaches to human sentence processing, in terms of the serial and the parallel processing accounts of sentence comprehension. Then, the chapter evaluated the validity of these two approaches to explain the fMRI findings of phrasal segmentation the current study provided. Finally, the chapter provided the proposal that phrasal segmentation reflects the parallel architecture of language processing in the brain. The chapter claimed that phrasal segmentation is universally associated with language processing.

Finally, in Chapter 7, this book, in conclusion, has reviewed our study, considering the future direction for further research of phrasal segmentation.

So far, throughout the discussion in this study, this book has sought to achieve the goals this book presented in Section 1.2 in Chapter 1. This book has successfully accomplished the first goal to directly investigate the on-line processing operation of phrasal segmentation and its underlying neural correlates, using fMRI techniques. In Chapter 4 & 5, this book specified the bimodal effect of phrasal segmentation and the related processing domain and region of phrasal segmentation in the brain. With regard to the second goal, this book argued the effect and the nature of phrasal segmentation and predicted proper directions of the study of phrasal segmentation within the framework of human sentence comprehension. This study of phrasal segmentation exclusively dealt with the issue of phrasal segmentation when we understand normally structured, meaningful, simple sentences. However, in sentence production, we can easily visualize the scene when we group words together phrase-by-phrase into sentences. This book was not able to look at the issue of phrasal segmentation when we speak or write. The processing operations of phrasal segmentation during on-line sentence production will be one challenging filed for further investigations. The issue of interface rules to mediate each linguistic source of information is also another challenging goal for the research of phrasal segmentation. This book hopes to open up a new field of such challenging studies of human language.

References

Aaronson, D. & Scarborough, H. S. (1977). Performance theories for sentence coding: Some quantitative models. *Journal of Verbal Learning and Verbal Behavior*, 16, 277–303.

Amano, S. & Kondo, T. (2003). *Nihongo no goi tokusei, dai ikki & dai niki* [Lexical properties of Japanese] [CD-ROM] (Vols. 1 & 2). Tokyo: Sanseido.

Amaro, Jr. S. & Baker, G. J. (2006). Study design in fMRI: Basic principles. *Brain and Cognition*, 60, 220–232.

Anderson, J. R. (2000). *Cognitive psychology and its implications* (5th ed.). New York, NY: Worth Publishers.

Badre, D. & Wagner, A. D. (2007). Left ventrolateral prefrontal cortex and the cognitive control of memory. *Neuropsychologia*, 45, 2883–2901.

Bandettini, P. A., Wong, E. C., Hinks, R. S., Tikofsky, R. S., & Hyde, J. S. (1992). Time course EPI of human brain function during task activation. *Magnetic Resonance in Medicine*, 25, 390–397.

Beckman, M. E. & Edwards, J. (1990). Lengthening and shortening and the nature of prosodic constituency. In J. Kingston & M. E. Beckman (Eds.), *Papers in laboratory phonology I. Between grammar and the physics of speech* (pp. 152–178). Cambridge, UK: Cambridge University Press.

Belin, P., Zatorre, R. J., Lafaille, P., Ahad, P., & Pike, B. (2000). Voice-selective areas in human auditory cortex. *Nature*, 403, 309–312.

Belin, P., Zatorre, R. J., & Ahad, P. (2002). Human temporal-lobe response to vocal sounds. *Cognitive Brain Research*, 13, 17–26.

Bentin, S., Mouchetant-Rostain, Y., Giard, M. H., Echallier, J. F. & Pemier, J. (1999). ERP manifestations of processing printed word at different psycholinguistic levels: time course and scalp distribution. *Journal of Cognitive Neuroscience*, 11, 235–260.

Binder, J. R., Frost, J. A., Hammeke, T. A., Bellgowan, P. S. F., Springer, J. A., Kaufman, J. N., & Possing, E. T. (2000). Human temporal lobe activation by speech and nonspeech sound. *Cerebral Cortex*, 10, 512–528.

Binder, J. R., McKiernan, K. A., Parsons, M. E., Westbury, C. F., Possing, E. T., Kaufman, J. N., & Buchanan, L. (2003). Neural correlates of lexical access during visual word recognition. *Journal of Cognitive Neuroscience*, 15, 372–393.

Bokde, A. L. W., Tagamets, M. A., Friedman, R. B., & Horwitz, B. (2001). Functional interactions of the inferior frontal cortex during the processing of words and word-like stimuli. *Neuron*, 30, 609–617.

Boland, J. E. & Cutler, A. (1996). Interaction with autonomy: Multiple output models and the inadequacy of the Great Divide. *Cognition*, 58, 309–320.

Bookheimer, S. (2002). Functional MRI of language: New approaches to understand the cortical organization of semantic processing. *Annual Review of Neuroscience*, 25, 151–188.

Bookheimer, S. Y., Zeffiro, T. A., Blaxton, T. Gaillard, W., & Theodore, W. H. (2000). Activation of language cortex with automatic speech tasks. *Neurology*, 55, 1151–1157.

Boomer, D. S. (1965). Hesitation and grammatical encoding. *Language and Speech*, 8, 148–158.

Broca, P. (1861). Perte de la parole, remollissement chronique et destruction partielle du lobe anterieur gauche du cerveau [Remarks on the localization of the ability of articulated language and a case report of aphasis]. *Bulletin Des Societés Anatomiques de Paris*, 2, 330–357.

Brockway, J. P. (2000). Two functional magnetic resonance imaging f(MRI) tasks that may replace the gold standard, Wada testing, for language lateralization while giving additional localization information. *Brain and Cognition*, 43, 57–59.

Brodmann, K. (1909). *Vergleichende lokalisationslehre der grosshirnrinde: in ihren principien, dargestellt auf grund des Zellenbaues* [Comparative Localization. Evidence for the Cortex, Explained and Depicted by Cell Structure]. Leipzig, Germany: Johann Ambrosius Barth Verlag.

Brown, C. M. & Hagoort, P. (1993). The processing nature of the N400: Evidence from masked priming. *Journal of Cognitive Neuroscience*, 5, 34–44.

Brown, C. M. & Hagoort, P. (1999). *Neurocognition of language*. Oxford, UK: Oxford University Press.

Buchanan, T. W., Lutz, K., Mirzazade, S., Specht, K., Shah, N. J., Zilles, K., & Jäncke, L. (2000). Recognition of emotional prosody and verbal components of spoken language: An fMRI study. *Cognitive Brain Research*, 9, 227–238.

Buchsbaum, B. R., Hickok, G., & Humphries, C. (2001). Role of left posterior superior temporal gyrus in phonological processing for speech perception and production. *Cognitive Science*, 25, 663–678.

Burton, M. W., Small, S. L., & Blumstein, S. E. (2000). The role of segmentation in phonological processing: An fMRI investigation. *Journal of Cognitive Neuroscience*, 12, 679–690.

Buxton, R. B., Uludag, K., Dubowitz, D. J., & Liu, T. T. (2004). Modeling the hemodynamic response to brain activation. *NeuroImage*, 23 (Supplement), S220–S223.

Buxton, R. B., Wong, E. C., & Frank, L. R. (1998). Dynamics of blood flow and oxygenation changes during brain activation: The balloon model. *Magnetic Resonance in Medicine*, 39, 855–864.

Bybee, J. (2001). *Phonology and language use*. Cambridge, UK: Cambridge University Press.

Caplan, D. (1987). *Neurolinguistics and linguistic aphasiology: An introduction*. Cambridge, UK: Cambridge University Press.

Caplan, D. (2004). Functional neuroimaging studies of written sentence comprehension. *Scientific Studies of Reading*, 8, 225–240.

Caplan, D., Alpert, N., & Waters, G. (1999). PET studies of syntactic processing with auditory sentence presentation. *NeuroImage*, 9, 343–351.

Carreiras, M., Vergara, M., & Barber, H. (2005). Early event-related potential effects of syllabic processing during visual word recognition. *Journal of Cognitive Neuroscience*, 17, 1803–1817.

Catani, M., Jones, D. K., & ffytche, D. H. (2004). Perisylvian language networks of the human brain. *Annals of Neurology*, 57, 8–16.

Chee, M., Caplan, D., Soan, C., Sicram, N., Tan, E., Thiel, T., & Weekes, L. (1999). Processing of visually presented sentences in Mandarin and English studied with fMRI. *Neuron*, 23, 127–137.

Chee, M. W. L., Weekes, N., Lee, K. M., Soon, C. S., Schreiber, A., Hoon, J. J., & Chee, M. (2000). Overlap and dissociation of semantic processing of Chinese characters, English words, and pictures: Evidence from fMRI. *NeuroImage*, 12, 392–403.

Chein, J. M., Fissell, K., Jacobs, S., & Fiez, J. A. (2002). Functional heterogeneity within Broca's area during verbal working memory. *Physiology & Behavior*, 77, 635–639.

Chomsky, N. (1980). *Rules and representations*. Oxford, UK: Basil Blackwell.

Chomsky, N. (1995). *The Minimalist Program*. Cambridge, MA: the MIT Press.

Chomsky, N. & Halle, M. (1968). *The sound pattern of English*. New York: Harper & Row.

Christophe, A., Gout, A., Peperkamp, S., Morgan, J. (2003). Discovering words in the continuous speech stream: The role of prosody. *Journal of Phonetics*, 31, 585–598.

Clifton, Jr., C., Carlson, K., & Frazier, C. (2002). Informative prosodic boundaries. *Language and Speech*, 45, 87–114.

Cohen, L. & Dehaene, S. (2004). Specialization within the ventral stream: The case for the visual word form area. *NeuroImage*, 22, 466–476.

Cohen, L., Dehaene, S., Naccache, L., Léhericy, S., Dehaene-Lambertz, G., Hénaff,

M.-A. & Michel, F. (2000). The visual word form area: Spatial and temporal characterization of an initial stage of reading in normal subjects and posterior split-brain patients. *Brain*, 123, 291–307.

Connoly, J. F. & Phillips, N. A. (1994). Event-related potential components reflect phonological and semantic processing of the terminal words of spoken sentences. *Journal of Cognitive Neuroscience*, 6, 256–266.

Cooke, A., Zurif, E. B., DeVita, C., Alsop, D., Koening, P., Detre, J., Gee, J., Pinango, M., Balogh, J., & Grossman, M. (2001). Neural basis for sentence comprehension: Grammatical and short-term memory components. *Human Brain Mapping*, 15, 80–94.

Coulson, S., King, J. W., & Kutas, M. (1998). Expect the unexpected: Event-related brain response to morphosyntactic violations. *Language and Cognitive Processes*, 13, 21–58.

Crocker, M. W. (1996). Computational psycholinguistics: An interdisciplinary approach to the study of language. Dordrecht, NL: Kluwer.

Crocker, M. W. (1999). Mechanisms for sentence processing. In S. Garrod & M., Pickering (Eds.), *Language processing* (pp. 191–232). Hove, East Essex, UK: Psychology Press.

Crocker, M. W. (2005). Rational models of comprehension: Addressing the performance paradox. In A. Cutler (Ed.), *Twenty-first century psycholinguistics: Four cornerstones* (pp. 363–380). Mahwah, NJ: Lawrence Erlbaum Associates, Publishers.

Culham, J. C. (2006). Functional neuroimaging: Experimental design and analysis. In R. Cabreza & A. Kingstone (Eds.), *Handbook of functional neuroimaging of cognition* (pp. 53–82). Cambridge, MA: the MIT Press.

Culicover, P. W. (2009). *Natural language syntax*. Oxford, UK: Oxford University Press.

Culicover, P. W. & Jackendoff, R. (2005). *Simpler syntax*. Oxford, UK: Oxford University Press.

Culicover, P. W. & Jackendoff, R. (2006). The simpler syntax hypothesis. *TRENDS in Cognitive Sciences*, 10, 413–418.

Cunillera, T., Gomila, A., & Bodríguez-Fornells, A. (2008). Beneficial effects of word final stress in segmenting a new language: Evidence from ERPs. *BNC Neuroscience*, 9, 1–10.

Cunillera, T., Toro, J. M., Sebastián-Gallés, N., & Bodríguez-Fornells, A. (2006). The effects of stress and statistical cues on continuous speech segmentation: An event-related brain potential study. *Brain Research*, 1123, 168–178.

Curtin, S., Mintz, T. H., & Christiansen, M. H. (2005). Stress changes the representational landscape: Evidence from word segmentation. *Cognition*, 96, 233–262.

Curtis, C. E. & D'Esposito, M. (2006). Functional neuroimaging of working memory. In

R. Cabreza & A. Kingstone (Eds.), *Handbook of functional neuroimaging of cognition* (pp. 269–306). Cambridge, MA: the MIT Press.

Cutler, A. (1990). Exploiting prosodic probabilities in speech segmentation. In G. T. M. Altmann (Ed.), *Cognitive models of speech processing: Psycholinguistic and computational perspectives* (pp. 105–121). Cambridge, MA: the MIT Press.

Cutler, A. (1994). The perception of rhythm in language. *Cognition*, 50, 79–81.

Cutler, A. (1999). Prosodic structure and word recognition. In A. D. Friederici (Ed.), *Language comprehension: A biological perspective* (2nd ed., pp. 41–70). Berlin, Germany: Springer-Verlag.

Cutler, A. & Clifton, Jr., C. (1999). Comprehending spoken language: A blueprint of the listener. In C. M. Brown & P. Haroort (Eds.), *The Neurocognition of language* (pp. 123–166). Oxford: Oxford University Press.

Cutler, A., Dahan, D., & Van Donselaar, W. (1997). Prosody in the comprehension of spoken language: A literature review. *Language and Speech*, 40, 141–201.

Cutler, A. & Otake, T. (1994). Mora or morpheme? Further evidence for language specific listening. *Journal of Memory and Language*, 33, 824–844.

Daikoku, K. (1995). Môra-ni taisuru ishiki-wa kana-moji-no yomi-syûtoku-no hitsuyô-jyôken-ka? [Is awareness of morae a requisite for acquisition of kana reading?] *The Japanese Journal of Psychology*, 66, 253–260.

Dapretto, M. & Bookheimer, S. Y. (1999). Form and content: Dissociating syntax and semantics in sentence comprehension. *Neuron*, 24, 427–432.

Davidson, R. J., Jackson, D., & Larson, C. L. (2000). Human electroencephalography. In J. T. Cacioppo, G. Bernston, & L. Tassinary (Eds.), *Principles of psychophysiology* (2nd ed., pp. 27–52). New York: Cambridge University Press.

Davis, E. P., Bruce, J., Sydney, K., & Nelson, C. A. (2003). The X-trails: Neural correlates of an inhibitory control task in children and adults. *Journal of Cognitive Neuroscience*, 15, 432–443.

Démonet, J-F, Thierry, G., & Cardebat, D. (2005). Renewal of the neurophysiology of language: Functional neuroimaging. *Physiological Reviews*, 85, 49–95.

Dominey, P. F., Hoen, M., Blanc, J. M., & Lelekov-Boissard, T. (2003). Neurological basis of language in sequential cognition: Evidence from simulation, aphasia, and ERP studies. *Brain and Language*, 86: 207–225.

Dronkers, N. F., Wilkins, D. P., Van Valin Jr., R. D., Redfern, B. B., & Jaeger, J. J. (2004). Lesion analysis of the brain areas involved in language comprehension. *Cognition*, 92, 145–177.

Embick, D., Marantz, A., Miyashita, Y., O'Neil, W., & Sakai, K. (2000). A syntactic specialization for Broca's area. *Proceedings of the National Academy of Sciences USA*, 97,

6150–6154.

Ferreira, F. (1993). Creation of prosodic structure during sentence production. *Psychological Review*, 100, 233–253.

Ferstl, E. C. & d'Arcais, G. F. (1999). The reading of words and sentences. In A. D. Friederici (Ed.), *Language comprehension: A biological perspective* (2nd ed., pp. 175–210). Berlin, Germany: Springer-Verlag.

Fiebach, C. J., Friederici, A. D., Müller, K., & von Cramon, D. Y. (2002). fMRI evidence for dual routes to the mental lexicon in visual word recognition. *Journal of Cognitive Neuroscience*, 14, 11–23.

Fiebach, C. J., Schlesewsky, M., Lohmann, G., von Cramon, D. Y., & Friederici, A. D. (2004). Revisiting the role of Broca's area in sentence processing: Syntactic integration versus syntactic working memory. *Human Brain Mapping*, 24, 79–91.

Fiez, J. A., Balota, D. A., Raichle, M. E., & Peterson, S. E. (1999). Effects of lexicality, frequency, and spelling-to-sound consistency on the functional anatomy of reading. *Neuron*, 24, 205–218.

Fiez, J. A. & Peterson, S. E. (1998). Neuroimaging studies of word reading. *Proceedings of the National Academy of Sciences of the United States of America*, 95, 914–921.

Fischler, I., Bloom, P. A., Chiders, D. G., Roucos, S. E., & Perry, N. W. Jr. (1983). Brain potentials related to stages of sentence verification. *Psychophysiology*, 20, 400–409.

Fletcher, P. C. & Henson, R. N. A. (2001). Frontal lobes and human memory: Insights from functional neuroimaging. *Brain*, 124, 849–881.

Flitch, W. T. (2005). Computation and cognition: Four distinctions and their implications. In A. Cutler (Ed.), *Twenty-first century psycholinguistics: Four cornerstones* (pp. 381–400). Mahwah, NJ: Lawrence Erlbaum Associates, Publishers.

Fodor, J. D. (1995a). Thematic roles and modularity. In T. M. Altman (Ed.), *Cognitive models of speech processing: Psycholinguistic and computational perspectives* (pp. 434–456). Cambridge, MA: the MIT Press.

Fodor, J. D. (1995b). Comprehending sentence structure. In L. R. Gleitman & M. Liberman (Eds.), *Language* (2nd ed., pp. 209–246). Cambridge, MA: the MIT Press.

Frazier, L. (1979). On comprehending sentences: Syntactic parsing strategies. Doctoral dissertation, University of Connecticut.

Frazier, L., Carlson, K., & Clifton, C. Jr. (2006). Prosodic phrasing is central to language comprehension. *TRENDS in Cognitive Sciences*, 10, 244–249.

Frazier, L., Clifton, C. Jr., & Carlson, K. (2004). Don't break, or do: Prosodic boundary preferences. *Lingua*, 114, 3–27.

Friederici, A. D. (1995). The time course of syntactic activation during language processing: A model based on neuropsychological and neurophysiological data. *Brain and Language*, 50, 259–281.

Friederici, A. D. (1999). The neurobiology of language comprehension. In A. D. Friederici (Ed.), *Language comprehension: A biological perspective* (2nd ed., pp. 265–292). Berlin, Germany: Springer-Verlag.

Friederici, A. D. (2002). Towards a neural basis of auditory sentence processing. *TRENDS in Cognitive Sciences*, 6, 78–84.

Friederici, A. D. (2004). Processing local transitions versus long-distance syntactic hierarchies. *TRENDS in Cognitive Sciences*, 8, 245–247.

Friederici, A. D. (2005). Neurophysiological markers of early language acquisition: from syllables to sentences. *TRENDS in Cognitive Sciences*, 9, 481–488.

Friederici, A. D. & Alter, K. (2004). Lateralization of auditory language functions: A dynamic dual pathway mode. *Brain and Language*, 89, 267–276.

Friederici, A. D., Hahne, A., & Mecklinger, A. (1996). Temporal structure of syntactic parsing: Early and late event-related brain potential effects. *Journal of Experimental Psychology: Learning, Memory, and Cognition*, 22, 1219–1248.

Friederici, A. D. & Kotz, S. A. (2003) The brain basis of syntactic processes: Functional imaging and lesion studies. *NeuroImage*, 20, S8–S17.

Friederici, A. D., Pfeifer, E., & Hahne, A. (1993). Event-related brain potentials during natural speech processing: Effects of semantic morphological and syntactic violations. *Cognitive Brain Research*, 1, 157–176.

Friederici, A. D., Ruschemeyer, S-A., Hahne, A., & Fiebach, C. J. (2003). The role of left inferior frontal and superior temporal cortex in sentence comprehension: Localizing syntactic and semantic processes. *Cerebral Cortex*, 13, 170–177.

Friederici, A. D. & Wessels, J. M. I. (1993). Phonotactic knowledge of word boundaries and its use in infant speech perception. *Perception and Psychophysics*, 54, 287–295.

Friston, K. J., Zarahan, E., Josephs, O., Henson, R. N., & Dale, A. M. (1999). Stochastic designs in event-related fMRI. *NeuroImage*, 10, 607–619.

Gabrieli, J. D., Poldrack, R. A., & Desond, J. E. (1998). The role of left prefrontal cortex in language and memory. *Proceedings of the National Academy of Sciences of the United States of America*, 95, 906–913.

Garrod, S. & Pickering, M. J. (1999). Issues in language processing. In S. Garrod & M. J. Pickering (Eds.), *Language processing* (pp. 1–11). Hove, East Essex, UK: Psychology Press.

Gee, J. P. & Grosjean, F. (1983). Performance structures: A psycholinguistic and linguistic appraisal. *Cognitive Psychology*, 15, 411–458.

Geers, A. E. (1978). Intonation contour and syntactic structure as predictors of apparent segmentation. *Journal of the Acoustical Society of America*, 4, 273–283.

Gerken, L., Jusczyk, P. W., & Mandel, D. R. (1994). When prosody fails to cue syntactic structure: 9-month-olds' sensitivity to phonological versus syntactic phrases. *Cognition*, 51, 237–265.

Giraud, A. L. & Price, C. J. (2001). The constraints functional neuroimaging places on classical models of auditory word processing. *Journal of Cognitive Neuroscience*, 13, 754–765.

Gleitman, H. (1986). *Psychology* (2nd ed.). New York: W. W. Norton & Company.

Glover, G. H. (1999). Deconvolution of impulse response in event-related BOLD fMRI. *NeuroImage*, 9, 416–429.

Grodzinsky, Y. & Friederici, A. D. (2006). Neuroimaging of syntax and syntactic processing. *Current Opinion in Neurobiology*, 16, 240–246.

Grosjean, F., Grosjean, L., & Lane, H. (1979). The patterns of silence: Performance structures in sentence production. *Cognitive Psychology*, 11, 58–81.

Grossman, M., Koening, P., DeVita, C., Glosser, G., Alsop, D., Detre, J., & Gee, J. (2002). Neural representation of verb meaning: An fMRI study. *Human Brain Mapping*, 15, 124–134.

Gunji, T. (2002). *Tango to bun-no kôzô*, [Word and sentence structure]. Tokyo: Iwanami Press.

Hagoort, P. (2003a). Functional brain imaging. In W. J. Frawley (Ed.), *International encyclopedia of linguistics* (2nd ed., pp. 142–145). New York: Oxford University Press.

Hagoort, P. (2003b). How the brain solves the binding problem for language: A neurocomputational model of syntactic processing. *NeuroImage*, 20, S18–S29.

Hagoort, P. (2005a). On Broca, brain, and binding: A new framework. *TRENDS in Cognitive Sciences*, 9, 416–423.

Hagoort, P. (2005b). Broca's complex as the unification space for language. In A. Cutler (Ed.), *Twenty-first century psycholinguistics: Four cornerstones* (pp. 157–172). Mahwah, NJ: Lawrence Erlbaum Associates, Publishers.

Hagoort, P. (2008). The fraction of spoken language understanding by measuring electrical and magnetic brain signals. *Philosophical Transactions of the Royal Society B*, 363, 1055–1069.

Hagoort, P., Brown, C. M., & Osterhout, L. (1999). The neurocognition of syntactic processing. In C. M. Brown & P. Hagoort (Eds.), *The Neurocognition of language* (pp. 271–316). Oxford: Oxford University Press.

Hagoort, P., Hald, L., Bastiaansen, M., & Petersson, K. M. (2004). Integration of word meaning and world knowledge in language comprehension. *Science*, 304, 438–441.

Hagoort, P. & van Berkum, J. (2007). Beyond the sentence given. *Philosophical Transactions*

of the Royal Society B, 362, 801–811.
Hagoort, P., Wassenaar, M., & Brown, C. M. (2003). Syntax-related ERP-effects in Dutch. *Cognitive Brain Research*, 16, 38–50.
Hahne, A. & Friederici, A. D. (2002). Differential task effects on semantic and syntactic processes as revealed by ERPs. *Cognitive Brain Research*, 13, 339–356.
Harley, T. (2001). *The psychology of language* (2nd ed.). Hove, East Essex, UK: Psychology Press.
Heim, S. (2005). The structure and dynamics of normal language processing: Insights from neuroimaging. *Acta Neurobiologiae Experimentalis*, 65, 95–116.
Hickok, G., Buchsbaum, B. R., Humphries, C., & Muftuler, T. (2003). Auditory-motor interaction revealed by fMRI: Speech, music, and working memory in area Spt. *Journal of Cognitive Neuroscience*, 15, 673–682.
Hoeks, J. C. J., Stowe, L. A., & Doedens, G. (2004). Seeing words in context: The interaction of lexical and sentence level information during reading. *Cognitive Brain Research*, 19, 59–73.
Homae, F., Hashimoto, R., Nakajima, K., Miyashita, Y., & Sakai, K. L. (2002). From perception to sentence comprehension: The convergence of auditory and visual information of language in the left inferior frontal cortex. *NeuroImage*, 16, 883–900.
Homae, F., Yahata, N., & Sakai, K. L. (2003). Selective enhancement of functional connectivity in the left prefrontal cortex during sentence processing. *NeuroImage*, 20, 578–586.
Inagaki, K., Hatano, G., & Otake, T. (2000). The effect of Kana literacy acquisition on the speech segmentation unit used by Japanese young children. *Journal of Experimental Child Psychology*, 75, 70–91.
Ingram, J. C. L. (2007). *Neurolinguistics*. Cambridge, UK: Cambridge University Press.
Inkelas, S. & Zec, D. (1990). *The phonology-syntax connection*. Chicago, IL: University of Chicago Press.
Inui, T., Otsu, Y., Tanaka, S., Okada, T., Nishizawa, S., & Konishi, J. (1998). A functional MRI analysis of comprehension processes of Japanese sentences. *Neuro Report*, 9, 3325–3328.
Ischebeck, A. K., Friederici, A. D., & Alter, Kai (2008). Processing prosodic boundaries in natural and human speech: An fMRI study. *Cerebral Cortex*, 18, 541–552.
Jackendoff, R. (1987). *Consciousness and the computational mind*. Cambridge, MA: the MIT Press.
Jackendoff, R. (1992). *Languages of the mind*. Cambridge, MA: the MIT Press.
Jackendoff, R. (1999). The representational structures of the language faculty and their interactions. In C. M. Brown & P. Hagoort (Eds.), *The Neurocognition of language*

(pp. 37-79). Oxford, UK: Oxford University Press.
Jackendoff, R. (2002). *Foundations of language*. Oxford, UK: Oxford University Press.
Jackendoff, R. (2010). *Meaning and the Lexicon*. Oxford, UK: Oxford University Press.
Jarvella, R. J. (1971). Syntactic processing of connected speech. *Journal of Verbal Learning and Verbal Behavior*, 10, 409-416.
Johnson, E. K. & Jusczyk, P. W. (2001). Word segmentation by 8-month-olds: When speech cues more than statistics. *Journal of Memory and Language*, 44, 548-567.
Johnson, E. K. & Jusczyk, P. W., Cutler, A., & Norris, D. (2003). Lexical viability constraints on speech segmentation by infants. *Cognitive Psychology*, 46, 65-97.
Jusczyk, P. W. & Aslin, R. N. (1995). Infants' detection of the sound patterns in fluent speech. *Cognitive Psychology*, 29, 1-23.
Jusczyk, P. W., Houston, D. M., & Newsome, M. (1999). The beginnings of word segmentation in English-learning infants. *Cognitive Psychology*, 39, 159-207.
Just, M. A. & Carpenter, P. A. (1980). A theory of reading: From eye fixations to comprehension. *Psychological Review*, 87, 329-354.
Just, M. A., Carpenter, P. A., Keller, T. A., Eddy, W. F., & Thulborn, K. R. (1996). Brain activation modulated by sentence comprehension. *Science*, 274, 114-116.
Just, M. A., Carpenter, P. A., & Woolley, J. D. (1982). Paradigms and processes in reading comprehension. *Journal of Experimental Psychology: General*, 111, 228-238.
Kaan, E. & Swaab, T. Y. (2002). The brain circuitry of syntactic comprehension. *TRENDS in Cognitive Sciences*, 6, 350-356.
Kooijman, V., Hagoort, P., & Cutler, A. (2005). Electrophysiological evidence for prelinguistic infants' word recognition in continuous speech. *Cognitive Brain Research*, 24, 109-116.
Kubozono, H. (1998a). *Onseigaku, oninron*, [Phonetics and phonology]. Tokyo: Kuroshio Press.
Kubozono, H. (1998b). *Nihongo-no onsei*, [Japanese speech sound]. Tokyo: Iwanami Press.
Kuperberg, G. R., Holcomb, P. J., Sitnikova, T., Greve, D., Dale, A. M., & Caplan, D. (2003). Distinct patterns of neural modulation during the processing of conceptual and syntactic anomalies. *Journal of Cognitive Neuroscience*, 15, 272-293.
Kuperberg, G. R., McGuire, P. K., Bullmore, E. T., Brammer, M. J., Rabe-Hesketh, S., Wright, I. C., Lythgoe, D. J., Williams, S. C. R., & David, A. S. (2000). Common and distinct neural substrates for pragmatics, semantics, and syntactic processing of spoken sentences: An fMRI study. *Journal of Cognitive Neuroscience*, 12, 321-341.
Kuperberg, G. R., Sitnicova, T., Caplan, D., & Holcomb, P. J. (2003). Electrophysiological distinctions in processing conceptual relationships within simple sentences. *Cognitive*

Brain Research, 17, 117–129.

Kuriki, S. & Murase, M. (1989). Neuromagnetic study of the auditory responses in right and left hemispheres of the human brain evoked by pure tones and speech sounds. *Experimental Brain Research*, 77, 127–134.

Kutas, M. & Federmeier, K. D. (2000). Electrophysiology reveals semantic memory use in language comprehension. *TRENDS in Cognitive Sciences*, 4, 463–470.

Kutas, M., Federmeier, K. D., & Sereno, M. I. (1999). Current approaches to mapping language in electromagnetic space. In C. M. Brown & P. Hagoort (Eds.), *The neurocognition of language* (pp. 359–392). Oxford, UK: Oxford University Press.

Kutas, M. & Hillyard, S. A. (1980a). Reading senseless sentences: Brain potentials reflect semantic incongruity. *Science*, 207, 203–205.

Kutas, M. & Hillyard, S. A. (1980b). Reading between the lines: Event-related brain potentials during natural speech processing. *Brain and Language*, 11, 354–373.

Kutas, M. & Hillyard, S. A. (1983). Event-related potentials to grammatical errors and semantic anomalies. *Memory and Cognition*, 11, 539–550.

Kutas, M. & Hillyard, S. A. (1984). Brain potentials during reading reflect word expectancy and semantic association. *Nature*, 307, 161–163.

Kutas, M. & Van Petten, C. K. (1994). Psycholinguistics electrified. In M. A. Gernsbacher (Ed.), *Handbook of psycholinguistics* (pp. 83–143). San Diego, CA: Academic Press.

Kutas, M., Van Petten, C. K., Kluender, R. (2006). Psycholinguistics electrified II(1994–2005). In M. A. Gernsbacher & M. Traxler (Eds.), *Handbook of psycholinguistics* (2nd ed., pp. 659–724). San Diego, CA: Academic Press.

Kwong, K. K., Belliveau, J. W., Chesler, D. A., Goldberg, I. E., Weisskoff, R. M., Poncelet, B. P., Kennedy, D. N., Hoppel, B. E., Cohen, M. S., Turner, R., Cheng, H. M., Brady, T. J., & Rosen, B. R. (1992). Dynamic magnetic resonance imaging of human brain activity during primary sensory stimulations. *Proceedings of the National Academy of Sciences USA*, 89, 5675–5679.

Lasnik, H. (1995). The forms of sentences. In L. R. Gleitman & M. Liberman (Eds.), *Language* (pp. 283–310). Cambridge, MA: the MIT Press.

Lichtheim, L. (1885). On aphasia. *Brain*, 7, 433–485.

Lieu, Y. & Perfetti, C. A. (2003). The time course of brain activity of reading English and Chinese: An ERP study of Chinese bilinguals. *Human Brain Mapping*, 18, 167–175.

Loubinoux, I., Carel, C., Alary, F., Boulanouar, K., Villard, G., Manelfe, C., Rascol, O., Celsis, P., & Collet, F. (2001). Within-session and between-session reproducibility of cerebral sensorimotor activation: A test-retest effect evidenced with functional magnetic resonance imaging. *Journal of Cerebral Blood Flow and Metabolism*, 21, 592–607.

Marslen-Wilson, W. D. (1973). Linguistic structure and speech shadowing at very short latencies. *Nature*, 244, 522–523.

Marslen-Wilson, W. D. (1975). Sentence perception as an interactive parallel process. *Science*, 198, 226–228.

Masuoka, T. (1997). Bunpô no kihon gainen 1 [Basic concept of grammar 1]. In T. Masuoka, Y. Nitta, T. Gunji, & S. Kinsui (Eds.), *Gengo-no-kagaku 5 Bunpô, [Linguistic sciences Vol. 5 Grammar]* (pp. 41–78). Tokyo: Iwanami Press.

Masuoka, T. & Takubo, Y. (1992). *Kiso nihongo bunpô*, [Basic grammar of Japanese]. Tokyo: Kuroshio Press.

Matthew, H. D. & Johnsrude, I. S. (2003). Hierarchical processing in spoken language comprehension. *Journal of Neuroscience*, 23, 3423–3431.

Mayer, M., Alter, K., & Friederici, A. (2003). Functional MR imaging exposes differential brain responses to syntax and prosody during auditory sentence comprehension. *Journal of Neurolinguistics*, 16, 277–300.

McCandliss, B. D., Cohen, L., & Dehaene, S. (2003). The visual word form area: Expertise for reading in the fusiform gyrus. *TRENDS in Cognitive Sciences*, 7, 293–299.

McNealy, K., Mazziotta, J. C., Dapretto, M. (2006). Cracking the language code: Neural mechanisms underlying speech parsing. *The Journal of Neuroscience*, 26, 7629–7639.

Mesulam, M.-M. (1990). Large-scale neurocognitive networks and distributed processing for attention, language, and memory. *Annals of Neurology*, 28, 1013–1052.

Mesulam, M.-M. (1998). From sensation to cognition. *Brain*, 121, 1013–1052.

Moro, A., Tettamanti, M., Perani, D., Donati, C., Cappa, S. F., & Fazio, F. (2001). Syntax and the brain: Disentangling grammar by selective anomalies. *NeuroImage*, 13, 110–118.

Müller, O. & Hagoort, P. (2006). Access to lexical information in language comprehension: Semantics before syntax. *Journal of Cognitive Neuroscience*, 18, 84–96.

Näätänen, R. (2001). The perception of speech sounds by human brain as reflected by the mismatch negativity (MMN) and its magnetic equivalent (MMNm). *Psychophysiology*, 38, 1–21.

Näätänen, R., Lehtokoski, A., Lennes, M., Cheour, M., Huotilainen, M., Iivonen, A., Vainio, M., Aluku, P., Ilmonieni, R. J., Luuk, A. Allik, J., Sinkkonen, J. & Alho, K. (1997). Language-specific phoneme representations revealed by electric and magnetic brain responses. *Nature*, 385, 432–434.

National Institute for Japanese Language. (2004). *Bunrui goi hyô* [Word list by semantic principles]. Tokyo: Dai Nippon Tosho.

Neville, H. J., Nicol, J., Brass, A., Forster, K. I., & Garret, M. F. (1991). Syntactically based

processing classes: Evidence from event-related brain potentials. *Journal of Cognitive Neuroscience*, 3, 151–165.
Ni, W., Constable, R. T., Mencl, W. E., Pugh, K. R., Fulbright, R. K., Shaywitz, B. A., Gore, J. C., & Shankweiler, D. (2000). An event-related neuroimaging study distinguishing form and content in sentence processing. *Journal of Cognitive Neuroscience*, 12, 120–133.
Ogawa, S. & Lee, T. M. (1990). Magnetic resonance imaging of blood vessels at high fields: In vivo and in vitro measurements and image simulation. *Magnetic Resonance in Medicine*, 16, 9–18.
Ogawa, S., Lee, T. M., Kay, A. R. & Tank, D. W. (1990). Brain magnetic resonance imaging with contrast dependent on blood oxygenation. *Proceedings of the National Academy of Sciences USA*, 87, 9868–9872.
Ogawa, S., Tank, D. W., Menon, R., Ellermann, J. M., Kim, S. G., Merkle, H., & Ubergil, K. (1992). Intrinsic signal changes accompanying sensory simulation: Functional brain mapping with magnetic resonance imaging. *Proceedings of the National Academy of Sciences USA*, 89, 5951–5955.
Okada, K., Smith, K. R., Humphries, C., & Hickok, G. (2003). Word length modulates neural activity in auditory cortex during covert object naming. *NeuroReport*, 14, 2323–2326.
Oldfield, R. C. (1971). The assessment and analysis of handedness: The Edinburgh inventory. *Neuropsychologia*, 9, 97–113.
Osterhout, L. & Holcomb, P. A. (1992). Event-related potentials elicited by syntactic anomaly. *Journal of Memory and Language*, 31, 785–806.
Osterhout, L. & Mobley, L. A. (1995). Event-related potentials by failure to agree. *Journal of Memory and Language*, 34, 739–773.
Otake, T., Hatano, G., Cutler, A., & Mehler, J. (1993). Mora or syllable? Speech segmentation in Japanese. *Journal of Memory and Language*, 32, 258–278.
Palolahti, M., Leino, S., Jokela, M., Kopra, K., & Paaviliainen, P. (2005). Event-related potentials suggest early interaction between syntax and semantics during on-line sentence comprehension. *Neuroscience Letters*, 384, 222–227.
Pannekamp, A., Toepel, U., Alter, K., Hahne, A., & Friederici, A. D. (2005). Prosody-driven sentence processing: An event-related brain potential study. *Journal of Cognitive Neuroscience*, 17, 407–421.
Partee, B. (1975). Montague grammar and transformational grammar. *Linguistic Inquiry*, 6, 203–300.
Perfetti, C. A. (1999). Comprehending written language: A blue print of the reader. In C. M. Brown & P. Haroort (Eds.), *The Neurocognition of language* (pp. 167–208).

Oxford, UK: Oxford University Press.
Pickering, M. J. (1999). Mechanisms for sentence processing. In S. Garrod & M., Pickering (Eds.), *Language processing* (pp. 123–153). Hove, East Essex, UK: Psychology Press.
Pinker, S. (1987). The bootstrapping problem in language acquisition. In B. MacWhinney (Ed.), *Mechanisms of language acquisition* (pp. 399–441). Hillsdale, NJ: Lawrence Erlbaum Associates.
Pinker, S. (1999). *Words and rules*. New York, NY: Basic Books.
Pinker, S. (2000). Language acquisition. In L. R. Gleitman & M. Liberman (Eds.), *Language* (2nd ed., pp. 135–182). Cambridge, MA: the MIT Press.
Poeppel, D., Yellin, E., Phillips, C., Roberts, T.P.L., Rowley, H.A., Wexler, K. & Marantz, A. (1996). Task-induced asymmetry of the auditory evoked M100 neuromagnetic field elicited by speech sounds. *Cognitive Brain Research*, 4, 231–241.
Poldrack, R. A., Wagner, A. D., Prull, M. W., Desmond, J. E., Glover, G. H., & Gabrieli, D. E. (1999). Functional specialization for semantic and phonological processing in the left inferior prefrontal cortex. *NeuroImage*, 10, 15–35.
Price, C. J. (2000). The anatomy of language: contribution from functional neuroimaging. *Journal of Anatomy*, 197, 335–359.
Price, C. J. & Devlin, J. T. (2003). The myth of the visual word form area. *NeuroImage*, 19, 473–481.
Price, C. J. & Devlin, J. T. (2004). The pros and cons of labeling a left occipitotemporal region: "The visual word form area." *NeuroImage*, 22, 477–479.
Price, C. J., Indefrey, P., & van Turennout, M. (1999). The neural architecture underlying the processing of written and spoken word forms. In C. M. Brown & P. Hagoort (Eds.), *The neurocognition of language* (pp. 211–240). Oxford, UK: Oxford University Press.
Price, C. J., Mummery, C. J., Moore, C. J., Frackowiak, R. S., & Friston, K. J. (1999). Delineating necessary and sufficient neural systems with functional imaging studies of neurophysiological patients. *Journal of Cognitive Neuroscience*, 11, 371–382.
Price, C. J., Wise, R. J. S., Warburton, E., Moore, C. J., Howard, D., Patterson, K., Frackowiak, R. S., & Friston, K. J. (1996). Hearing and saying: The functional neuroanatomy of auditory word processing. *Brain*, 119, 919–931.
Pulvermüller, F., Shtyrov, Y., Kujala, T. & Näätänen, R. (2004). Word-specific cortical activity as revealed by the mismatch negativity. *Psychophysiology*, 46, 106–112.
Pylkkänen, L., Stringfellow, A., & Marantz, A. (2002). Neuromagnetic evidence for the timing of lexical activation: An MEG component sensitive to phonotactic probability but not to neighborhood density. *Brain and Language*, 81, 666–678.

Raichle, M. E. (2003). Functional brain imaging and human brain function (miniseries). *Journal of Neuroscience*, 23, 3959–3962.

Raichle, M. E. (2006). Functional neuroimaging: a historical and physiological perspective. In R. Cabreza & A. Kingstone (Eds.), *Handbook of functional neuroimaging of cognition* (pp. 3–20). Cambridge, MA: the MIT Press.

Rayner, K. & Duffy, S. A. (1986). Lexical complexity and fixation times in reading. Effects of word frequency, verb complexity, and lexical ambiguity. *Memory and Cognition*, 14, 191–201.

Rodd, J. M., Davis, M. H., & Johnsrude, I. S. (2005). The neural mechanisms of speech comprehension: fMRI studies of semantic ambiguity. *Cerebral Cortex*, 15, 1261–1269.

Rogalsky, C. & Hickok, G. (2011). The role of Broca's area in sentence comprehension. *Journal of Cognitive Neuroscience*, 23, 1664–1680.

Rosen, B. R., Buckner, R. L., & Dale, A. M. (1998). Event-related functional MRI: Past, present, and future. *Proceedings of the National Academy of Sciences of the United States of America*, 95, 773–780.

Rösler, F., Friederici, A. D., Pütz, P., & Hahne, A. (1993). Event-related brain potentials while encountering semantic and syntactic constraint violations. *Journal of Cognitive Neuroscience*, 5, 345–362.

Ruschemeyer, S-A., Zysset, S., & Friederici, A. D. (2006). Native and non-native reading of sentences: An fMRI experiment. *NeuroImage*, 31, 354–365.

Saffran, J. R., Aslin, R. N., & Newport, E. L. (1996). Statistical learning by 8-month-old infants. *Science*, 274, 1926–1928.

Saffran, J. R., Newport, E. L., & Aslin, R. N. (1996). Word segmentation: The role of distributional cues. *Journal of Memory and Language*, 35, 606–621.

Sanders, L. D. & Neville, H. J. (2003). An ERP study of continuous speech processing: I. segmentation, semantics, and syntax in native speakers. *Cognitive Brain Research*, 15, 228–240.

Sanders, L. D., Newport, E. L., & Neville, H. J. (2002). Segmenting nonsense: An event-related potential index of perceived onsets in continuous speech. *Nature Neuroscience*, 5, 700–703.

Scerif, G., Kotsoni, E., & Casey, B. J. (2006). Functional neuroimaging of early cognitive development. In R. Cabreza & A. Kingstone (Eds.), *Handbook of functional neuroimaging of cognition* (pp. 351–378). Cambridge, MA: the MIT Press.

Schafer, A. J., Speer, S. R., Warren, P., & White, S. D. (2000). Intonational disambiguation in sentence production and comprehension. *Journal of Psycholinguistic Research*, 29, 169–182.

Selkirk, E. O. (1984). *Phonology and syntax: the relation between sound and structure.* Cambridge, MA: the MIT Press.

Shieber, S. & Johnson, M. (1993). Variations on incremental interpretation. *Journal of Psycholinguistic Research,* 22, 287–318.

Shukla, M., Nespor, M., & Mehler, J. (2007). An interaction between prosody and statistics in the segmentation of fluent speech. *Cognitive Psychology,* 54, 1–32.

Silva-Pereyra, J., Rivera-Gaxiola, M., & Kuhl, P. K. (2005). An event-related brain potential study of sentence comprehension in preschoolers: Semantic and morphosyntactic processing. *Cognitive Brain Research,* 23, 247–258.

Steinhauer, K., Alter, K., & Friederici, A. D. (1999). Brain potentials indicate immediate use of prosodic cues in natural speech processing. *Nature Neuroscience,* 2, 191–196.

Steinhauer, K. & Friederici, A. D. (2001). Prosodic boundaries, comma rules, and brain responses: The closure positive shift in ERPs as a universal marker for prosodic phrasing in listeners and readers. *Journal of Psycholinguistic Research,* 30, 267–295.

StGeorge, M., Kutas, M., Martinez, A., & Sereno, M. (1999). Semantic integration in reading: Engagement of the right hemisphere during discourse processing. *Brain,* 122, 1317–1325.

Stowe, L. A., Haverkort, M., & Zwarts, F. (2005). Rethinking the neurological basis of language. *Lingua,* 115, 997–1042.

Stowe, L. A., Paans, A. M. J., Wijiers, A. A., & Zwarts, F. (2004). Activation of "motor" and other non-language structures during sentence comprehension. *Brain and Language,* 89, 290–299.

Strangman, G., Culver, J. P., Thompson, J. H., & Boas, D. A. (2002). A qualitative comparison of simultaneous BOLD fMRI and NIRS recordings during functional brain activation. *NeuroImage,* 17, 719–731.

Suci, G. (1967). The variability of pause as an index of units in language. *Journal of Verbal Learning and Verbal Behavior,* 6, 26–32.

Swaab, T., Brown, C., & Hagoort, T. (2003). Understanding words in sentence contexts: The time course of ambiguity resolution. *Brain and Language,* 86, 326–343.

Talairach, J. & Tournoux, P. (1988). *Co-Planar stereotaxic atlas of the human brain.* Stuttgart: George Thieme Verlag.

Taraban, R. & McClelland, J. R. (1988). Constituent attachment and thematic role assignment in sentence processing: Influence of content-based expectations. *Journal of Memory and Language,* 25, 597–632.

Thompson-Schill, S., Aguirre, G., D'Esposito, M., & Farah, M. (1999). A neural basis for category and modality specificity of semantic knowledge. *Neuropsychologia,* 37, 671–676.

Trueswell, J., Tanenhaus, M. K., & Garnsey, S. (1994). Semantic influence on parsing: Use of thematic role information in syntactic disambiguation. *Journal of Memory and Language*, 33, 285–318.

Turken, A. U. & Dronkers, N. F. (2011). The neural architecture of the language comprehension network: converging evidence from lesion and connectivity analyses. *Frontiers in Systems Neuroscience*, 5, 1–20.

Tyler, L. K. & Marslen-Wilson, W. D. (1977). The on-line effects of semantic context on syntactic processing. *Journal of Verbal Learning and Verbal Behavior*, 19, 528–553.

Van Berkum, J. J. A., Brown, C. M., & Hagoort, P. (1999). Early referential context effects in sentence processing: Evidence from event-related brain potentials. *Journal of Memory and Language*, 41, 147–182.

Vandenberghe, R., Nobre, A. C., & Price, J. (2002). The response of left temporal cortex to sentence. *Journal of Cognitive Neuroscience*, 14, 550–560.

Van den Brink, D. Brown, C. M. & Hagoort, P. (2006). The cascaded nature of lexical selection and integration in auditory sentence processing. *Journal of Experimental Psychology: Learning, Memory and Cognition*, 32, 364–372.

Van den Brink, D. & Hagoort, P. (2004). The influence of semantic and syntactic context constraints on lexical selection and integration in spoken-word comprehension as revealed by ERPs. *Journal of Cognitive Neuroscience*, 16, 1068–1084.

Van Petten, C. (1993). A comparison of lexical and sentence-level context effects in event-related potentials. *Language and Cognitive Processes*, 8, 485–531.

Van Petten, C., & Bloom, P. (1999). Speech boundaries, syntax and the brain. *Nature Neuroscience*, 2, 103–104.

Van Petten, C., & Luka, B. J. (2006). Neural localization of semantic effects in electromagnetic and hemodynamic studies. *Brain and Language*, 97, 279–293.

Vigneau, M., Beaucousin, V, Hervé, P. Y., Duffan, H., Crivello, F., Houdé, O., Mazoyer, B., & Tzourio-Mazoyer, N. (2006). Meta-analyzing left hemisphere language areas: Phonology, semantics, and sentence processing. *NeuroImage*, 30, 1414–1432.

Vouloumanos, A. Kiehl, K. A., Werker, J. F., & Liddle, P. E. (2001). Detection of sounds in the auditory stream: event-related fMRI evidence for differential activation to speech and nonspeech. *Journal of Cognitive Neuroscience*, 13, 994–1005.

Wagner, A. D., Pare-Blagoev, E. J., Clark, J., & Poldrack, R. A. (2001). Recovering meaning: Left prefrontal cortex guides controlled semantics retrieval. *Neuron*, 31, 329–338.

Wernicke, C. (1874). *Der Aphasische Symptomencomplex* [*The Aphasic Symptom Complex*]. Breslau: Cohn and Weigert.

Williams, L. M., Phillips, M. L., Brammer, M. J., Skerrett, D., Lagopoulos, J., Rennie, C,

Bahramali, H., Olivieri, G., David, A. S., Peduto, A., & Gordon, E. (2001). Arousal dissociates amygdale and hippocampal fear responses: Evidences from simultaneous fMRI and skin conductance recording. *NeuroImage*, 14, 1070–1079.

Wingfield, A. (1975). The intonation-syntax interaction: Prosodic features in perceptual processing of sentences. In A., Cohen & S. G., Nooteboom (Eds.), *Structure and process in speech perception of sentences* (pp. 146–160). Berlin: Springer-Verlag.

Wise, J. S. R. & Price, C. J. (2006). Functional neuroimaging of language. In R. Cabreza & A. Kingstone (Eds.), *Handbook of functional neuroimaging of cognition* (pp. 191–227). Cambridge, MA: the MIT Press.

Appendix A: List of Sentence Stimuli

(1) Experimental Condition (120 stimuli):
Non-Segmented Congruent Stimuli (30 stimuli)
1 せいとはしょんぼりとじゅぎょうにでた
2 こどもはこわごわみずにはいった
3 がかはえらそうにでしにはなした
4 いしゃははっとよていにきづいた
5 かえるはちゃぽんとみずにもぐった
6 あいつはとてもおかねにきたない
7 てんちょうはやたらかねにこまかい
8 おとうとはいちばんさけにつよい
9 おまえはやたらおれにあつかましい
10 むすめはとくにじかんにきびしい
11 さいばんかんがでんしゃにのった
12 おかあさんがせいせきにあきれた
13 しょうがくせいがふとんにはいった
14 はかせがともだちにはなしかけた
15 しんかんせんがとうきょうについた
16 ははがともだちにおかねをかした
17 おじがおばにでんごんをつたえた
18 ちちがいなかにてがみをおくった
19 あにがきんじょにみやげをくばった
20 おとうとがきんぎょにえさをやった
21 おもてでいぬがひとにかみついた
22 かぶきできゃくがやくしゃにみとれた
23 やまできこりがかみなりにあった

24 てじなでかみがおさつにかわった
25 くじでちちにしょうひんがあたった
26 しまのかげにふしぎなふねがある
27 つくえのしたにくろいかさがある
28 うちのそばにせまいあきちがある
29 そらのかなたにくらいほしがある
30 たかのあしにするどいつめがある

Segmented Congruent Stimuli (30 stimuli)
1 おんなは　いそいそ　いえに　かえった
2 べんごしは　ようやく　えきに　ついた
3 おとうとは　しぶしぶ　でんわに　でた
4 えものは　まんまと　わなに　はまった
5 ちちは　あわてて　かいしゃに　もどった
6 あには　たいへん　かぞくに　やさしい
7 むすこは　すごく　はいくに　くわしい
8 きみは　へんに　ひとに　なれなれしい
9 かぜは　なんとも　ほほに　ここちよい
10 おやは　いちいち　こどもに　うるさい
11 おとこのこが　わたしに　あやまった
12 じゅけんせいが　かみさまに　いのった
13 こうはいが　せんぱいに　えんりょした
14 きょうだいが　ゆうえんちに　でかけた
15 こどもが　すいそうに　みずを　いれた
16 せんせいが　せいとに　ほんを　あげた
17 しゅじんが　きゃくに　めがねを　わたした
18 ともだちが　たにんに　うそを　ついた
19 たびびとが　しょうねんに　えを　みせた
20 おとこが　かべに　らくがきを　かいた
21 やまで　たぬきが　きつねに　であった

22 やまみちで　くるまが　たにに　おちた
23 ひとごみで　こどもが　みちに　まよった
24 しあいで　みかたが　てきに　まけた
25 よせんで　あにが　さんいに　はいった
26 うみの　そばに　きれいな　しろが　ある
27 こころの　すみに　ふるい　きずが　ある
28 やまの　てっぺんに　たかい　きが　ある
29 にわの　すみに　あかい　つばきが　ある
30 となりの　いえに　ひろい　にわが　ある

Non-Segmented Incongruent Stimuli (30 stimuli)
 1 かのじょはゆっくりちゃわんにおちた
 2 からすはつるりとかぜにふるえた
 3 めいじんはそっとめにかみついた
 4 かべははきはきしゃちょうにしゃべった
 5 あいつはすらすらおれにわめいた
 6 りんごはたしょうれいぎにきびしい
 7 たしざんはじつにのどにやさしい
 8 たいようはいきなりかみにあつい
 9 こうえんはみょうにもぐらにちかい
10 ろうかはわずかにごみにさびしい
11 げんかんがざぶとんにぶつかった
12 こうこうせいがねこにしみついた
13 きょうりゅうがようふくにはきかえた
14 れいぞうこがへやにとじこもった
15 とけいがさんりんしゃにまたがった
16 けいさつがわににじゅうしょをきいた
17 けいじがちゃわんにかぎをあずけた
18 ねこがさかなにねごとをたのんだ
19 さるがいすにきゅうりょうをはらった

20　はしごがかべにおつりをわたした
21　ふろばでせっけんがゆにおぼれた
22　げしゅくでつくえがてにまきついた
23　へやではしらがまどにかみついた
24　つりでえさがさかなにつかまった
25　しけんでじゅんいがしたにあがった
26　はしのしたにじょうずなはながある
27　くものなかにりっぱなみせがある
28　なべのあいだにふといがけがある
29　さかなのほねにほそいあしがある
30　うまのはねにきいろいくびがある

Segmented Incongruent Stimuli (30 stimuli)
1　おとこは　びゅうびゅう　かいしゃに　いった
2　ちちは　こっそりと　ふゆに　かくれた
3　あには　とことこ　つくしに　のぼった
4　すいかは　しっかり　からすに　さわった
5　ふぐは　ぺこぺこ　しゃしょうに　どなった
6　あねは　すこし　おんせんに　つめたい
7　ぼくは　かなり　おんがくに　わるい
8　みずむしは　ちょっと　けんこうに　よい
9　ほねは　いやに　せなかに　なつかしい
10　いとこは　まるごと　げんきに　つらい
11　ちんぴらが　かたつむりに　からんだ
12　おぼうさんが　ほこりに　じまんした
13　せんすいかんが　じめんに　もぐった
14　おかあさんが　ごはんに　だきついた
15　ひきだしが　こいぬに　もぐりこんだ
16　ちじが　だいじんに　くうきを　うった
17　うしが　らくごかに　くぎを　おしえた

18 すずめが　たまごに　ひなを　かえした
19 なかまが　ひみつに　みみを　しゃべった
20 うえきが　おゆに　ぼうずを　そそいだ
21 そらで　じてんしゃが　みぎに　まがった
22 こやで　いるかが　ひつじに　さけんだ
23 かわで　たこが　さわぎに　ふりむいた
24 じしんで　ゆかが　つくえに　たおれた
25 いりぐちで　とが　そでに　はさまった
26 びんの　そこに　まるい　しかくが　ある
27 たきの　さきに　ながい　ほくろが　ある
28 みちの　はずれに　ふるい　むらが　ある
29 えのぐの　なかに　しろい　うでが　ある
30 きりんの　くびに　ながい　きばが　ある

(2) Control Condition (60 stimuli):
Non-Segmented Control Stimuli (30 stimuli)
1 れっしゃはようやくえきについた
2 くるまはずけずけしゃこにはいった
3 てがみはどうやらあいてにとどいた
4 ぼくはちやほやともだちにはなした
5 せけんはやっぱりひとにつめたい
6 おとこはぎゅっとうでにいやしい
7 かいいぬはわりとえさにうるさい
8 じてんしゃはよくうみにむずかしい
9 えんがわはとってもひるねによい
10 おくじょうはかなりかいぎにわるい
11 かがくしゃががっかいにさんかした
12 だいがくせいがけんきゅうかいにでた
13 えんそうかいがとこやになげいた
14 げいじゅつかがいなかにひっこした

15　だいがくががくせいにふりむいた
16　しゃいんがかいしゃにでんわをかけた
17　うぐいすがすずめにぐちをいった
18　あにがせんせいにほんをかえした
19　たべすぎがねぶそくにてをふった
20　ごうとうがけいさつにせをむけた
21　やねでみみずがすあなにはいった
22　にかいでかぞくがぼくにどなった
23　やくしょでえがあいさつにこたえた
24　みちではいしゃがいしにつまづいた
25　まちでこうがいがいえになやんだ
26　まどのふちにちゃいろいわくがある
27　こうばんのそばにいたいきがある
28　みずのなかにふしぎないしがある
29　ふすまのうらにふるいいすがある
30　くびのまわりにくろいてんがある

Segmented Control Stimuli (30 stimuli)
1　せいとは　すらすら　といに　こたえた
2　おとこは　すっかり　てに　つかまった
3　おとうとは　ぼそぼそ　あねに　はなした
4　あには　ぐつぐつと　いもうとに　きいた
5　きみは　べらべら　かのじょに　しゃべった
6　ふうふは　のんびり　さけに　つかった
7　かのじょは　さすがに　ことばに　つよい
8　あいは　ものすごく　こいに　せつない
9　ほんは　とても　せいとに　ありがたい
10　かいじゅうは　すこし　しょくじに　せまい
11　かいさいしゃが　いしゃに　あいさつした
12　かいぬしが　かいいぬに　しかられた

13　けいさつが　かいぞくに　つかまった
14　きゃくが　やくしゃに　わらいかえした
15　うでどけいが　べんとうに　しゃべった
16　えんそうしゃが　かんせいに　こたえた
17　でんしゃが　えきいんに　きっぷを　みせた
18　ふくろうが　ひなに　えさを　はこんだ
19　ころしやが　かたなに　たまを　いれた
20　せいじかが　ししゃに　こえを　かけた
21　やきもちが　とりもちに　えを　かいた
22　たんぼで　たにしが　つちに　もぐった
23　げんかんで　きが　いぬに　かみついた
24　ざしきで　ねこが　こたつに　はいった
25　じこで　えきが　でんしゃに　ぶつかった
26　まちで　かいしゃいんが　さぎに　あった
27　あしの　さきに　ほそい　いりぐちが　ある
28　つくえの　はしに　くろい　すじが　ある
29　かいだんの　うえに　ひろい　はが　ある
30　ちの　はてに　ふしぎな　せかいが　ある

Appendix B: Sample List of Stimulus Presentation (Event Related Design)

null_¥¥xx.xxx   0

                         0
                         0
「い」

じこで　えきが　でんしゃに　ぶつかった
やまでみみずがあなにはいった
しゃいんがかいしゃにでんわをかけた
あしの　さきに　ほそい　いりぐちが　ある
きみは　べらべら　かのじょに　しゃべった
けいさつが　かいぞくに　つかまった
にかいでかぞくがぼくにどなった
てがみはどうやらあいてにとどいた
つくえの　はしに　くろい　すじが　ある
こうばんのそばにいたいきがある
あにがせんせいにほんをかえした
かいさいしゃが　いしゃに　あいさつした
くるまはずけずけしゃこにはいった
たべすぎがねぶそくにてをふった
かいぬしが　かいいぬに　しかられた

null_¥¥xx.xxx

　　　　　　　　　　　　　　　　　　0

意味

やまできこりがかみなりにあった
おやは　いちいち　こどもに　うるさい
さるがいすにきゅうりょうをはらった
おじがおばにでんごんをつたえた
あには　とことこ　つくしに　のぼった
みずむしは　ちょっと　けんこうに　よい
おとうとは　しぶしぶと　でんわに　でた
つりでさかながえさにつかまった
いりぐちで　とが　そでに　はさまった
null_¥¥xx.xxx
おとうとはいちばんさけにつよい
さかなのほねにほそいあしがある
くじでちちにしょうひんがあたった
おとこのこが　わたしに　あやまった
こころの　すみに　ふるい　きずが　ある
げんかんがざぶとんにぶつかった
むすめはとくにじかんにきびしい
あねは　すこし　おんせんに　つめたい
きりんの　くびに　ながい　きばが　ある
ふろばでせっけんがゆにおぼれた
からすがつるりとかぜにふるえた
おとうとがきんぎょにえさをやった
null_¥¥xx.xxx
じしんで　ゆかが　つくえに　たおれた
おぼうさんが　ほこりに　じまんした
びんの　そこに　まるい　しかくが　ある

きみは　へんに　ひとに　なれなれしい
こやで　いるかが　ひつじに　さけんだ
おもてでいぬがひとにかみついた
おかあさんがせいせきにあきれた
おばあさんがごはんにだきついた
えのぐの　なかに　しろい　うでが　ある

null_¥¥xx.xxx
null_¥¥xx.xxx
「い」

まどのふちにちゃいろいわくがある
ぼくはちやほやともだちにはなした
null_¥¥xx.xxx
かいだんの　うえに　ひろい　はが　ある
うぐいすがすずめにぐちをいった
でんしゃが　えきいんに　きっぷを　みせた
れっしゃはようやくえきについた
あいは　ものすごく　こいに　せつない
まちで　かいしゃいんが　さぎに　あった
くびのまわりにくろいてんがある
えんそうしゃが　かんせいに　こたえた
ふくろうが　ひなに　えさを　はこんだ
げんかんで　きが　いぬに　かみついた
やくしょでえがあいさつにこたえた
おとこは　すっかり　てに　かみついた
おとうとは　ぼそぼそ　あねに　はなした
null_¥¥xx.xxx

null_¥¥xx.xxx

意味

あいつはとてもおかねにきたない
null_¥¥xx.xxx
となりの いえに ひろい にわが ある
かのじょはゆっくりちゃわんにおちた
そらのかなたにくらいほしがある
はかせがともだちにはなしかけた
しあいで みかたが てきに まけた
かえるはちゃぽんとみずにもぐった
つくえのしたにくろいかさがある
いとこは まるごと げんきに つらい
けいさつがわににじゅうしょをきいた
うちのそばにせまいあきちがある
null_¥¥xx.xxx
そらで じてんしゃが みぎに まがった
おんなは いそいそ いえに かえった
みちの はずれに ふるい みみが ある
おまえはやたらおれにあつかましい
めいじんはそっとめにかみついた
あいつはすらすらおれにわめいた
かぜは なんとも ほほに ここち よい
げしゅくでつくえがてにまきついた
かわで たこが さわぎに ふりむいた
null_¥¥xx.xxx
ろうかはわずかにごみにさみしい
おとこは びゅうびゅう かいしゃに いった
さいばんかんがでんしゃにのった
いしゃははっとよていにきづいた

こどもはこわごわみずにはいった
すいかは　しっかり　からすに　さわった
すずめが　たまごに　ひなを　かえした
りんごはたしょうれいぎにきびしい
ひきだしが　こいぬに　もぐりこんだ

null_¥¥xx.xxx
null_¥¥xx.xxx
「い」

かいいぬはわりとえさにうるさい
ころしやが　かたなに　たまを　いれた
みちではいしゃがいしにつまづいた
ごうとうがけいさつにせをむけた
ふうふは　のんびり　さけに　つかった
みずのなかにふしぎないしがある
だいがくががくせいにふりむいた
やきもちが　とりもちに　えを　かいた
だいがくせいがけんきゅうかいにでた
ちの　はてに　ふしぎな　せいかいが　ある
せいじかが　しじしゃに　こえを　かけた
おくじょうはかなりかいぎにわるい
ざしきで　ねこが　こたつに　はいった
null_¥¥xx.xxx
でんしゃはよくうみにむずかしい
げいじゅつかがいなかにひっこした

null_¥¥xx.xxx

0

意味

こうえんはみょうにもぐらにちかい
へやではしらがまどにかみついた
やまの　てっぺんに　たかい　きが　ある
null_¥¥xx.xxx
よせんで　あにが　さんいに　はいった
しけんでじゅんいがしたにあがった
なかまが　ひみつに　みみを　しゃべった
ひとごみで　こどもが　みちに　まよった
たきの　さきに　ながい　ほくろが　ある
なべのあいだにふといがけがある
ちちがいなかにてがみをおくった
たいようがいきなりかみにあつい
やまみちで　くるまが　たにに　おちた
null_¥¥xx.xxx
とけいがさんりんしゃにまたがった
せんすいかんが　じめんに　もぐった
こどもが　すいそうに　みずを　いれた
ちちは　あわてて　かいしゃに　もどった
あには　たいへん　かぞくに　やさしい
せいんせいが　せいとに　ほんを　あげた
きょうだいが　ゆうえんちに　でかけた
えものは　まんまと　わなに　はまった
null_¥¥xx.xxx
ははがともだちにおかねをかした
しまのかげにふしぎなふねがある
たびびとが　しょうねんに　えを　みせた
てじなでかみがおさつにかわった
やまで　たぬきが　きつねに　であった
うまのはねにきいろいくびがある
うえきが　おゆに　ぼうずを　そそいだ

Appendix B: Sample List of Stimulus Presentation (Event Related Design)   209

ちじが　だいじんに　くうきを　うった
ちんぴらが　かたつむりに　からんだ
あにがきんじょにみやげをくばった
null_¥¥xx.xxx

null_¥¥xx.xxx
null_¥¥xx.xxx
「い」

かのじょは　さすがに　ことばに　つよい
まちでこうがいがいえになやんだ
うでどけいが　べんとうに　しゃべった
たんぼで　たしが　つちに　もぐった
null_¥¥xx.xxx
ほんは　とても　せいとに　ありがたい
えんそうかいがとこやになげいた
かがくしゃががっかいにさんかした
かいじゅうは　すこし　しょくじに　せまい
あには　ぐつぐつと　いもうとに　きいた
きゃくが　やくしゃに　わらいかえした
せけんはやっぱりひとにつめたい
おとこはぎゅっとうでにいやしい
せいとは　すらすら　といに　こたえた
えんがわはとってもひるねによい
ふすまのうらにふるいいすがある

null_¥¥xx.xxx

0

意味

うみの そばに きれいな しろが ある
たしざんはじつにのどにやさしい
おとこが かべに らくがきを かいた
にわの すみに あかい つばきが ある
きょうりゅうがようふくにはきかえた
しんかんせんがとうきょうについた
せいとはしょんぼりとじゅぎょうにでた
はしごがかべにおつりをわたした
ふぐは ぺこぺこ しゃしょうに どなった
はしのしたにじょうずなはながある
しゅじんが きゃくに めがねを わたした
うしが らくごかに くぎを おしえた
ぼくは かなり おんがくに わるい
べんごしは ようやく えきに ついた
null_¥¥xx.xxx
くものなかにりっぱなみせがある
こうせいがねこにしみついた
ほねは いやに せなかに なつかしい
むすこは すごく はいくに くわしい
ねこがさかなにねごとをたのんだ
けいじがしゃもじにかぎをあずけた
たかのあしにするどいつめがある
null_¥¥xx.xxx
こうはいが せんぱいに えんりょした
かぶきできゃくがやくしゃにみとれた
れいぞうこがへやにとじこもった
しょうがくせいがふとんにはいった
がかはえらそうにでしにはなした
ともだちが たにんに うそを ついた
じゅけんせいが かみさまに いのった

Appendix B: Sample List of Stimulus Presentation (Event Related Design)   211

ちちは　こっそりと　ふゆに　かくれた
てんちょうはやたらかねにこまかい

                                            0
                                            0
                                            0
"xx.xxx" "Bbxx"   ;
"お疲れ様でした"   ;

Note.
The sentences presented in the comprehension task included both semantically congruent (Congruent) and incongruent (Incongruent) sentences: 60 semantically congruent and 60 incongruent sentences. The sentences presented in the control task (Cont) also included both semantically congruent and incongruent sentences: 30 semantically congruent and 30 incongruent sentences. Each sentence in each task was pseudo-randomly ordered. The sentences in each task were divided into 4 blocks respectively: 30 sentences in each comprehension block and 15 sentences in each control block. Then each comprehension and control block was combined in alternation as a series of 8 blocked tasks.

日本語の読者のための内容紹介

1. はじめに

　本書は、人間が文を理解するときに、脳がどのようにことばの処理に関わっているのかを、脳科学の装置と手法を使って明らかにした本です。本書では、人間が文を理解するときに、語をより大きな言語単位（本書では、句）にまとめたり、語よりも大きな言語単位（同じく、句）にまとめながら区切るという能力の存在を、fMRI を使った脳活動の計測から明らかにします。本書は、文理解という言語に関わる課題について、これまでの言語学、言語処理、心理言語学、神経心理学、神経言語学の各分野の言語研究の知見を取り上げ、検討しながら、fMRI による脳活動の計測の実験（本書では、2 つの実験行っています）を行い、その結果から、人間の文理解処理時に、語をより大きな言語単位にまとめたり、区切るという能力の所在（脳の神経基盤）を明らかにします。その上で、人間の言語に経験的に観察される普遍的現象とこれを支える能力について、神経心理学的視点からの最新の言語研究の成果をもとに、理論的枠組に基づく言語研究と実証的成果に基づく言語研究の接点を探っていきます。

2. Phrasal segmentation とは聞きなれない言葉ですが？

　Phrasal segmentation ということばは、まだ、多くの人にとって、なじみがないことばであることと思います。そこで、本書の内容の紹介をはじめる前に、まず、本書の書名にも登場し、文中にも出てくる、

phrasal segmentation ということばの内容と定義の説明しておきたいと思います。

最初に phrasal segmentation の語義について触れておきます。Phrasal とは、「句」をさす phrase にちなんだ語です。ですから、phrasal は「句の、句に関する」という内容をさします。そして、segmentation は、「分節（化）」をさします。したがいまして、phrasal segmentation とは、文字どおりで言うと、「句分節（化）、句への分節（化）」をさすことばということになります。

次に、phrasal segmentation ということばがさす内容についてですが、本書では、phrasal segmentation とは、文字どおりのごとく、もっぱら「句分節（化）、句への分節（化）」だけをさすことばとしては登場しません。本書の phrasal segmentation は、phrase（句）（断わりのない限り、本書では、phrase（「句」）は、「統語句」をさします）の単位への、「文から句への分節（化）」、そして、「語から句への群化」の両方をさすことばとして登場します。ですから、本書の phrasal segmentation は、字句どおりの「句分節（化）、句への分節（化）」をさす一方で、「句への群化」をさすことばということになります。少しややこしいですが、本書では、phrasal segmentation とは、断わりのない限り、「句への分節と群化」の両方をさすことばとして登場します。さらに、「分節」、あるいは、「群化」のどちらか一方について述べる必要がある場合には、どちらであるか断わりをつけています。

ところで、今度は、「分節（化）」とは、「群化」とは一体何のことかと、またあらたな疑問が出てくることと思います。「分節（化）」とは、文字どおり「区切ること」で segmentation をさします。一方、「群化」とは、「まとめること」で grouping のことをさします。本書では、segmentation（「分節」）は、文を句という単位の語のまとまりごとに切り分ける能力、切り分けるという処理をさし、grouping（「群化」）は、語を複数語あわせて句という単位の語のまとまりに語をまとめる能力、まとめ

る処理をさします。そして、「句単位の分節（化）」と「句単位の群化」の両方の能力、それらの能力に基づくことばの処理を、phrasal segmentation ということばを使ってさすようにしています。

　では、どうして、何のためにわざわざ phrasal segmentation ということばを使うのか、その理由は3つあります。1つめは、本書を執筆した時点では、「句単位の分節（化）」、「句単位の群化」の能力と処理をさす適切なことば、表現がみあたらなかったということ。そして、2つめは、「分節（化）」をさす segmentation という語が言語に関する研究のさまざまな場面で使われていて、そのままでは混乱が生じること（例えば、「分節音（segment）」、「語の分節（word segmentation）」、そして、「分節（の）（segmental）」という語にいたってはさまざまな言語の能力、言語の現象の記述に幅広く関わって使用されています）。最後に、3つめは、segmentation だけでは、「区切る」ということへの限定した意味合いが強くなり、「群化」の意味合いが無くなってしまうという懸念があったということ。これら3つの理由から、本書では、「句への分節」と「句への群化」の両方の内容を端的に言い表すための術語として、phrasal segmentation ということばを採用しました。

　したがいまして、phrasal segmentation とは、本書では、「句単位の分節（化）」、「句単位の群化」の能力と処理をさす術語ということになります。というわけで、本書のタイトルにある Japanese phrasal segmentation とは、「日本語の句分節（群化と分節）」をさすことになり、タイトルの *fMRI Study of Japanese Phrasal Segmentation: Neuropsychological Approach to Sentence Comprehension* とは、「fMRI を使用した日本語の句分節・群化処理の研究：文理解への神経心理学からのアプローチ」というような内容になります。

3. Phrasal segmentation と人間のことばの能力

　では、本題の本書で取り上げた phrasal segmentation の研究の紹介をいたします。

　人間にはことばの能力が備わっていて、人間はことばを使ってコミュニケーションを行います。しかし、人間によって行われる、ことばを使ったコミュニケーションは、個々の語をばらばらに並べて行われるのではなく、一定の規則（文法）に従って、語を組み合わせてひとまとまりにした文を使って行われます。語がまとまって文になることで、文は、あるまとまった内容を持ち、形の上でも意味の上でも1つの完結したことばの単位となり、人間のことばのコミュニケーションの主役として働くようになります。したがって、人間によることばを使ったコミュニケーションは、いくつかの語をまとめ合わせて文を作る能力、そして、いくつかの語をまとめ合わせてできた文を理解する能力を前提にして成り立っているといえます。

　しかし、人間が語から文を作るという行為においては、一瞬にしていくつかの語からひとまとまりの文をまとめ上げることができるというようなことは、現実的には、比較的短い定型的な表現を除いては、あまり見当たりません。むしろ、いくつかの語をまとめて、句を作り、さらに、いくつかの句を1つの文にまとめながら、文を作り出すことが普通です。話者が、長い文のまとまりを一瞬にして手持ちの語彙から作り出すというようなことは、人間の一時に操作できる情報量、一時に留め置くことができる記憶容量の制約（いわゆる、ワーキングメモリの制約）から見ても、現実的ではありません。また、人間は、語をならべて際限なく長い文を作り出すこともできますが、際限なく長い文が、語から一瞬にして出来上がるというようなこともありそうには思えません。むしろ、際限なく長い文は、1語1語からいきなり出来上がるのではなく、語をより大きな単位（句）にまとめながら、出来上がっていくと考える方

が自然に思えます。したがって、人間が、語から文を作るという行為は、語をいくつかの語のまとまりである句にまとめながら、さらに、句から、句のまとまりである文を作るという行為に他ならないと見ることができます。

　一方、文を理解するときには、文をいきなり１語１語に分解するのではなく、文よりも小さなことばの単位である、句の単位の語のまとまり(構成素)を文から切り出し、句どうしの関係から、文の意味を理解するということが行われていると見ることができます。聞いたり読んだりして文を理解するときには、１語１語が聴覚や視覚を通じて時間順に(時系列に沿って)取り込まれ、取り込まれた複数の語は順にまとまりとなって、最後には１まとまりの文として認識されると考えることができます。つまり、人間によることばのコミュニケーションでは、文を使って話したり書いたりする場合には、語をいくつかの語にまとめながら文を作り出し、また、文を使って聞いたり読んだりして理解する場合には、文の中からいくつかの語のまとまりを切り出しながら文を理解しているということができます。

　例えば、

（１）　僕は昨日雑誌を買った。

という文は、

（２）　僕は　昨日　雑誌を　買った。

という語のまとまりの単位(句の単位)で、左から右に時系列順にアウトプット(出力)され、文が作られ、また、同じく、左から右の時系列順に文はインプット(入力)として取り込まれ理解されます。

　もちろん、

（3）　僕　は　昨日　雑誌　を　買った。

という左から右への時系列順の語から文のアウトプット、インプットや、

（4）　ぼ　く　は　き　の　う　ざ　っ　し　を　か　っ　た。

という左から右への時系列順の音声（モーラ）単位の文のアウトプット、インプットも想定できます。

　確かに一見すると、(3)は、「語→文」の生成、理解で、(4)は、語よりもさらに小さな音（モーラ）の単位からの文の生成、理解（「モーラ→文」の生成、理解）に見えます。しかし、実際に(3)と(4)を読んで内容を理解しようとすれば、(3)は、実は、「語→句→文」の経路を経た文理解に他ならず、(4)も、実は、「モーラ→語→句→文」の経路であって、(3)も(4)も、(2)を経て、つまり、「句」のまとまりを介して（句の処理経路を経た）文の理解であることに気がつくことと思います。つまり、(2)、(3)、(4)の一見したところの違いは、表記上の分節（分節単位、分節レベル）の違いを示すに過ぎず、いずれの場合も、全体を１つの文として発話したり、理解したりしようとすれば、いずれも「句」の処理経路が介在するという点は同じです。したがって、文を作り出す場合には、「語から句へのまとめ上げ」（「句単位の群化」）が介在し、文を理解する場合には、「文から句の切り出し」（「句単位の分節（化）」）が介在していることになります。こうした「語から句へのまとめ上げ」（「句単位の群化」）や「文から句の切り出し」（「句単位の分節（化）」）の能力の存在は、(1)を一定のまとまりに分節することを尋ねた場合の結果の自然さ、不自然さの判断では、(2)への分節が、(3)や(4)への分節に比べると、最も自然に思えることの自覚（直観、intuition）がわたしたちのなかに共通に存在することからも明らかなことといえます。

4. Phrasal segmentation と脳における言語の処理

　前節で述べたとおり、人間がことばを使ってコミュニケーションを行う場合には、語を、句や文のようなより大きなことばの単位にまとめるという行為、また、文のようなより大きなことばのまとまりのなかから、より小さなことばのまとまりを切り出すという行為を行います。このことは、ことばによるコミュニケーションでは、例えば、人間が発話したり書いたりして、ことばで表現するときには、１つ１つの語から、いきなり大きなことばの単位である文を作り出すわけではなく、１つ１つの語を、いくつかの文よりも小さなことばの単位（本書では、「句（統語句）」）にまとめ、いくつかの句をさらに１つの文にまとめるという行為を行っているということ、そして、聞いたり話したりして、ことばの内容を理解するときには、いきなり大きなことばの単位である文から、１つ１つの語に切り分けて文の内容を理解しているわけではなく、文よりも小さく、１つ１つの語よりも大きなことばの単位（同じく、「句（統語句）」）を取り出し、それぞれの句の意味と句どうしの文法関係から、文全体の内容を理解していることを示しています。

　語がまとまって句になり、句がまとまって文になるという言語現象は、言語学の分野では、統語論を中心に研究が進み、個々の語が複数の語にまとまるという言語現象は広く取りあげられ、例えば、生成文法のミニマリスト・プログラムでは、Merge（併合）という操作の中で論じられています。また、経験的事実をとおして語と文の関係を見た場合にも、語がまとまって１つの文になるという言語現象、語をまとめて１つの文を作ったり、文を語のまとまりに分けて理解したりするという人間のことばの能力は、個別の言語によらず、人間の言語に共通して、普遍的にあらわれ、観察される言語現象であり、ことばの生成や理解に関わる基盤的な能力の１つであるように見受けられます。したがって、言語の理論的枠組をとおしての観察からも、経験的事実から見ても、語

を句にまとめたり、語のまとまりである句を切り出したりして、文を作り、理解する、人間のことばの能力とそうした能力に基づく処理が、人間の文生成、文理解に強く反映されていることは事実と考えて差し支えないようです。
　こうした人間のことばの現象、能力は、特に近年では、脳の機能との関わりから、その実在が論じられるようになり、言語学の分野でも、ことばの現象、能力は、心的に実在する存在として、その存在が脳に求められるということがさかんに論じられるようになってきました。また、最近では、実際に脳の機能を計測することで、ことばの現象、能力を、健康な人間のからだに危害を加えないで（「非侵襲的(non-invasive)」といいます）人間の脳の活動を通して確かめることが可能になってきました。そうすると、適切な方法、装置を使用することで、phrasal segmentation についても、その存在を脳に求め、その存在の根拠や脳の神経的基盤についても、脳の機能の計測を通して観察し、議論することが十分に可能になるということになります。しかも、そうして観察した人間の言語現象や能力の様子は、実験装置を使いながらも、かなりの精度で、人間の日常の言語の処理やそれを支える言語の能力を直接的に反映した結果として取り出すことが可能です。
　しかし、現時点では、語を句にまとめたり、句のまとまりを文から切り出したりする操作の様子や操作の基盤となる脳の働き（phrasal segmentation に関わる脳の働き）については、脳のことばに関わる機能の計測が進んだ現在でも、いまだ詳しいことはわかっていません。そうした能力の存在、能力に基づく処理の様子が、実際に脳にどのように具体的に反映され、人間の脳の活動の中にどのように現れるのか、そうした疑問を明らかにする研究の試み、例えば、Merge の操作を行う際の人間の脳の活動、言語情報処理を明らかにして、論じたというような研究も、その数は非常に少なく（現状では、皆無といって差支えない状態）、研究領域や研究手法も非常に限られた範囲にとどまっているというのが

現状です。

　そうした背景から、本書では、脳と言語の関わりに注目し、脳科学的な手法を取り入れて(本書では、そうした手法による言語研究へのアプローチを「神経心理学からのアプローチ(neuropsychological approach)」と呼んでいます)、人間が文を生成したり、理解するときの脳における言語の処理の様子を視覚化して測定し、phrasal segmentation(「句単位の分節(化)と群化」)に直接的に関わる脳の働きを明らかにし、文生成や文理解における phrasal segmentation の役割について論じていくこととします。特に、本書では、副題に sentence comprehension とあるように、文理解時の phrasal segmentation の処理について明らかにし、文理解における phrasal segmentation の役割について考えていくことにしました。

　人間が言語を処理するときには、通常、音声、統語、意味の各領域の情報が言語情報として関わっていることが知られています。脳の言語に関わる処理を調べてみても、音声、統語、意味のそれぞれの情報が関わっていて、しかも、各情報の処理は、処理情報ごとに異なっています。さらに、音声、統語、意味のそれぞれの言語情報の処理は、処理する言語の単位の大きさにより、例えば、語の処理と句の処理、文の処理とでは、脳の処理領域や処理のネットワークに違いがあることが知られています。また、同じ語でも、意味的情報を大きく担う語と統語的情報を大きく担う語とでは、脳内での処理の様子に違いが見られ、文でも、正しい文と誤りを含む文とでは、また、処理の様子が違ってきます。したがって、ひとくちに言語に関わる脳の処理といっても、その中味は様々で、具体的な言語に関わる脳の処理の様子の特定には、様々な言語に関わる現象や能力を個々に反映した課題を作り、1つ1つ測定データを積み上げることが必要で、そうした作業を経ることで、はじめて、脳の言語に関わる活動の様子が特定できることになります。

　これまで、人間の言語に関わる活動や能力は、左脳(右利きの人は、

特に、言語に関する処理の脳領域は左脳を中心として広がっていて)の
ブローカ野(前頭下部)、ウェルニッケ野(側頭後部)への集中した関与が
解剖学的データから裏付けられていましたが、現在では、そうした領域
の言語への関与は、言語情報や言語処理の内容の違いにより、さらに細
分化し、また、そうした領域以外の脳(左脳、右脳)の各領域の言語への
関与も詳しく明らかになってきています。そうしたこれまでの研究成果
を踏まえながら、本書は、音声、統語、意味の各言語情報の処理の特性
からも、phrasal segmentation に関わる脳での言語処理の様子について
明らかにすることができました。さらに得られた結果からは、文処理モ
デルとしてしばしば取り上げられる、直列処理モデル(serial model)と
並列処理モデル(parallel model)からの予測の妥当性についても検討し、
phrasal segmentation の研究から得られた最新の知見をもとに、各モデ
ルの人間の言語に関する処理のモデル、とりわけ、文理解処理のモデル
について、そのモデルとしての適合性、妥当性についても論じていま
す。詳しい成果については、ぜひ本文をお読みください。

5. fMRI による phrasal segmentation を行う脳活動の計測

　次に、本書で取り上げる phrasal segmentation の脳活動の計測の方法
について解説します。本書では、脳の活動の計測に fMRI という方法を
利用します。fMRI とは、functional magnetic resonance imaging の略で、
「機能的磁気共鳴画像法」とよばれる脳の活動を計測する方法です。ま
た、fMRI は、「機能的磁気共鳴画像法」を使って実際の脳活動の様子
を測定する装置のこともさすことがあります。ところで、人間が認知的
な活動(思考や言語を始めとする人間の大脳を中心とした脳の活動に由
来する活動のことを、認知的な活動、認知活動とよびます)を行ってい
るときの脳活動の様子の計測には様々な方法があります。そうした脳活
動の計測は、大きく2つにわかれ、1つは、脳の神経細胞の活動に由来

する脳からの電気的、或いは、磁気的信号をとらえて計測する方法、そして、もう１つは、神経細胞の活動に伴って生じる脳内の血流や代謝の変化をとらえて計測する方法があげられます（それぞれの計測方法、計測装置の詳しい内容については、本書の中で取り上げ、長所、短所、向き、不向きを含め、解説をつけています）。そして、fMRIは神経細胞の活動に伴って生じる脳内の血流の変化をとらえて、脳が認知的な活動（本書では、phrasal segmentation）を行う場合の活動の様子を明らかにするという、計測方法でいえば、後者の方法に相当します（fMRIの原理、測定方法については、本文を参照してください）。

　fMRIによる脳活動の計測では、通常、差分法（subtraction）とよばれる方法を使って、特定の認知活動に関わる脳活動の様子、脳の活動領域を特定します。差分法とは、１条件だけ異なる２種類の課題を与え、それぞれの脳活動の様子を計測し、異なる１条件を含む課題の脳活動の計測データから、異なる１条件を含まない課題の脳活動の計測データを減じる（差し引きする）ことで、異なる１課題に関わる脳活動の様子、脳の活動領域を特定するという方法です。そもそも、脳は、安静にしていても何らかの活動を行っていますので、ある１つの特定の課題だけからは、特定の認知活動に関連した脳活動を特定することは困難です。そのため、fMRIを使って可視化して脳活動を計測する場合は、差分という方法により、特定の認知活動に関わる脳活動、脳活動の領域を突き止めていくという方法を取ります。本書では、文を理解するときに、phrasal segmentationの処理を要求する課題と要求しない課題（正確には、phrasal segmentationの処理負荷が極端に低い課題）のそれぞれを行って、差分法により、phrasal segmentationに関わる脳活動の様子、活動領域を特定するという方法を採用しています（詳細は、本文をご覧ください）。

6. 各章の紹介

最後に本書の各章の紹介をします。本書は、全7章からなります。各章の概要は次の通りです。

第1章、Introductionでは、人間の発話や文理解が、語や句の単位に基づいて行われているという現象を取り上げ、語への分節については、その現象やメカニズムについての研究が進む一方で、phrasal segmentationの問題が未解決のままであることを述べ、研究への問題提起を行っています。

さらに、章末には、言語の脳科学的研究で用いられる様々な研究手法、術語、さらに、研究装置の仕組みや原理を解説したアルファベット順の用語集をつけました。Phrasal segmentationの研究だけでなく、言語に関わる現象や能力について、脳科学的手法を取り入れて言語の研究を始める方や脳科学関連の言語を扱った英語論文を読むには、便利な内容になっています。

第2章、Why Phrasal Segmentation?では、まず、人間のphrasal segmentationの能力の心的実在の証拠を、人間言語への直観と行動データに基づく実証的研究から提示しました。次に、phrasal segmentationと文処理モデルの関係を取り上げ、現在の文処理モデルでは、phrasal segmentationが全く位置付けられていない点を指摘しました。また、脳の神経生理学的反応に基づいた文処理モデルでも、phrasal segmentationに関わる言語の能力については未解明であることを指摘し、文処理の研究分野では、phrasal segmentationの問題に対する研究にはいまだ手が付けられていないことを示しました。そのうえで、phrasal segmentationという未開拓の研究の必要性を示しました。

加えて、本章では、脳活動の計測装置、計測手法、測定原理を解説し、それぞれの長所、短所について解説を加えました。この解説も、脳科学的手法を取り入れた言語研究や関連論文の研究には、便利な内容に

なっています。

　第3章、Human Language Processing in the Brainでは、phrasal segmentationの問題が、人間の言語処理に関わる脳内の処理の中でどう扱われるかを予測し、問題解明の方向性を示し、phrasal segmentationに関わる脳機能が、音韻、意味、統語の各情報の処理との関わりの中で、機能的に捉えられることの可能性を示しました。その上で、現在、有効な2つの文理解モデルの中で、phrasal segmentationの処理段階、脳内での処理領域がどの位置にあると考えられるか仮説を立て、fMRIによる実験から、2つの文理解モデル、直列処理モデル（serial model）と並列処理モデル（parallel model）の正当性、妥当性を明らかにすることが可能であると述べ、研究の目的を言明しました。

　第4章、Search for Phrasal Segmentation: Visual fMRI Studyでは、日本語の単文理解における、phrasal segmentationの脳内における処理段階、処理領域を明らかにする、視覚刺激を用いたfMRIによる実験を取り上げました。

　第5章、Search for Phrasal Segmentation: Auditory fMRI Studyでは、第4章と同じ条件の聴覚刺激を用いたfMRIによる実験を取り上げ、phrasal segmentationと脳の言語に関わる処理の関連が、視覚、聴覚にかかわらず普遍的に認められるかどうかを明らかにしました。

　第6章、What Happens with Phrasal Segmentation in the Brain, Then?では、2つの実験結果を受けて、phrasal segmentationが、視覚・聴覚のモダリティにかかわらず、普遍的な神経基盤を持つ言語処理能力であること、また、phrasal segmentationには、いくつかの特定の脳領域、言語情報の処理が関わることを指摘し、phrasal segmentationは、人間の文理解処理に、普遍的に関わる言語の能力、言語の処理段階であることを明らかにしました。その上で、本書のphrasal segmentationの研究結果が、JackendoffやCulicoverが言語理論に基づいて予測した言語処理モデルを、脳の活動を可視化して捉えたことで実証的に裏付ける結果と

なっていることを示しました。

第 7 章、Conclusion では、本書で得られた成果、そして課題をあげ、今後の phrasal segmentation の方向性を示し、各章を概観して、結びとしました。

7. おわりに

　本書は、人間が文を発したり、理解したりするときに、語をより大きな言語単位にまとめたり、区切ったりするという言語現象とそれを支える能力の基盤について、神経心理学的手法から新しいことばの知見を得ようとする試みです。ことばに関わる現象や能力については、経験的に見てどの言語にも共通に、普遍的に観察されるものが多くあります。そうした現象、能力のなかには、言語の関連研究分野では、経験的にその存在が確かめられてはいても、理論化や実証的検証がその途上にあるものも少なからず見受けられます。本書は、そうした言語の現象、能力の 1 つ、phrasal segmentation に理論化と実証的検証の光をあて、理論的枠組にもとづく言語研究と実証的言語研究との接点を見出そうとするものです。本書をとおして、理論的言語研究と実証的言語研究の共通の対話の場がさらに広がり、本書が、fMRI をはじめとした脳科学的手法にもとづく言語研究のナビゲーターになれば、筆者としては望外の幸せです。

Index

A
auditory areas 134
auditory experiment 83, 121

B
BA 44 68, 73
BA 44/45 73, 80
BA 47 74
BA 45 68
basal ganglia 101
bimodal brain functions 162
bimodal cortical activations 150, 157, 163
bimodal inconsistent distribution 156
block design 63
BOLD effect 63
bootstrapping operation 169
Broca's area 67

C
Closure Positive Shift (CPS) 45
combinatorial 52
Congruent 89, 123
Cont 89, 124
core linguistic information 39, 153

D
different degree of specialization 159

E
ELAN 44
electroencephalography (EEG) 40
event related brain potential (ERP) 41
event-related design 63, 64
evoked magnetic field (EMF) 41

F
fMRI 62, 63, 222
functional relationship 76
functional specialization 82, 146, 150

G
grouping 214

I
IFG 80
immediacy 50
Incongruent 89, 123
incongruent sentence processing 103, 138
inconsistency in segmentation 6
integration 79
interaction 79
interactive 47
interface operations 167
intuition of language 31
intuitive knowledge of phrasal segmentation 33
ITG 81

L
LAN 44
left pars orbitalis 112, 147, 158
left STG 155
lemma information 52
linguistic information 36, 37
local phrase structure building 80

M
M100 42
magnetic event related field (MERF) 41
magnetoencephalography

(MEG) 40, 41
meaningful groupings 32
Merge 165, 219
mismatch negativity
  (MMN) 42
modality independent 144
MTG 81

N

N150 42
N320 43
N350 43
N400 43, 117
neuropsychological
  approach 221
non-invasive 220
Non-seg 89, 123
non-segmented condition
  11, 84

O

OT 62

P

P600 43
parallel 47
Parallel Architecture 167
parallel models 39
parallel processing 81, 87,
  113, 159, 166
pars opercularis 158
pars orbitalis 101, 102,
  104, 108, 109, 136, 137,
  139, 143, 155

pars triangularis 101, 108,
  155, 158
perisylvian language areas
  67
PET 62
phrasal segmentation 3,
  214, 221
processing level 38, 40
processing operations 157
prosodic bootstrapping
  hypothesis 7
prosodic information 3, 6,
  7, 144
prosodic phrase boundaries
  4
prosodic phrasing 45

R

region of interest (ROI)
  approach 17, 65
representational level 38,
  39, 40
ROIs 65, 98, 133

S

Seg 89, 123
segmentation 214
segmentation problem 2
segmented condition 11, 84
semantic domain 113
semantic information 158
semantic integration 112,
  114, 146
semantic violations 103,
  115, 138, 148
serial 47
serial models 39
serial processing 81, 87, 159
seriality 50
STG 80
STS 98
subtraction 65, 223
subtraction method 15
syntactic domain 113
syntactic information 159
syntactic phrase boundaries
  4
syntax-first 47

T

temporal pole 99, 136,
  137, 139, 143, 155

U

Unification Model 50

V

ventral pathway 155
violation paradigms 162
visual experiment 83, 87
voxelwise approach 65

W

Wernicke's area 67
word segmentation 3
working memory 84, 92,
  126

【著者紹介】

大嶋 秀樹(おおしまひでき)

香川県出身。同志社大学文学部英文学科卒業。東北大学大学院国際文化研究科(言語コミュニケーション論講座)博士後期課程修了。博士(国際文化)(東北大学)。現在、滋賀大学教育学部英語教育講座准教授。

〈主な著書・論文〉

"Assessing communicative writing proficiency: An expert rater's decision making when scoring EFL compositions," *Annual Review of English Language Education in Japan (ARELE)* 13: 81–90 (2003). "Cortical mechanisms of segmentation in visual sentence comprehension of Japanese Kana," *NeuroImage* 31, Supplement 1, S116 (2006). "Cortical mechanisms of segmentation in Japanese auditory sentence comprehension," *NeuroImage* 36, Supplement 1, S50 (2007).

Hituzi Linguistics in English No. 18

fMRI Study of Japanese Phrasal Segmentation
Neuropsychological Approach to Sentence Comprehension

発行	2013年2月27日 初版1刷
定価	15000円+税
著者	Ⓒ 大嶋秀樹
発行者	松本 功
印刷所	三美印刷株式会社
製本所	三省堂印刷株式会社
発行所	株式会社 ひつじ書房
	〒112-0011 東京都文京区千石 2-1-2 大和ビル 2F
	Tel.03-5319-4916 Fax.03-5319-4917
	郵便振替 00120-8-142852
	toiawase@hituzi.co.jp　http://www.hituzi.co.jp/

ISBN978-4-89476-595-5　C3080

造本には充分注意しておりますが、落丁・乱丁などがございましたら、小社かお買上げ書店におとりかえいたします。ご意見、ご感想など、小社までお寄せ下されば幸いです。

脳からの言語研究入門　最新の知見から研究方法まで
　　横山悟著　　定価 2,200 円 + 税

近年、脳機能計測技術の発達により、人間の言葉・言語を使っているときの脳活動を画像化しようという研究が増えてきている。本書は、脳からの言語研究に興味を持つ学生及び研究者を対象に、脳機能計測を用いた言語研究の最新の知見概説と、実際に人文系の学生・研究者が脳からの言語研究を行う際に、具体的に何から始めればいいのか、何を準備してどうすればデータ解析結果が得られるのか、の説明までを網羅した入門書。

言語・脳・認知の科学と外国語習得

東北大学言語認知総合科学 COE 論文集刊行委員会編　　定価 4,600 円＋税

東北大学における COE プログラム「言語・認知総合科学戦略研究教育拠点」での研究教育活動の成果をまとめた論文集である。収録論文を「言語の多様性と普遍性」、「言語を学ぶ脳」、「言語のモデルと外国語習得」の 3 部構成として編纂した。

第 1 部
連鎖推移と言語接触のインターフェイス（井土慎二）
南アジア諸語における非顕在的動作主構文（パルデシ・プラシャント）
日中語の名詞修飾構文の機能類型論（王路明）
コーパスデータに基づいた韓国語の「것이다(KES-ITA)」の用法（金廷珉）
終結語尾と終助詞に見る話し手の心的態度（平香織）

第 2 部
日本語短距離かき混ぜ文の脳内処理機構（金情浩）
脳内における日本語文理解モデル（横山悟）
バイリンガルの脳内言語処理（鄭嫣婷）
言語・非言語コミュニケーションに関与する神経基盤（佐々祐子）

第 3 部
中国語を母語とする日本語学習者における格助詞「を」「に」の習得過程（蘇雅玲）
多少の「も」の意味論と多義性（中村ちどり）
第二言語学習におけるアウトプットの役割（鈴木渉、板垣信哉）
言語認知処理における言語形態情報の影響（白晨、岩崎祥一）

刊行案内

Hituzi Linguistics in English No.12
Detecting and Sharing Perspectives Using Causals in Japanese
宇野良子 著
978-4-89476-405-7　定価 12,000 円 + 税

Hituzi Linguistics in English No.13
Discourse Representation of Temporal Relations in the So-Called Head-Internal Relatives
石川邦芳 著
978-4-89476-406-4　定価 9,400 円 + 税

Hituzi Linguistics in English No.14
Features and Roles of Filled Pauses in Speech Communication
A corpus-based study of spontaneous speech
渡辺美知子 著
978-4-89476-407-1　定価 11,000 円 + 税

Hituzi Linguistics in English No.15
Japanese Loanword Phonology
The Nature of Inputs and the Loanword Sublexicon
六川雅彦 著
978-4-89476-442-2　定価 12,000 円 + 税

Hituzi Linguistics in English No.16
Derivational Linearization at the Syntax-Prosody Interface
塩原佳世乃 著
978-4-89476-485-9　定価 12,000 円 + 税

Hituzi Linguistics in English No.19
Typological Studies on Languages in Thailand and Japan
宮本正夫・小野尚之・Kingkarn Thepkanjana・上原聡 編
978-4-89476-607-5　定価 9,000 円 + 税